FAR TORTUGA

by Peter Matthiessen

Bantam Windstone Books
Ask your bookseller for the books you have missed

AT PLAY IN THE FIELDS OF THE LORD
    by Peter Matthiessen
THE BELL JAR by Sylvia Plath
THE BOOK OF DANIEL by E. L. Doctorow
CANCER WARD by Alexander Solzhenitsyn
THE CONFESSIONS OF NAT TURNER
    by William Styron
DARKNESS VISIBLE by William Golding
DELTA OF VENUS Erotica by Anaïs Nin
THE END OF THE ROAD by John Barth
FAR TORTUGA by Peter Matthiessen
THE FIRST CIRCLE by Aleksandr I. Solzhenitsyn
THE FLOATING OPERA by John Barth
GILES GOAT-BOY by John Barth
THE GOLDEN NOTEBOOK by Doris Lessing
GOODBYE, COLUMBUS by Philip Roth
THE LONG MARCH by William Styron
LOST IN THE FUNHOUSE by John Barth
THE MEMOIRS OF A SURVIVOR by Doris Lessing
THE MIDDLE GROUND by Margaret Drabble
MY LIFE AS A MAN by Philip Roth
NIGHT OF THE AUROCHS by Dalton Trumbo
ONE DAY IN THE LIFE OF IVAN DENISOVICH
    by Alexander Solzhenitsyn
PORTNOY'S COMPLAINT by Philip Roth
SET THIS HOUSE ON FIRE by William Styron
THE SNOW LEOPARD by Peter Matthiessen
SOMETIMES A GREAT NOTION by Ken Kesey
THE STONE ANGEL by Margaret Laurence
THE SUMMER BEFORE THE DARK
    by Doris Lessing
V. by Thomas Pynchon
VISION QUEST by Terry Davis
A WEAVE OF WOMEN by E. M. Broner
WELCOME TO HARD TIMES by E. L. Doctorow
WHEN SHE WAS GOOD by Philip Roth

FAR TORTUGA

Peter Matthiessen

BANTAM BOOKS
Toronto • New York • London • Sydney

FAR TORTUGA

*A Bantam Book / published by arrangement with
Random House, Inc.*

PRINTING HISTORY

Random House edition published April 1975

2nd printing . . . . May 1975		4th printing . . . . June 1975
3rd printing . . . . June 1975		5th printing . . . . July 1975
	6th printing . . . August 1975	

Book-of-The-Month Club edition published April 1975

2nd printing . . . . July 1975	3rd printing . . September 1975

Bantam edition / April 1976

2nd printing . . . . April 1976	4th printing . . November 1976
3rd printing . . . . June 1976	5th printing . . . August 1979

Bantam Windstone edition / November 1981

*Bantam Books are published by Bantam Books, Inc. Its trade-
mark, consisting of the words "Bantam Books" and the por-
trayal of a rooster, is Registered in U.S. Patent and Trademark
Office and in other countries. Marca Registrada. Bantam
Books, Inc., 666 Fifth Avenue, New York, New York 10103.*

PRINTED IN THE UNITED STATES OF AMERICA

15 14 13 12 11 10 9 8 7 6

FOR MARIA

ACKNOWLEDGMENTS

This book required and received unusual care and attention from all involved in it, and I am very grateful to such friends as Judy Gimblett for expert typing of the interminable drafts; Candida Donadio, the book's agent, for her fearless advocacy in the marketplace; copy editor Lynn Strong for her concern, patience and unfailing intuition; and Kenneth Miyamoto, the book's designer, whose fine work speaks here for itself.

Especially I wish to thank my editor, adversary and long-time friend, Joe Fox; we have been through hell together.

Death, Thou comest
When I had Thee least in mind.

—*Everyman*

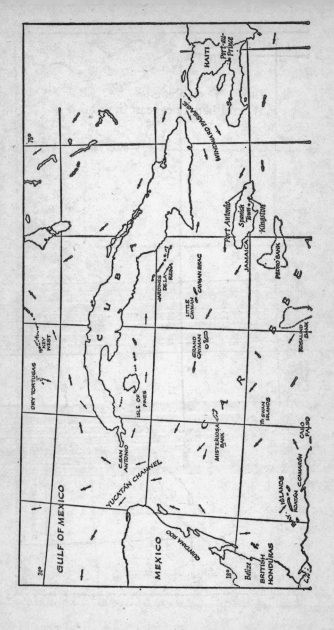

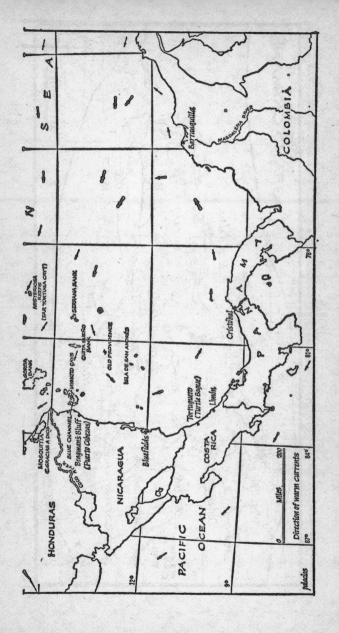

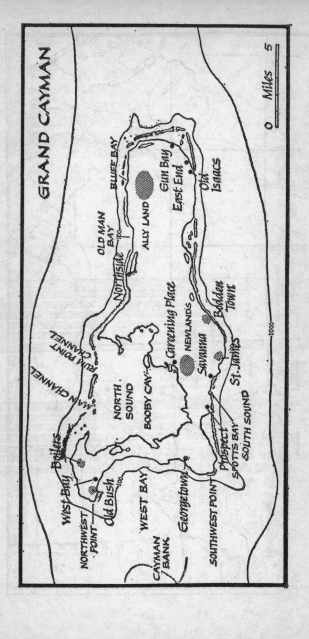

GRAND CAYMAN

0   Miles   5

BLUFF BAY

OLD MAN BAY

NORTHSIDE

Ally Land

Gun Bay

East End

Old Isaacs

Careening Place

NEWLANDS

Bodden Towne

SAVANNA

St. James

SOUTH SOUND

Prospect

SPOTTS BAY

SOUTHWEST POINT

Georgetown

WEST BAY

Old Bush

NORTHWEST POINT

West Bay

Boilers

CAYMAN BANK

RUM POINT CHANNEL

MAIN CHANNEL

NORTH SOUND

BOOBY CAY

100

1000

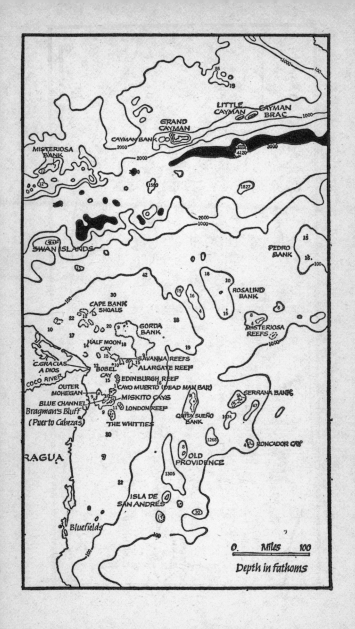

In terms of distance from the nearest land, the most isolated point in the Caribbean is a group of ocean islands south of Cuba. On a voyage north from Panama to Hispaniola, according to the journal kept in 1503 by Ferdinand Columbus, "we were in sight of two very small and low islands, full of tortoises, as was all the sea about, insomuch that they look'd like little rocks, for which reason those islands were called Tortugas." Later, these islands were confused with Far Tortuga, called Misteriosa *by the Spanish, a remote cay on the outer banks off Nicaragua that is not to be found on modern charts; Far Tortuga may have worn away in hurricane, leaving only submerged reef, but it seems more likely that this cay was a mere dream and legend of the turtle men.*

Eventually, Columbus' islands became known as the Caimans, Caymanos, and Cayman Islands, from the Carib caiman, *or "crocodilian." (Sir William Dampier, who visited Grand Cayman in 1675–76, mentions the presence of crocodiles on the surface at West Bay.) In the late seventeenth century, the Caymans were a common ground for sea rovers of all nations, who came there mainly for* tortugas; *these green sea turtles, which could be kept alive on deck, supplied fresh provender for the pillage of the Caribbean.*

Apart from their turtles, the barren islands were considered worthless, and no country bothered to claim them until 1655, when England seized Jamaica from Spain. The British regarded the turtle cays as outposts of the larger island, and acquired them officially in 1670 by the provisions of the Treaty of

Madrid. In this same year, the Spanish of Cuba burned twenty wood huts at "Caimanos" in an effort to suppress its raffish settlement of castaways, freebooters and deserters from the British army in Jamaica; these punitive raids, which continued for a century, have never been forgiven to this day.

In 1677, Dutch pirates taking water in the islands left behind a few blacks seized from a French slaving ship burned at Haiti, and some of these Africans mixed with the whites to form the ancestral population. By the time the first true settlers arrived at Grand Cayman, in the early eighteenth century, the green turtles were so depleted that ships no longer came to hunt them, and the Caymanians themselves were scouring the south coast of Cuba and the islands called Jardines de la Reina, where the turtle fishery was eked out with brigandage. Apparently they had retained their "turbulent disposition," for as late as 1798, Grand Cayman was called a "pirate's nest" by the Cubans, who appealed to Madrid to wipe it off the earth: "The islet is inhabited by a handful of lawless men who bear the name and carry on the trade of fisher-folk, but who are in reality nothing more than sea-robbers. The island constitutes their lair, and it is the place where they hide their ill-gotten gains." The pirate Neale Walker frequented the island, and Edward Thatch, the notorious "Blackbeard," once "took a small turtler" at Grand Cayman, though what fate is implied by "took" is not recorded. Without question it was a ruffianly place. As Bunce observes in Sir Walter Scott's The Pirate: *"Is he dead? It is a more serious question here than it would be on the Grand Caymains . . . where a brace or two of fellows may be shot in the morning and no more heard of, or asked about them than if they were so many wood pigeons."*

In the nineteenth century, the only marked change in island customs was the reduction of piracy to the "wrecking business"—luring ships onto the reefs, premature salvage and the like—and the transfer of the turtle fishery from south Cuba to the Miskito Cays off

Nicaragua, with a resultant occupation by Caymanians not only of that coast but of the remote cays from Old Providence, a Colombian possession, north to the Bay Islands of Honduras. Miskito Indians, who were expert turtle fishermen, were conscripted for the crews (Dampier had taken a Miskito harpooner on his voyage to the Celebes) and there occurred a small reverse migration of these Indians to Grand Cayman: even today, in the faces of the turtle men, a strain of Indian is quite apparent. But contact with the outside world was small, and declined still further as the nineteenth century came to an end. The Caymans lay across the trade winds, near old sailing routes, but with the advent of steam and swift straight courses, the passing ship was rarely more than a faint smudge on the encircling horizon.

Daybreak.

At Windward Passage, four hundred miles due east, the sun is rising. Wind east-northeast, thirty-eight knots, with gusts to forty-five: a gale.

Black waves, wind-feathered. White birds, dark birds.

The trade winds freshen at first light, and the sea rises in long ridges, rolling west.

Sunrise at longitude 76, 19 degrees north latitude.

Sunrise at longitude 77.

Sunrise at the lesser Caymans. Horizon rises from horizon. To the westward, Grand Cayman is gray; its high cumulus, visible to migrant birds a hundred miles away, is a gray-pink.

The sun, coming hard around the world: the island rises from the sea, sinks, rises, holds.

Daybreak at Gun Bay Village, at East End. Parted, the Antilles Current caroms on the reef. The new light turns the sea from black to blue, the surf from gray to white, the hulks high on the reef from rust to black.

Sunrise at Old Isaacs (Isaac Bawden, deserter, first known settler; dates obscure). The sun kindles the thatch of hip-roofed cottages, built at East End since early days. Sand road, white pickets, periwinkle; white sand yards bordered with pink conchs.

Cock crow.

Wind and cloud sail down the island, east to west. A sweet warm wind comes, sucking faint damp from the parched cactus and palmetto.

Sunrise in trackless Ally Land. New light strikes the blue spines of an iguana. Its chewing slows. Starting from its hole, a land crab pauses, then withdraws; a grain of earth rolls down into the hole.

Sunrise at Old Man, on the north coast. Blue shacks with dark shutters, closed.

Sunrise at Meagre Bay and Bodden Town, on the white road of coral marl that trails along the emerald sounds of the south shore. Fringing the sounds is the long reef, and beyond the reef, cold deep blues of the abyss.

Sunrise at Kitty Clover Land.

Sunrise at Newlands and Careening Place and Booby Cay.

Sunrise at Savanna. A lone dog on the road, stiff-legged. Poinsettia and jasmine, low white walls.

Green parrots cross the sunburst to the mango trees. Light polishes gray-silver cabin sides, glows in the bolls of the wild cotton, shines the dun flanks of a silken cow in pastures of rough guinea grass; a gumbo limbo tree, catching up sun in red translucent peels of shedding bark, glows on black burned-over ground between gray jutting bones of ocean limestone.

New sun on a vermilion fence. Breadfruit and tamarind.

Cock crow.

Sunrise at Spotts Bay and Matilda Pond. In a woman's tongue tree, the dawn wind passes and racketing pods fall still.

Sunrise at Prospect, on South Sound, abandoned since the Hurricane of '32. The Prospect Church decays in an old orchard, grown over now by seaside wood; the roof of the church is wind-slotted, battered by gales. Lizards scatter in the leaves and sun-spots that stray in the church door, and a hermit crab, snapped shut, rocks minutely in the silence.

In the graveyard behind the falling church grows oleander and white frangipani. On the ironshore below, incoming seas burst through black fissures in the rock, and black crabs scutter.

SACRED

TO THE MEMORY

OF

WILLIAM PARCHMENT

BORN

16TH DECEMBER 1924

PERISHED

APRIL 1968

ON THE MISKITO BANKS

The quai at Georgetown.

Shade trees, a small waterfront of green and pink pastels. Soft air of sunrise. Birdsong and a bicycle bell. Sweet rot, tin roofs, bougainvillaea.

Cock crow.

Three walking figures and a dog.

Black palm fronds stir against the eastern light: a hard glitter in the dew on leaf and tin where the sun pierces burning trees. Hard sun, high wind, high morning cumulus that draws swift shadows across the quai and dampens clacking palm fronds with a shower. A bird voice and sweet flower smells blow over Hanging Point into the ocean.

Clear of the land, the clouds string out and dissipate in the emptiness to westward, where the rain returns into the sea.

Figures beneath an almond tree observe the distant rain. Though the water at quaiside, in the lee, is clear and still, the green schooner offshore swings on her mooring. Beyond, the water shades from emerald to gray to the hard blue of the Antilles Current which mounts in shimmers to the sea horizon, rolling away west toward Quintana Roo.

*Small motor vessels of several hundred tons
may berth alongside a rough wharf at George-
town, Grand Cayman, the capital of the
Islands. Docking facilities are poor.
There are reasonably frequent services to
Tampa and Miami, Florida; Kingston,
Jamaica; and the Bay Islands,
Republic of Honduras.*

A big man in a turquoise shirt forsakes the figures by the almond tree. He steps backward, his voice rising. In his left hand, he carries a cardboard suitcase; in his right, a string bag of green mangoes. He rolls down to the quaiside, hailing an old man across the wind.

... a fair wind for de Cays, den, Copm Teddy!

The old man waits for the wind to ease before making his answer; he does not raise his head. Steadily he pares the skin from night-blue tuna. The fish, set out in a rigid row, have long lean wings that hold the ocean light.

You sailin late, Byrum! Get more wind den turtle, in de May time!

On the quai, a weathered sign reads WELCOME. Behind the sign, old boat ribs rise from a graveyard of dead oil drums, rust-gutted. Under the quai, in a slip blasted from black ironshore of fossil coral, is a Cayman catboat, an open boat like the whaleboat of other days that can be rigged quickly as a sloop. A small black man, barefoot, in ragged clean white T-shirt and blue denims cut off as shorts, is rolling a blue drum across the beach of coral and concrete that adjoins the slip. At quaiside, where he brakes the drum, its rumble dies in a thick slosh of oil.

The man in the turquoise shirt lays his suitcase flat and sets the mango bag on top.

What say, mon? Easy, mon! I give you a hand dere with dat drum!

Dat okay—I got dis by myself. Long's he don't squish dat sailor in de boat, Speedy doin fine!

Call dat a sailor? Dat old Vemon! What say, Vemon?

A man is slumped in the bilges of the catboat. His rags are nondescript in color; on his head sits a striped engineer's cap and on otherwise bare feet are old black shoes, well-rotted by salt water. Upright in his lap is a bottle with a yellow label: SAINT CECILIA RUM. The man's chin rests on the gunwale of the boat, and he stares into the shallows of the small cove called Hogsty Bay.

On the bottom, the flayed skin of an angelfish is yellow-gray, shaped like a face. Through a faint rainbow of petroleum, the white sand is scattered with cans and bottles in welt-colored crusts of coralline algae, and sand-shrouded old conchs, each with a hole knocked in the whorl, and white coral skeletons poxed with red hydrozoans.

A tubeworm blows its ghostly waste. In the small surge of tropic tides, as the bottom breathes, the faceless face rises and falls.

The catboat rolls and surges with the loading of the fuel drum; water laps against the quai. The drunk frowns, coughs and scratches, staring downward. He tries to spit; the spit hangs from his chin. Cursing, he wipes his mouth, then drains the bottle and dashes it into the water; the reef fish dart from point to point, in liquid sparkles.

butterfly fish

beau gregory

The bottle fills, and the yellow label shimmers; in the silence, in slow motion, the bottle sinks to the white sand, does a slow roll, and comes to rest beside the face-shaped skin.

Shuddering, the drunkard glowers at the small sailor in the T-shirt.

Black Honduran!

How dat go, Vemon?

Nemmine, mon, he don't bodder me. Speedy doin fine.

Goddom Vemon. (*sighs*) Dat de last fuel drum you got dere, Honduras?

Dat de last one.

Fueled up, Vemon? Well, let's go, den! Ready, Vemon? You got any last-minute engagements?

I waitin on *you*, Byrum! Ain't I settin in de boat? We goin to *sea*!

Byrum slings his gear into the boat. He winks at Speedy.

Dat a sailor talkin, hear de way he do? De thing
was, I had to give more sweetenin to my intended
dere, Miss Gwen—hey, mon?

Byrum socks Speedy on the arm.

Touchin de bun! Don't have none of dat down
in Honduras?

Oh, we *heard* about dat, I guess.

Heard about it! Dass all dem niggers do down dere
is coot! Goddom Honduras! Me and de Coptin,
we ain't never goin back dere in dis life, I tell
you dat!

You and de Coptin! Vemon, you don't shift you
ass, it gone get *wet!*

The reef fish jump as an oar blade darts downward—
choonk!—and parts the oil slick; tepid bubbles rise,
and a faint grating sound, as the oar probes for a footing in dead coral. The boat is shoved stern foremost
from the slip.

In the bow, Speedy mans the port oar; Byrum, astern,
mans the starboard. Vemon sits sullen in the bilges.

The boat slides across the harbor toward the green
schooner. At the commercial wharf, a crewman on the
motor vessel *Daydream* dumps slops into the harbor;
in the clear water, the stain rolls.

What say dere! We gone see you on de banks?

No, mon! Season done with, Byrum! De onliest one
you gone find out dere is Desmond Eden!

Copm Desmond! Mon, oh *mon!*

From the water between the catboat and the *Day-dream*, a man-o'-war bird snatches up bright entrails of a tuna, kept afloat by gas caught in the bladder. From the shore, in the new heat of growing morning, blow sweet market smells: fish, blossoms, rotted coconut, papaya, creosote.

BRING DAT BOAT ABOARD OF HERE!

Byrum bends to his oar; the sun dances on his turquoise shoulders.

Hear dat, Honduras? Old Raib jumpin already!

The *Lillias Eden*, formerly a schooner. Men move about her decks, which are littered with ship's stores, fuel and water drums, stove wood, fishing gear. On her stern a raw new deckhouse is still unpainted. Her rusty hull is worn near bare of its green paint; rope fenders sag, her shrouds are frayed, her taffrail broken.

Byrum whistles.

Mon! I never think she come home from Honduras lookin poor as dat!

You in de modern time, mon: sailin boat a thing of de past.

Well, all of de same, I be sorry to see dem motors. Dass de last one you lookin at dere. Dass de last of de old-time sailin fleet.

Mm-hm. I seen her de day she sail down to
Honduras. I workin dere in French Harbour,
y'know, into de drydock, and I seen her come in
dere under sail. In Roatán. In de Bay Islands.

Well, you know den, Honduras—

I called Speedy. Cause I fast, mon. Very, very fast.

Okay den, Speedy, you see for yourself how very
bad she look now with de masts half sheared away,
and dat goddom deckhouse dat she got dere place
of de fo'c's'le.

Dass right. Modern time, mon.

De fashion dat domn thing tacked on dere! Look
like a outhouse! Look like a goddom *Jamaica* boat,
and dass de truth. *(sighs)* How come you sign on,
mon? Don't like dry-dockin?

Oh, I like it very fine. But den Old Doddy dere,
he kept after me cause he short-handed.

You gone find out why Raib short-handed!

Huh! Byrum go crew for Copm Raib cause he got
fired off de *Adams*—

I go crew cause I gots to eat, same as dis Vemon
gots to drink! I a big mon, and I gots to eat! *(strokes
violently)* Down on de banks, may be hard farins,
but mostways you has something to eat, even
if it nothin better'n hox-bill or barra!

Dass it. So one day I say, Speedy-Boy, you best
cotch turtles one time in dis life just so you know it.

Might cotch turtle, but dis ain't de number one
boat. Dey heard about de *A.M. Adams* down dere
in Honduras? *(whistles)* Sweet Christ, look at dis
turtler we got here! Got hisself another bottle!

What dat you said, Byrum?

I say I s'prise de old bastard sign you on again, Vemon, must be he desperate! Goddom Raib dere, he do better with dis vessel runnin *tourists* den sailing away down to de Cays. *(shouts)* LAST OF DE CAYMAN SCHOONERS! HOPPY SAILS AROUND DE ISLAND! SEE COPM RAIB AVERS AT WEST BAY! But he such a domn stubborn mule, ain't nothin you can tell him—

Vemon sits up, spilling rum.

You watch your mouth! Copm Raib hear you talkin into dat manner, he gone change your speech!

It *your* mouth need de watchin, Vemon. All de rum runnin out. *(quietly)* Dey only de one way de Coptin gone to hear something, and dass when you tell him. And you just de mon to do a job like dat—

Easy, mon. He only drunk—

He hidin behind dat. Dis Vemon is a pretty one, y'know—

I knowed Copm Raib gone forty year, and never a wry word!

You gone get a wry word, Vemon, you don't hide dat rum! Dis ain't no kind of Jamaica boat, mon, ever'body drunk aboard and all of dat! Dis a *turtle* schooner, mon!

You tellin *me* dat, dat help build dat vessel thirty year ago, right dere in de yard of Elroy Arch! Me 'n Elroy 'n Seth 'n Fossie, and Jim Arch!

I didn't think you ever be sober enough to 'member so much as dat, Vemon. You quite a fella, Vemon.

You think you somebody cause you went crew on de *A.M. Adams!* But I got *papers!* You can go right up dere to United States and ask if Vemon Dilbert Evers got he seaman's papers, able-bodied seaman! Ask Copm Gene on de *Tropic Breeze!* Goddom sonofabitch! I tellin you—

A silence as Byrum rests his oar; the catboat is gliding up under the hull. Byrum places a big hand on Vemon's shoulder.

No, *I* tellin *you*: shut dat dirty mouth or you goin over de side!

Mon, mon. We ain't even put to sea yet.

BRING DAT BOAT ABOARD OF HERE! DAT DE LAST BOAT!

C'mon Buddy! Throw de line down, boy, we comin up!

Byrum and Speedy bend a rope sling to the fuel drum, which is hoisted aboard: the pulley is rigged to the end of the foremast boom, and lines of a second pulley are reeved through blocks high on the foremast.

On the blue morning sky above, a heavy-headed man lays big hands on the rails.

Come up, den, Vemon! Dese fellas ain't paid to h'ist you!

Dass okay, Copm Raib—we got'm.

Copm Raib? I comin, Copm Raib! You a hard mon, Copm Raib!

Goddom it to hell, if he too drunk to get hisself
aboard of here, den hook dat hook into his pants
and hike him up ass foremost, cause dat de way dat
fool proceedin through dis life!

Byrum whistles for the sling, pointing at Vemon, who
has folded his arms across his chest.

What say, Byrum!

What say, Will! Give us a hand with dis turtler
here!

The men on deck grasp Vemon and haul him aboard;
he puts his feet down gingerly on deck, brushing himself off. Now Byrum's head appears over the rail.

Dis de right boat? Don't look like de *Eden* to *me*!

How you been keepin, Byrum?

Not bad, Will. How yourself?

Dere he is! Big Byrum! What say, mon!

What say, Athens! I pleased to meet you again!
How you been feelin?

Well, I *feelin*, dass about it.

Byrum, whistling, takes his suitcase aft into the deckhouse.

The Captain passes a propeller down to Speedy, who
is stowing oars under the catboat thwarts.

You fit dis propeller to de shaft while Will
filin de pin!

Okay, Doddy!

Raib Avers is a broad strong man in his middle fifties.
His iron hair is patched with white, his bare feet are
thick and brown, and his bold nose, in a leather face
both wide and lean, has the cast of a full-blood Indian. Lines of merriment seam his face, but his eyes,
discolored by sea weather, have a mean squint.

Byrum, hitching at his pants, appears on deck. He has
put away his turquoise shirt and now wears khaki.
With the Captain, he watches Speedy pull the catboat
aft along the hull and tie it to the rudder shaft under
the stern.

See dat black fella, Byrum? I gone make a first-class
turtler out dat fella, cause he willin. And he
smart. (*laughs*) Had to go all de way to Honduras
to find a fella meets dat description in *dese*
goddom days.

I seen'm on de quai. Tell me nemmine, he hondle
dat oil drum by hisself. Little fella like dat—
he *strong*!

Dass right. When dat boy say he do something,
he *do* it.

Beneath the stern, a face bursts from the water. The
face contemplates Byrum and the Captain, then disappears again, the black rump rolling on the emerald
surface.

NAME OF VESSEL:	*LILLIAS EDEN*
BRITISH REGISTRY:	129459
BUILDER:	N. Elroy Arch, Georgetown, Grand Cayman
RIGGED:	Schooner
STEM:	Spoon
STERN:	V
BUILD:	Carvel
NO. BULKHEADS:	3
FRAMEWORK AND DESCRIPTION OF VESSEL:	Wood Commercial
LENGTH:	59.6 (from fore part of stem to the aft side of the head of the stern post)
BREADTH:	18.1
SHIP'S ARTICLES:	*LILLIAS EDEN* Off. No. 129459; Gross 76.84; Net 69.89

Signatures	Age	Nationality	Next of Kin	Last Ship
Raib Avers	54	B.W.I	Ardith A. (wife) West Bay	*Eden*
William Parchment	44	B.W.I.	Reaby B. (wife) West Bay	*Eden*
Byrum Powery Watler	30	B.W.I.	Deloris Ebanks (sister) West Bay	*C.J. Sulphur Queen*
Vemon Dilbert Evers	48	B.W.I.	Malvena Bodden (mother) Bodden Town	*Eden*
Wodie Greaves	43	B.W.I.	James Conally (brother) East End	*Lydia Wilson*
Athens Ebanks	29	B.W.I.	Mabel E. (wife) Georgetown	*Cayman Gal*
Jim Eden Avers	17	B.W.I.	Ardith A. (mother) West Bay	*Eden*
Junior Bodden	32	Span. Honduras	Pansy B. (wife) French Hbr. Roatán	*Bonnie Jay*
Miguel Moreno Smith	28	(unknown)	(unknown)	*Desirade*

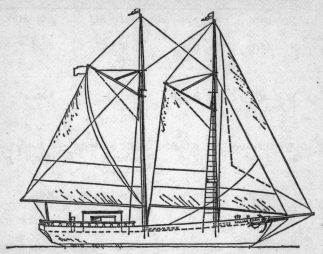

Common roof of deckhouse extended aft and to sides of vessel, providing sun and rain shelter

Shortened mainmast (boom removed) with scuttlebutt lashed to foot of mast

Engine controls tacked temporarily to housing

Taffrail

Wheel

Deckhouse

Compass in binnacle box

New housing for wheel and controls —not completed

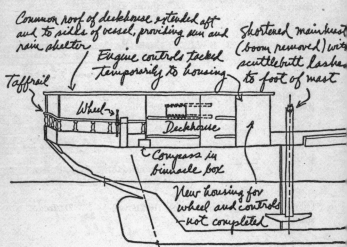

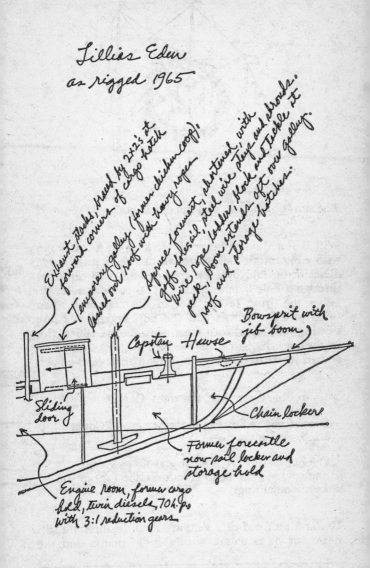

Lillias Eden
as rigged 1965

Exhaust stacks, braced by 2×2's at forward corners of cargo hatch

Temporary galley (former chicken coop) lashed over roof with heavy rope

Spruce foremast, shortened, with gaff foresail, steel wire stays and shrouds. Wire rope ladder, block and tackle it peak, boom extends aft over galley roof and storage hatches.

Bowsprit with jib boom

Capstan Hawse

Sliding door

Chain lockers

Former forecastle now sail locker and storage hold

Engine room, former cargo hold, twin diesels, 70 h.p. with 3:1 reduction gears

·2·

The sun is high now, and the day is hot.

Will is seated on the taffrail, working on a cotter pin with a big rattail file. Byrum adjusts the scuttlebutt, a diesel drum laid over on its side; water is dippered through a hole hatchet-hacked in its rusty surface. He lashes the drum to the foot of the mainmast, then turns to help Athens and the boy Buddy, who are stowing salt, sugar, corn meal, flour, beans, coffee, rice in the forward hatch. As the burlap sacks tumble together, motes of dust rise in the sun shaft of the hold.

... trouble down dere, dat right, Copm?

Dass what I tell'm, Copm Raib: me and Copm Raib, we ain't *never*—

Get out de way, Vemon! Just cause you went one voyage with me to Honduras don't mean you *know* something!

Under his striped cap, Vemon's small features are still neat, but he is gaunt, with spindle shanks and the hunch of an old man. His eyes are meat-colored and do not hold, and his teeth are rotted out of his tattered skull. Mouth a black hole, he backs off with a big circular step, bones jerking; regaining his balance, he salutes.

... come out of it all right, dat what dey sayin.

I ain't owin *dem* nothin, Byrum!

No, no, Copm, course not, only just watch out you don't go dere again or dey shoot you in de back, bein dey so angry with you.

I ain't *never* goin back! In dat country—Sponnish Honduras and den Nicaragua I talkin about— dey don't care about life!

Me and de Coptin—

Goddom it, Vemon, if you sober enough to talk, you sober enough to work! Now dese two *guardias*, dere was a fight, and one *guardia* tell de woman of de other one dat he gone slit her throat. So de other one decide he gone ambush dis fella next mornin, by de dock. Right across from where dis vessel were hauled out. So dis mon were called in to get his breakfast, an he shot'm. Once in de shoulder, knock him down into de water, and den he poke his head around under de dock and shoot'm three more time, and de last one get'm in de neck!

I guess *dat* scuttled him, okay.

Well, dat be one hell of a breakfast! *(laughs)* Dat show you what kind of fella dey have in de lands of de Sponnish, where dey call you in to get your breakfast and den shoot you! I mean to say, dat one hell of a breakfast! Call you in dere ...

Slowly, Raib stops speaking. His smile dies, his eyes tighten to a squint, and a low growl starting in his throat forms gradually into words: God *domn!*

A man has emerged from the engine hatch; he glances at the crew, then turns away, as if their work did not concern him. He has the feral air of a *bandito*, with sideburns, mustachio, bold gold teeth, hide sombrero with rawhide chin strap and rim stitching. He is in rags—torn, oil-soaked T-shirt, torn striped-pajama pants patched with heavier materials than itself, and pointed shoes without laces or socks. One sallow hip protrudes from the torn pants seat, and a brown cigarillo, rolled by hand, sits extinguished in his mouth.

Dass him! Dass de one! Call hisself Brown, but he one of dem goddom Sponnish! Dat bent shaft, dat were nothin but faulty installation of de port engine by dat hombre dere! Tell me he engineer, and den he go and do a job like dat!

Though the Captain takes no pains to lower his voice, the man in the sombrero is expressionless; he gazes without interest at the island.

Dass him! He stupid! Dat de mon! He stupid as a goat!

Byrum and Athens fit a kerosene light into the binnacle; Vemon bends over them, hands on knees, trying to steady himself. Eventually the wheel is to be placed in the new pilot's cabin, overlooking engine house, deck and sea, but for the moment in remains in its old position in the stern.

Now dat is a hell of a arrangement. Dat is a *hell*
of a arrangement, dat is. De mon at de helm
cannot even see where de ship *goin*! On all de boats
I ever sailed on, I never seen nothin to beat *dat*!

He say he gots to leave it dat way, Byrum, bein he so
broke. Spent all his money up down in Honduras,
poor fella. Say he got to get a pile of turtle to pay
for de next part of de job.

Well, dat is bullshit, Athens! All de money de mon
made smugglin up dere to Cuba, buyin dem
Cuban sharkskin? All dem years of runnin guns
all over de Caribbean Sea?

All of de same, we gone make dis voyage with a
bent shaft on de port engine, and with no cook,
and with dis wheel in dis crazy way where de
helmsman can't see nothin but straight up de
bunkey of de fellas layin in dere berths—

Byrum straightens up.

No *cook*?

ASK ONE OF DEM TO RIG A LANTERN,
AND LOOK AT DAT! TWO OF DEM
DOIN IT, AND A THIRD ONE LOOKIN
ON!

We tryin to figure dis arrangement you got here,
Copm—

Nemmine dat! It go fine if de mens know dere
job! But we ain't never gone to sail if you fellas
hang around back here!

Propeller done now, Copm!

The Captain turns to glare at Will.

Heave up de anchor, den! We don't get underway, we gone lose a day's fishenin on de banks, and de season gettin away from us already! Go on dere, Buddy! You fella Brown, turn dem engines over, till we see de vibration! Wait now! Get dat boat aboard of here!

Speedy has brought the catboat alongside. Pulleys lowered from foremast and boom are hooked to ring bolts in the catboat's bow and stern; they shriek as the boat is hoisted from the water. Byrum holds her clear of the hull by bracing an oar against the thwarts, careening the boat well over on her side so that her keel is high enough to clear the rails as she is swung inboard and lowered to the deck. The sun glistens on the green algaic slime that fouls her bottom. The boat is lashed down on her side, keel outboard, to conserve deck space.

Get on dere, Buddy! Get on dat windlass with de rest!

Copm Raib? Reportin for duty, Copm Raib!

Whirling, Raib bangs into Vemon, who is pitching up and down the deck. Vemon retreats. The Captain follows.

I reportin to work here, Copm Raib!

What you got into dat shirt?

Raib shoots his hand into Vemon's shirt and jerks the bottle out; they watch a button roll on edge across the deck.

Copm Raib—

Raib hurls the bottle out over the harbor.

> Goddom fool! Ain't you fool enough already
> without dat?

Vemon trembles. Fingering his shirt, he shakes his
head violently back and forth, eyes closed.

> No, brother! I goin back ashore! Copm Raib? Now
> hear me, brother—I *needs* dat to tide me over! I
> can't sail with you! You gots to put me ashore!

Vemon abandons his shirt; his hands wave, finger
bones spread. Raib grasps his scrawny arm and propels
him aft down the companionway and into the deckhouse.

> In dis goddom lot I got two drunkards, one thief,
> and five idiots, dass what I got!

The crew mutters.

> Well, he lucky he got *dat* much, flyin up de way he
> do—
>
> One of us got to be thief and idiot both, cause countin
> de boy dey only seven here!
>
> Got no cook, Athens say—

The men glance at the Captain's son, Jim Eden Avers,
known as Buddy, a thin-limbed boy of seventeen who
wears a long-billed cap on his long head.

Buddy looks away.

The windlass is an old-time oak-and-iron barrel drum cranked by hand levers. Byrum and the ragged man called Brown pump the port lever, Speedy and Athens Ebanks the starboard. As the heavy anchor chain clanks aboard, the mate, Will Parchment, rakes it clear of the windlass with an iron hook. In oversized blue pants, Buddy bends forward, as if he were helping, but there is nothing for him to do. His finger trails across the windlass baseplate: LUNENBURG FOUNDRY CO.

. . . Lunenburg? De *Bluenose,* mon! Lunenburg, Novy Scotia! Dat were de home port of de *Bluenose!*

Dat be a good name for Vemon—Blue Nose!

De *Bluenose!* Dat were de most famous of all de fishin schooners, mon! Won all de races! And dis vessel dat you standin on, she modeled after her! Dis vessel, and de *Goldfield,* and de *Lydia Wilson,* and den de *A.M. Adams!* De spoon bow—

Will straightens, pointing toward the south shore of the town.

No, mon. All dem vessels was built by Elroy Arch right dere behind dat grape tree where I pointin at, and dey were modeled after de old *Noonan.* De *Angeline Noonan,* dat were brought here in 1932. And de *Noonan* were a Gloucesterman, off de Grand Banks!

Will, de *Noonan* were in de *Bluenose* style!

Noonan! Bluenose! Out of *Lunenburg!*

Call it Goony Burg, de way dey make dis
windlass . . . fuckin mon-killer.

The anchor looms and washes free. In the white marl
sliding off the fluke, a polychaete worm, transparent,
reflects a sun-spot in its blood; at the surface it writhes
once and is snatched by a long houndfish, drawn by
the roil in the harbor water.

PUT DEM ENGINES INTO GEAR!

Lumber stored here for
making turtle racks in
hold

Deckhouse quarters
for six (ventilation by two
ports in hull side)

Food storage hatch

Upper/lower
berths

Binnacle
box

Upper/lower
berths

Wheelhouse
(incomplete)

Outline of common
roof

Auxiliary fuel
and water

Main cargo hold
(now engine room)

Lillias Eden, stem to stern

Two upper and lower berths against bulkhead

Hatch covers for main cargo hold: wood for galley fuel stacked on top

Cathead for securing kedge and chain.

Galley

Bilge pump

Catboats secured on deck (balanced on bilge)

Oh, de fact dat de *Noonan* were built after de lines of de *Bluenose*, and she were *American*-built, y'know—dat was supposed to mean something. (*grunts*) In dem days America was so far away dat dey thought it must be something grand. De *Noonan* sunk six years after she got here, and de Yankee owners seen quite clear dat it were only Cayman care and Cayman knowledge dat was keepin her afloat in dem six years. Dat goddom Yankee oak never stood up; her timbers was rotten from her keelson to her waterway! Dat is why de next boat dey had built was built in Cayman. Cayman mahogany. Dey went to work and built a vessel for Caymans dat were very well suited to de purpose of de Grand Banks.

No good, huh?

Well, I wouldn't say dat much, Speedy. De Cayman vessel is built very well. Used mahogany, and den ironwood, fiddlewood, pompero—all dem good old woods dat used to grow right in de island. (*suddenly excited*) I seen dis vessel slickin along at thirteen knots! Thirteen!

Ain't much of a harbor in Cayman, from what I seen. Ain't like French Harbour. In de Bay Islands.

In Cayman, Speedy, if a heavy storm strike dere, you be very lucky if you save your vessel. Dat place in de North Sound, dat de only place. Deep water right up to de mangroves. (*whistles*) Oh, mon. It astonishin to know de quantity of wind dat's in a hurricane, and what a hurricane can do ...

Athens Ebanks sinks down on the wheel cable housing and takes the spokes of an ancient wooden helm. Like Vemon, he is thin and soiled. He coughs constantly, and sucks cheap cigarettes. The nostrils flare in a nose that looks pushed back; he has buckteeth and a weedy mustache. He wears his cap so that its bill sticks straight out to one side of his head, and his shirt, undershirt, baggy pants all flap and fly, as if he were coming apart—even his shoes flap—but invariably his collar is tight-buttoned, as if this one button held him together. Whenever possible he is asleep, slumped, seated, sprawled, coiled, curled or prone.

Beside him, Speedy gazes at the shore; he turns a small brown wrinkled fruit in his black hand.

In dis season I got plantains. In Roatán. Banana. Plantains. Yams. In de Bay Islands. I got it made, mon. And I don't have to go lookin for my job. Ever'body after Speedy, cause he fast, mon, very very fast . . .(sighs) How you feelin?

Okay. Pretty good.

Can't leave it behind you on de dock, I guess.

I feelin better.

Well, dass very fine. Like dis nice niece-berry? Dis a very fine little fruit. Come from your own island. Come from de island of Grand Cayman.

Um-hm.

In de Bay Islands, call dat sapodilla. From de dilly tree.

FORWARD ON DE PORT! BACK ON DE STARBOARD!

3:34 P.M.: the *Lillias Eden* turns slowly in a circle. The starboard engine is shifted to neutral, then forward gear, and water spins along the hull. The vessel makes headway, moving offshore.

YOU, WILL! AND BYRUM! RIG DE
FORES'L!

Dark coral heads sink away into the deeps, and the
water changes from emerald to dark green.

Port, Athens!

PORT!

Due south and steady!

STEAD-DAY!

The harbor, no more than a shallow bight on the
western shore, flattens out against the island as the
pastels of Georgetown drop away. The *Eden* trudges
down to Southwest Point, where the coast bends eastward. At Pull-and-Be-Damned, the black bone of a
wreck bursts from bright surf on the fringing reef.

Stowaway! Copm Raib? We got a stowaway!

The Captain goes forward to the fo'c's'le hatch.

Ain't us he hidin from. COME OUT DEN,
WODIE! No, mon, ain't us. He hidin from de
constables of Bodden Town. Want *dis* fella for
murder. (*grins*) Dass de kind of crew you gets dese
goddom days, yah mon! A thief, two drunkards and
a murderer—all de rest is merely idiots!

The men come forward one by one.

A figure emerges from the hatch. Though he is black,
the man's hair and skin are whitish; in the twilight he

looks silver. He dusts himself, and a mist of white blows away on the sea wind; he laughs a high sweet laugh. In the dry whiteness of his face, which has caked where he has sweated, his mouth looks raw and wet. He is barefoot, in clownish pants too small for him and a bright checkered vest cut from coarse sacking. One eye is blind.

> See dat, Copm Raib? I makin myself a pretty shirt out some dem old flour sacks where I was layin! Passin de time, y'know!

The Captain grunts.

> Maybe some you fellas knowin Wodie Greaves— he one dem duppies from down East End. (*winks at Wodie*) And dis is what calls dereself a crew! Dey ain't much, Wodie, but I intendin to make turtlers out of dem, so don't go murderin too many in de night!

Wodie Greaves comes forward. In an unlined face that has not aged, the good eye is round and open and the smile is new.

> How do. I pleased to meet you.

The men do not take Wodie's hand. Wodie turns toward the Captain, who is laughing.

> Now, Copm Raib, maybe dese fellas do not know dat I am no murderer, and do not know dat you could be teasin dem along. De constables of Bodden Town, dey only wishin to take me into custody to protect me from dem dat wished me hurt. But I sayin to myself, now, Wodie Greaves, you might's well sail down to de Cays, make a penny to get on with life till times go better.

Northeast trades, and casuarinas on the leeward strand, bent away into the west; over Prospect Church veer frigate birds on long black wings. Beyond Prospect, misted by sea spume, Bill Eden Point and Old Jones Bay sink away into the land.

The island turns.

The *Eden* passes from the lee into the white-capped stone-blue chop of the deep ocean.

A wash of white: a wave rises high on the port bow, hangs, slaps, collapses. Bright brown sargassum weed sails by, and a flying fish skips free of the bow, skidding away on thin clear wings into the blue oblivion.

To the west, migrating land birds, spinning north.

Athens, at the helm, is dozing. Vemon is snorting in his bunk. Raib and Brown stare fixedly into the engine hold; they run the new engines at half speed. Watching his father, Buddy Avers lies on a soft coil of old rope, his hands in an attitude of prayer beneath his cheek. Squatted by the galley, washing coffee cups in a galvanized tin cup, Speedy chatters to himself. On the galley roof, Wodie Greaves sings "Yellow Bird" as he sews his checkered shirt.

Byrum and Will, forward, have hoisted the stunted foresail and the jib, to take advantage of the wind; the sails are grimy, and the foresail has a big patch of dark material under the gaff. Gazing upward at the sails and the blue Caribbean sky, Will lets his pinched face crack open in a grin, ignoring the oil stink on the wind eddies, and the vibration beneath his hard bare feet.

Eden like a wild horse, Byrum. Got to hang *on* to her.

Not no more. She make eight with a fair wind and both dem diesels, she be doin good.

Mon, I seen dis vessel average eleven mile an hour for two-twenty mile, all de way down to de banks! Good stiff boat! See dat? Don't throw big sheets of spray every time she roll; she behave nice in any kind of sea.

Well, she a good boat in a quarterin sea, I say dat much. She ride better den de *A.M. Adams;* she ride more straight.

Oh, she a pretty little vessel, mon! Every frame in her Cayman mahogany, every one.

Cupping the rain water in the port catboat, Byrum washes the rope tar from his hands. Will splashes water on his face, but on an instinct straightens slowly and gazes back toward the island. In the ocean sun, the old rain glistens on his cheeks. The permanent tobacco bulge in Will's jaw gives his face an odd mis-shapen cast; his rare smile, smiled shyly, bares his stained bent teeth.

Byrum? See dis port boat? She a new boat but she leakin. And dat is because we never took de time to put flowers on de bow before we launched her.

Know something else? We sailin on a Saturday, with a new moon.

Will Parchment nods.

I told him best wait and sail tomorrow, but he say de season gettin away from us already.

Yah, mon. We sailin very late. De *Adams* out dere somewhere in de Cays, but she must be pretty nearly set to sail for home.

In round-rimmed hat of tattered palm thatch, sky-colored jerkin without sleeves and dungarees torn off like britches at the knee, the barefoot mate looks like a sailor of Old Isaac's time; Byrum, in sneakers and clean khakis and an oil-stained khaki visor cap with emblem of gold anchors crossed on black, is a modern seaman of the merchantmen. Will is a white man, weathered for his age, knotty and wizened. Byrum looks younger than his thirty years; in whitish skin he has the features of a black man, and his gat teeth are helter-skelter in his jaw. From Byrum, everything spills out; he has a big voice, big teeth, big nose, big ears, big wrists and hands, and big pigeon-toed feet.

A.M. Adams, mon! I bet she got better den three hundred turtle right dis minute!

He stands beside Will, who is still gazing off into the north. The wind nags at the tatters of Will's hat.

Land sunk out already, Byrum.

She sunk out?

Yah, mon. Land sunk out. All dese years I seen dat Old Rock sink away, and still I wonderin if I ever see her rise again.

Byrum relieves Athens at the helm, as Venus rises.

Dere de evenin star.

Twilight. The men squat in a semicircle at the galley door. Their forks click on tin plates of beans and rice and each has a mug of coffee at his feet.

Vemon appears in the companionway. The sea has sent him reeling off rails, fuel drums, cabin side. Hurting his arm, he looks confused, then curses. At a fuel drum, he clings, panting, glaring at the rest; his shapeless pants snap thinly in the wind.

Look what comin! Smelled de food and out it come!

Smelled dat de work was done, most likely—
what say, Vemon!

I say SHIT! *Dat* what I say!

Dat *his* message, dat he give his shipmates

                              had enough of

your bad mouth down to Honduras!

Ain't nobody call me for my supper, Copm Raib, dat de kind of ship dis is!

Arms folded across his chest, Vemon is pitched by the sea into the galley door. He is shoved out again by Speedy.

You want supper I give it to you, but get your ass out dis galley!

Listen to dat! Black Honduran! Tellin me what I must do!

Dass right! Black Honduran!

Speedy de cook, he got de right—

No, mon! I cook dis evenin so we can eat, but I never sign on as no cook!

Dass what *he* think! Raib got *dat* fella fooled *good*!

Anyways it mighty fine.

Athens belches.

I never knowed dat black people could cook. (*winks*) Dey ain't nothin dat dis Speedy-Boy can't do!

Speedy pushes a plate of food against Vemon's chest.

Well, my father he left my mother, and den she went down to de copra plantation. When I were six; I were de oldest one. So I learn to cook: call dat school days, mon. With me it were do or die.

Where your partner? Don't he eat? I knowed he didn't talk, but don't he eat?

Brownie? He layin down dere in his bunk. He come when he get hungry.

Copm say in de ship's articles dey calls him Smith.

Sometime Smith. Sometime Brown. I calls him Brownie. He show up dere in Roatán a few years back, after de hurricane. Plenty like Brown down along de Sponnish shores, don't come from no place—more and more, like, seem to me.

Dass right. Plenty like dat. No home, no name, got no people anyplace. Just livin along.

Used to be nobody knew his doddy, but now dere's plenty dat don't know dere *mother*. Modern time, mon.

Dass right. Just livin along.

So den Brown had no job to speak about, so he come along with me. We learn cotch turtle. And sometimes maybe rig us a few nets, go back to Roatán, cotch couple turtle dere. Green turtle. In de Bay Islands.

Green turtle! What *you* know about it? Mon know about green turtle got to be a turtler! And de turtler come from Grand Cayman!

Hush up, Vemon.

The man called Brown appears on deck; the crew falls silent. He gapes and stretches, then strikes a pose with hands on hips, rocking a little on spread feet, pelvis cocked forward, sombrero tipped down onto his nose. The Captain glares at him.

Well, come along dere, Brownie!

Brown saunters over to the galley, and Speedy fixes him a plate; Speedy says something quiet, and after a moment the man shrugs. He flips his sombrero to the back of his dark head and squats down on his heels to eat. He chews slowly for a little while, then raises his head to speak, but since his mouth is full of food, his utterance is lost. Fork at his mouth, he looks slowly from man to man; uncomfortable, they nod and look away, then get up one by one and scrape their plates over the side and dump them into the galvanized tub before moving aft to the stern.

Brown squats by the galley door, eating alone. In the dark wind overhead, the canvas mutters. The mast rolls.

Speedy rigs a bucket to a line and drops it into the black sea; it draws a phosphorescent streak through the night plankton. He splashes salt water into a tub and tosses after it a cake of mustard-colored soap.

Buddy brings Byrum a plate of food and a mug of coffee, and relieves him at the wheel.

Where de hell de bacon? Don't we got meat aboard of here?

Will lights the kerosene lantern in the binnacle. The light dimly illuminates the bunks, which are littered with clothes, sacks, a small duffel and a cardboard suitcase. Vemon has the upper bunk on the port side, Athens the lower; Will and Byrum are upper and lower to starboard. The forward bunks, running transversely across the back wall of the wheelhouse, are occupied by Raib and Buddy. Speedy bunks with Brown down in the engine room.

Where dat Wodie sleepin? In de fo'c's'le?

Yah. Look to me like he some kind of Jonah.

No, mon. He a very nice fella. Kind of fufu, but he ain't too fool to work with.

Athens and Vemon crawl full-clothed into their berths and curl around the litter: Athens does not remove his cap. His cigarette glows in the darkness; he is smoking as he sings.

I knowed by de way you hold me, darlin ...

Don't all dat smokin make you cough?

I coughed every day of my life. I used to it. I be coughin in de grave.

Well, lend me a cigarette—we partners, ain't we?

Here, goddom it—

Never *could* keep money, y'know. Prob'ly you too young to 'member de time when Vemon Dilbert Evers could had bought dat whole stretch of West Bay Beach, from de marl pit in Georgetown to de graveyard in West Bay! I had me dat chance in life and den I lost it. Dat six miles of beach weren't worth nothin den. Old Honey, she say, Precious—

Precious?

Hon say to me, Precious, dat old sand ain't never gone to do you one bit of good. I say, Hon, when all my money gone and I am old, I still have dat land, and it better'n nothin. Why, boy, if I knew den what I know now! You hear me, Athens? If I had bought dat beach before de Yankees got to it, I'd be a millionaire! (*sighs*) And now I gettin old, and I got nothin.

Precious! Dat old whore never call him Precious in her life. Call him a lot of things but never call him dat! To hear dis fool run on like dis dat never owned a catboat, even, let alone de money to buy dat beach—

Copm Raib?

Oh, mon, de black mon dat woman took up with were ugly as a gorilla, and she a white woman, mon, so dis upset poor Vemon dere. Dat day in de Standard Bar, Vemon were drunk and usin his mouth de way he do, so dis black fella, he toss some alcohol on our poor old shipmate dere and toss a match after dat, to sot'm on fire, see if dat shut'm up. Well, it were shortly after Vemon left de hospital dat he ask to sail with me down to Honduras. He were very drunk dat day, too, and he told me he not goin to sail away from home without a case of rum, and after dat he told me dat he had papers, and dat a seaman dat had papers ought to get an extra half share, and I told him he could take dem papers—

I hearin you, Copm Raib!

Dass good! Might learn something!

I had good jobs and plenty! Steamshippin! Had my papers, and I been to other parts! Stead of signin on with you, I'd of done better to go up dere to United States, see if dey couldn't use a good mon up *dat* way—

You *had* good jobs, dat is right, in de days dat you could still hondle yourself and call yourself a deckhand! But de only jobs you gone get now is with domn fools like me dat take you along just to give you a rest from your own self!

I 'preciate dat, Copm Raib! I—

You 'preciate dat enough to do your work? Cause no mon here gone corry you, by Jesus!

A silence. Raib looks around him.

Buddy? You standin de first watch tonight?
Well, speak up, boy, you feelin seasick? Cause
on watch you gots de men's life in your hands, dey
ain't no lyin down. Dis here a empty part of de
bleak ocean, but dey could be a trader goin across
from de Windwards over to Belize, and dis vessel
ain't got runnin lights and all like dat to let'm know
dat fools is comin at'm out de dark, you hear me
now? You hear me?

No runnin lights, no, and no fire equipment, no life
jackets, no nothin—

Hear de way he shout? He scare'm fore he learn'm.

You fellas best listen here and stop dat mutterin!
I gone tell you a old-fashion story about standin
watch, and den I ain't gone to speak about dis
motter any more. In de days of my youth was dis
turtle coptin, a MacTaggart, I believe, dat dey call
him Fightin Mac. And dis vessel had a cargo of
turtle for Port Antonio. And he speakin to his crew
like I speakin to you now. So he say, dis is God's
own sailin ship, so when I gives an order, I don't
want to see no mon walk or run, I want to see him
fly dere, like a angel. (*laughs*) Like a *angel*! But
dere was dis little Miskita Indian, and dis Indian
fell alseep durin de time of his watch. And dere
come down a press of wind, and because dis vessel
was not steered in de proper fashion, de bow was
drawed under, and one of de crew was washed over
de side, and drownded. Got a mouthful of sand, as
de old people say.

A long pause.

A mouthful of sand.

The Captain looks from man to man.

Well, Fightin Mac, he made dis little Indian stand a forty-eight-hour watch, and all of dis time he beat'm with a knout of rope. So when dey come ashore dere, in Jamaica, dis little Indian, he went to de insane asylum—*dass* de kind of shape dat poor fella was in after his voyage with Fightin Mac . . . Now dat is a old-fashion story, and I hopes dat you fellas reap some sense from it. Cause I only sayin what is fair when I say you ain't much of a crew. I got to *make* a crew out of dis lot, and I mean to do it.

See, Buddy? Dat de north star. Goes very bright, and den she fades again, every four days. Dat is one thing you can count on. Everything else in this goddom world changin so fast dat a mon cannot keep up no more, but de north star is always dere, boy, de cold eye of it, watchin de seasons come and go.

Abruptly, Raib stands and turns his back upon his son and, hands in pockets, swaying with the ship, gazes northward up the silver wake.

It were watchin on de night dat you were borned, and it be watchin when dat night comes dat you die.

Polaris

·3·

wind

black clouds across the stars

night squalls

Speedy relieves Buddy.

Wodie relieves Speedy.

Vemon relieves Wodie.

In the sun's imminence, the horizon to the east expands, and high in the west, toward Swan Island, a lone cloud following the night is turning pink.

During the night, a migrant swallow has come aboard. Borne back toward the south, it bills water from a vibrating puddle of fresh rain in the rim of a fuel drum.

The wind has slackened but the daybreak sky is a dead yellow that turns the sea to glimmering gray. Bruised masses shroud the sun, and an iron gleam is cast on the wet surface of the deck.

Trousers hanging, rubbing his eyes with fists, Raib appears in the doorway of the deckhouse and gazes balefully to windward. The sea, roiled suddenly by squall, turns a soft black. Soon rain is pelting on the deckhouse roof, running off in wind-whipped strings. Raib cups it in his hand and splashes his face, then drinks some, gasping.

I tellin you, Vemon, to drink fresh rain dat way is something *good*. Better den rum, darlin.

Dass what dey call fair-weather rain! After *dat* rain come fair weather!

Raib, who has turned away, whirls back.

Fair-weather rain! Listen to dat! De wind gone rise again today, and be just as bad again tomorrow! *Mon!* I suppose you too drunk to see de sky last evenin? We gone to have *wind*, mon!

Vemon retracts his neck into his bony shoulders. A limp collar much too big for him and the big striped cap that presses down his ears makes the helmsman's neck look thin and unprotected. Though sober now, he is still shaky. He gums and mutters, sucking his lower lip; he hums and curses, casting dark looks at the world from beneath his cap.

WIND!

The wind rises as the morning grows, to twenty knots or better, blowing crests off the big seas that cross the small bows of the *Eden*. The broken blues are flecked with torn sargassum.

Dat gulfweed never die, y'know—dat same piece dere were floatin by in Guineaman times, when old Neale Walker sunk de *Genoese* on de Pedro Bank.

In the wheelhouse, the Captain stares into the south. On the floor, Buddy sits reading, his back to the deck-house wall. Beside Buddy is a red scholar's bag of imitation leather.

I were not lookin for dis wind, I tellin you dat.

Vemon call dat rain fair-weather rain—

Fair-weather rain! You hear me, boy? Don't listen to dat fool—he fill your head with trash! De weather is something dat is too important to be a fool about if you wants to keep your life on de bleak ocean! (*somberly*) I 'spect you to watch dat sky very careful dis evenin, and tell me what you read dere.

I try to, Papa.

Tryin not enough if a *hurricane* comin down on you, I tell you dat! You got to *do* it!

Raib bangs the bulkhead with the flat of his palm, then speaks again.

When de sun's goin down on de horizon, a turtler must look out to de sunset. Supposin you havin a red sunset, and when you look back into de east, you see red above de blue. Well, dat is good weather: moderate weather or calm. Blue above de red means blusterous weather, prob'ly squally or plenty of breeze, and if you see it real gray, dat means blusterous weather, too. Red evenin sky and underneath is dark—well, dat is good red weather.

Raib turns to face the boy for the first time, and now his voice is quiet and intense.

Now where de wind will be blowin *from* depend on de way dat de stars hang. If de Milky Way hang on a northeasterly-south-southwesterly range across de sky, dere will come a southeasterly wind. East-to-southeasterly wind. If you see her range more southeasterly and northwesterly, dat means a north-easterly wind. And if she rangin almost west to east, de wind will be southwesterly . . .

This is the U.S. Weather Station at Swan Island. Here is the report: For the Southwest Caribbean, winds east and southeast, nineteen to twenty-five knots, through Monday. State of the sea: choppy. Barometric pressure at sea level: twenty-nine decimal nine nine and steady.

Got a radio, huh—*dat* something new!

It new, okay, but it don't *send*. Dey messages comin at me from all over de goddom Caribbean, but come down to *sendin,* de sonofabitch is quiet as a conch!

Raib turns in time to see Byrum wink at Athens. Byrum clears his throat as Athens grins.

One time I was over to Swan Island; went up dere to de weather station. Couldn't come near, dem Yankees got so many bad dogs to keep you off.

Spies, mon. Got spies in Caymans, too, most likely.

What dey spy on Swan Island? De sprat birds? Used to be de Glidden family raise plenty nice cattle over dere—now de Yankees in dere with bad dogs!

Bad dogs protect de spies, mon. One thing spies don't like, and dat is people spyin on dem. Oh, dey *hates* dat, mon!

Well, what dem Yankees doin is, dey broadcastin to Cuba—we heard all dem spies yellin at de time of de Bay of Pigs. Got dem bad dogs dere to keep people off while dey tellin de Cubans what dey s'posed to be thinkin about Cuba. After dey gets done with dat, dey tell dem all about de land of de free and de home of de brave.

As Speedy watches, Will rigs trolling lines, baiting his hooks with strips of white sail canvas smeared with lard. The lines bend away to leeward, over the rolling wake, dipping and sailing in the wind. In the distance, northbound plover, dark and fast, beat across the long slow courses of the shearwaters.

Call dat a bait?

When I ain't got nothin better. *(sighs)* Copm Steadman dere on de *Majestic* used to say dat in de spring dey eat bird meat half de time, dey was so many of dem periodical birds comin aboard—snipes and all like dat. Now de people killin *everything*, and dey ain't nothin in de month of April but a few dem little swallers.

Maybe we get fish dis day, Mist' Will. You all set dere for de greediest one.

One time under sail, crossin de banks, we hit de tides correctly and we got three hundred pound of fish in one hour and a half. Three hundred pound, mon. On two lines. We got jacks, and den we got bonita, and den we got dorado, and den we got albacore.

Maybe de boat cotch better under sail. So quiet dat way—she just rush along.

De only thing is, now she go straight, she don't have to beat. If de wind be fair or no fair, she go straight. Dat right, Copm Raib?

Well, good men hard to get now for de sailin boat— de work is harder, and dey work in de night and in de day. De times is changin. You fellas wantin dis goddom progress cause you are lazy. I never wanted it some way, but I got to get on with life, so I make my peace with it.

Dass de way de world go—modern time, mon.

Modern time, huh? In de old days, I wouldn't have no eighteen children to rear up like I got now, cause a mon could count on de half of dem bein dead before de age of ten—only de strongest ones survivin. Now dey *all* survivin, just like Buddy dere. Call dat progress? Children by de litter—can't even remember de names! Buddy dere, he Wordsworth or Jim Eden—

Sonny is Wordsworth, Papa. I Jim Eden.

Contemplating his son, Raib nods his heavy head.

Jim Eden. Dass what de world calls *dat* one.

Dem Edens is kin to you, ain't dat so, Copm?
Desmond and all dem?

No, mon! We ain't no kind of kin to Desmond
Eden!

The swallow flutters in the water on the drumhead.
Soon it rises and circles out onto the sky, then skims
back again, hanging in the air one moment before
settling on a crossbar of the shrouds. It preens its
breast and settles close, riding south into the wind.

Noon.

Athens relieves Will.

With a gaunt sextant, Raib takes a reading on the
angle of the sun with the horizon, then returns to the
deckhouse and pulls a book of tables and a hydro-
graphic chart from under his mattress. He spreads the
chart on the deckhouse floor. Its creases are worn and
greasy, and he moves carefully to keep it from falling
apart.

H.O. 394: Punta Herrero to Cabo Gracias a Dios.

On his knees, Raib traces his course with a thick
finger.

See dat, Athens? Sixteen degrees and 40 minutes.
And I right on de point, boy, right on de point!

Well, dass good. Better right on de point den right
on de reef, dass what Copm Desmond say.

Copm Desmond! De only one in Caymans calls him
dat is Desmond Eden!

Raib glares out the door, where Athens, staring away
outboard, is whistling. With Athens' head averted, the
bill of his cap is aimed straight at his Captain, who
grunts and bends his head again to his old chart.

We be comin up onto de Gorda Bank in a little
while. We pass Cay Gorda long about midnight.

Just so we pass it, Copm, dat is de main thing.

South of latitude 17, the *Eden* nears the continental
shelf. The sea color changes rapidly from the night
blue of the deeps to the dark smoky blue of fifty fathoms, then more rapidly still, in the next reach, to a
roiled aquamarine. The ship is one hundred and
twenty-five miles northeast of Cabo Falso, in Honduras.

. . . calls dis Misteriosa Bank. Cause dey can't find it.

How many times you sailed dis way, Byrum?
Misteriosa Bank over dat way westward, maybe a
hundred mile. Misteriosa Reef, *dat* is de place dat
nobody can find, cause it ain't on de charts at all.

Far Tortuga?

Far Tortuga is de cay dat rises on Misteriosa Reefs. Dem reefs ain't on de charts, but dere is vessels dat has come across dem all of de same! Oh yes!

Den why ain't dey reported?

Very difficult to report much when you havin a mouthful of sand, darlin. (*laughs*) Dem vessels gone!

All I sayin is, dis de most forsakenest domn part of all de oceans, dass what Copm Allie say—bad winds and bad currents and bad reefs.

Yah, mon. Say *dat* again, darlin. Three hundred mile north and south, from Cay Gorda to Turtle Bogue, and half of dat same distance eastward from de coast, out to Misteriosa Reef—all of dat is a bad place if de storm cotch you. In all of dat distance dere is not one light or one buoy or one marker in dat whole bleak ocean, and not one good harbor—

Bad place to go overboard, another thing. Dey shark dere of de biggest kind.

Hear dat? Oh, Byrum *hates* sharks, mon!

Buddy clears his throat.

Copm Desmond—

Copm Desmond?

Well, Papa, Desmond tellin dem dere on de quai about dis tiger shark come up alongside one de catboats of Copm Steadman Bodden. And de men seen he was as long as de catboat, and he foller dem, dis big black shark. So de fellas thrown him a hox-bill dat dey had drawn in de nets, and de shark take dat turtle in just one bite. And after dat de shark got excited and capsize de boat. So two de

fellas scromble up onto de keel, but de shark grob
de other mon dere, and dat were de end of him—

Dat is bullshit. Dey put all dem stories onto
Steadman now, just cause he dead. Desmond sayin
dat cause he think you child enough so you
believe'm.

Papa, dey was *men* dere listenin. I only snuck up
dere—

It don't pay to be such a booby all de time!

Well, I will say now, Copm, dere is one thing
Desmond know, and dat is shark.

DASS CAUSE HE A SHARK HISSELF! SHOW
ME DE MON DAT EVER HAD BUSINESS
WITH DESMOND EDEN AND NEVER
REAP NO HURT FROM IT!

A silence.

Byrum clears his throat to conceal a smile.

Y'see, Speedy, Desmond Eden were de main shark
fisherman of de island, but he shift; he try one thing
and if dat a failure, well, he gone again.

The Captain nods.

Tried murder once. (*laughs*) Good thing he shift
away from *dat*.

Well, Desmond turtlin again, Copm Raib—can't
do much hurt out in de cays.

And he loyal now to his family, Copm Raib!

He loyal cause he out here in de cays—ain't nothin here to coot! And de onliest reason he out here is cause if he were not, he be in jail!

In the bow, the silhouette of the windlass rolls, rises, falls, rolls, rises, falls. With each rise, its head soars on the southern skyline; with each fall, it shudders. Again the figure rises on the sky, and the ship gathers, bumping and creaking with old strains. On the wave's crest, in the beam wind, dry wisps of rigging fly at a sharp angle to the ship's direction; they point northwest by west, toward Yucatán.

The figure falls.

A hollow *boom*, a wash of seas; the tinware in the galley rings.

Raib points at Byrum.

Dem Yankees gone to change de ways of de whole island! Sweet Christ, an honest mon can't hardly find a fish no more along de island, dey so many of dem tourist boats foulin de sea! And de mon greasin de skids for dem is nobody else den Desmond Eden!

Raib stamps into the deckhouse, then reappears in the narrow doorway. He has knocked his straw hat off, baring a white line under his scalp. His breath is harsh and his voice ugly. He stoops to pick up his hat.

Copm Desmond! Oh, dere was a time it weren't like *dat*, I tellin you! A coptin were one of de island's best, he were not some goddom mongrel fella dat has to hide out down amongst de cays or dey put him in jail! *No*, mon! De *worst* of de island's men in dem days was a better mon den plenty dat I got sittin here dats calls dereself a crew.

Raib wipes his pale forehead and replaces his hat, re-pressing a bad smile. He looks his men over, then goes forward to the wheelhouse.

Athens and Byrum hoot into their hands.

Oh, mon. He say he hate Desmond for sellin out de island to de Yankees, but *dat* ain't de reason—

Mon, dey *both* pirates. Desmond talk de same way about him.

De reason is, dey two from de same pod. Copm Andrew Avers were not loyal to his family, and it were knowed to be a fact dat dis Creole woman had dis bush child by Copm Andrew—

Ssh! Not so loud, mon! (*pause*) Who tell you dat tale, Athens?

Desmond told me it! When he were drunk! He say, Bein an outside child don't bother me. De one thing in dis life dat I ashamed of is havin de same blood as dat high-minded bastard!

Byrum whoops.

Dat could be, mon, dat could be.

Oh, mon, dey both pirates! De only difference is, Desmond admit it.

Yah, mon! People sayin dat when Copm Andrew give her to Desmond, dis one here sot fire to de old *Clarinda* just to get his share of de insurance.

Well, Byrum, I do not believe dat Copm Raib would set fire to de *Clarinda*, for she were de Avers family vessel—

Will? What de hell you think paid for dem new diesels?

A silence.

Old Doddy. (*pause*) He treat me pretty fair so far.

Oh, yes. He not a hard fella to deal with until he got you where he want you; he very polite in his speech and all like dat. Dem West Bay pirates, dat be dere little way. Very agreeable. But you cotch more turtle den dey do, dey don't forgive dat—don't talk to you next mornin. No, mon. Oh, dey very agreeable so long as you leave de road clear for *dem*. (*coughs*) Raib ain't de only one.

Athens fingers the top button of his shirt, coughs again.

One time I was comin home on another vessel with a good cargo of turtle, we was way out dere north of Swan Island and broke down. And we fiddled and filed for a couple of days, and could not fix her. So dis was into de month of September, and dere was a hurricane reported down around de Windward Islands someplace, so we got on de radio for help. So de first to show up dere was another turtle boat, goin north. Well, dat West Bay coptin dat Byrum dere knows very well, he took a look into de situation, and he tell us den dat he would not take us in tow. No, mon. Say towin was too much strain on his engines. He offered to take de men off, but de vessel and her cargo could go to hell. Dis way, see, dere would be one less vessel in competition on de turtlin grounds. So we refused to abandon de vessel, and he was gettin set to leave us right dere in de way of de storm when de Administrator got him on de radio and told him if he abandon us before another vessel come to our assistance, den he better not come home to Cayman hisself. Dere was dis freighter comin, see. Well, by Christ you should had heard how he bitched at *dat*. He was hollerin dat dere was a hurricane on de way, and dat he had dis perishable cargo! (*spits*) Mon! I hope I get dat bastard in a tight spot one day. Cause dat were de first time any mon ever told me dat a turtle life were worth more den my own!

Modern time, mon. Every mon for hisself. Learn dat from school days.

Oo, *mon*. (*coughs*) I heard plenty in dis life dat I didn't like to hear, but never did I heard dat a turtle life were worth more den my own.

The gale wind on the port beam brings sheets of spray over the rails. In the ocean sun, the wet rust glitters. Sea minerals driven into the oaken deck have cured it hard, wood and iron becoming one, glinting with brine.

Truth. Dey is very hard-hearted fellas. I knowed one coptin dat got vexed cause he was asked by another vessel to drop off a ranger at Cay Gorda, and dat ranger happened to be de coptin's very own brother. So he said, How in de hell could I be responsible to collect dat mon if a storm come down, and him settin on dat rock dat is ninety miles north of Miskita Cay, and awash in time of storm? So I thought dat dis coptin meaned dat he would never risk his own brother into dat situation, but dis were not it at all; he just wanted a legal paper from dat owner sayin he were not responsible for de ranger's loss of life, y'see. Once he got dat paper, he would had dropped his brother off in hell.

Maybe he had more brothers den he knowed what to do with—

Dat could be, mon. Dat could be.

Latitude 18: the ship rolls south toward Central America.

Athens is yanked by the old wheel; he is half dozing. Raib and Brown stand at opposite ends of the new wheelhouse, looking down into the engine room. Will is perched on the slanted seat of the port catboat, caulking its seams. From the main cargo hold, Speedy, Byrum and Vemon heave up turtle nets, log floats and chunks of fossil coral used as net anchors. On deck, Wodie and Buddy stack the chunks on port and starboard side.

I thinkin dat dese old rocks was ballast. Call dem kellecks, huh?

Prob'ly de back-time people not speak English good as we do, Speedy, do dey say kellecks.

We ain't got dat word in Roatán. In de Bay Islands.

Dey *plenty* you ain't got in de Bay Islands, boy.

Why you act so disagreeable, Vemon? We gone make a first-class turtler out dis boy.

Dass right. I be very fine. Everybody tell you Speedy willin—he got a willin mind. (*nods*) I gots fifty-five acres in Roatán, mon. In de Bay Islands. And I got three cows. A mon dat got cows, he got it made. I got dis fifty-five acres dat I own all clear, got it cheap cause de people say dey ain't no water dere. Dass cause dey lazy. So one mornin I goes out dere with a shovel and at eight o'clock I starts to diggin and at two o'clock Speedy got water—*plop*! Right in de face!

Rigging a rope sling to a loose kelleck, Byrum jams it with a piece of seizing line.

Das what I told Copm Raib—when dat boy say he do something, he *do* it.

Wind. Faint reek of tar . . .

The rigging snaps and whistles. A loose kelleck rocks with the ship's roll, making small thumps on the oak deck. In the bow, the iron figure shudders with each *boom*; a roar and rush as the bow wave pours outboard and the ship reels back into the trough.

boom

. . . tellin you, boy, don't stack dem nets dat way!

How you want'm, Vemon?

Want'm? I want'm *right*, dass how I want'm! You gone be a *turtler*, boy, you gots to know how to hondle turtle *nets*. Cause de first thing about turtles, boy, is turtle *nets*!

You seen you can't humbug Speedy, so you tryin to pick on de boy, ain't dat right, Vemon?

Shit! For a mon dat got fired off de *Adams*—

How you feelin, Buddy?

I fine, thank you, Speedy.

Well, dass very fine.

Vemon relieves Athens.

Each little while the men haul in the trolling lines to clear them of drifting weeds. Byrum holds the canvas lure a moment, gazing north over the rolling wake; then he blinks, becomes aware of it again and loops it out into the sea.

Raib steps from the deckhouse, carrying the chart.

Who de fella got de watch? Byrum? Dis watch I bought—

Mine say five forty-three. And she a pretty good keeper.

Well, I be honest den, we ain't de proper distance. When I took dat position dere at noon, dis watch were wrong. So I lost de longitude.

Why de hell you buy a cheap old watch like dat, and no chronometer on de goddom vessel? Mon, oh mon. It like dat new radio-telephone you got dere!

Dass what I mean! I bought dat domn radio brand-new and she ain't worked yet! Not once!

Dass what I sayin—why you buy it if it don't work?

It brand-new, I tellin you! From out de store! If it don't work, den why de hell dey make it!

Copm Raib? If you don't know where we is, Copm Raib, den what we gone do? We can't heave to de way dat wind cuttin, not with dem currents, and Cay Gorda Reef—

What *you* know about it, Vemon? Shut up dat talk! How de hell a mon gone think with you runnin off like dat? Goddom fool! Now head her up a little, till I see what I must do!

Head her up!

Dass it—*steady*, you domn fool!

STEAD-DAY!

I say, Head her *up*! I never say, Head for Africa!

The sky is poised for the sudden dark. The swallow flutters up and down the deck, and Brown, amidships, catches it and tosses it high into the slipstream of the masts; it returns and he catches it again, and laughs. Again he throws it and again it returns; again he laughs. He casts it away, but this time the bird is caught by a wave leapt up along the hull and is sucked down and swept away into the wash.

. . . don't make dis course good, we not goin to make Cape Gracias tomorrow. And we don't make Cape Gracias tomorrow, we gone to miss a whole day fishenin.

And de season gettin late. Dem turtle gone to be headed southward. To de Bogue.

We mash up on Gorda Reef, you men ain't gone to bother yourselves about losin a day's *fishenin*, I tell you dat much! You gone to be bothered about losin your *lifes*, like plenty others from Caymans dat sailed down to de Cays. Yah, mon! A mouthful of sand, dat be your portion! (*glares*) I mean to say, men dat sailed down to dese reefs all de days of dere lifes, and dey askin me to run dese reefs which is mostly under de water! In de nighttime! In de dark!

With no proper bearins.

With no proper bearins! Dem is men dat can't learn nothin from de sea! Will Parchment settin right dere dat seen de *Majestic* mash up at Serrarers—

We only sayin—

Nemmine sayin, Byrum! Dey too many sayin too much aboard of here! (*pause*) Now, I want dis vessel steered offshore, into de southeast! Buddy, you jump forward dere and tell Brownie, cut de rpm to 1300, till I eats my supper and thinks what we must do. De rest of you fellas strike de mains'l and lash it good—just leave dat jib dere for a steady-sail. Dere plenty of breeze in de wind's eye yet, and maybe squalls.

A smoky sunset. Wind.

On the galley roof, Wodie lies upon his back, feet dangling down against the weathered boards of the galley wall. The black hairs on his leg are tight on his dark skin.

In the galley hut, in shadow, Speedy hunches on the ware chest that also serves as the cook's bench; there is headroom for a small man to sit upright. The galley was formerly a chicken coop, and the ship's ware is stacked in the hens' nesting boxes. Opposite, filling the fore wall of the hut, is a low stove forged of iron: the interior of the galley is soot-blackened from grease smoke. Heavy black pots on the ranges, plastic cups for salt and sugar. Speedy turns the sugar cup in his hand, wrinkles his nose; the dirty plastic has a gritty look and feel. He sets down the cup and wipes his fingertips on his denim shorts, as Athens watches.

Athens is leaned against the doorway, hands in pockets, fingering himself.

Over the sea wash and thump of rigging, the ring of tinware, the voices of Athens and Speedy come and go. Both talk quietly at once, in singsong.

                              seen a rat

     dirty, mon

                    food settin on de deck, mon

                                        roaches

                                             not
enough pans for one thing—no pots. I say, I give
you de best dat stove can do, but he
expect better den dat

                         got a demon, y'know. Mon dat
rage and laugh de way he do

                              come on hard with me,
I be hard right back. It like de way he treat his
boy dere—like he might treat some old kind of a
crab

     Oh, yes!

Wodie sits up, grinning. His single eye gives his quick
face a sweet and sad expression.

Dat was bad food, after dem storms. *Dat* was hard
farins. All de provision grounds uprooted, so de
women take and grate and beat all de cassava before
it spoil, cause cassava bread, dat keep a good long
while. Dey make sea grape wine and jelly, usin de
tamarind pulp for de preserves. We ate dem red
shanks, too—de crab. On lucky days we cotch red

rabbit, and den dere was parrot pot pie. And de men would go by boat to Colliers and Innerland, and Ally Land, Whitemud, all dem places, to find bullrush. Grate *dem* tubers, too, make fungie porridge out of dat, and save de trash of it for dumplins. Oh, mon! We children were glad to get *any* victuals in dose times. Hard farins, mon. Oh, yes! (*sings*) *If I had de wings of a dove* . . .

He lies back again, talking joyfully at the sky.

Oh, I know practically everything dat grows, cause I were reared up in de island, and by dat I come to know things. As a child, I made a little money plattin. Baskets. Hats. And weavin thatch rope, too. Sometime de mon cut palm tops for de family. (*sits up*) Mon puts his basket across his shoulder and puts his hands in front like dis (*gestures*), but a woman she cannot corry so, she corry it on her head.

Athens winks at Speedy, rolls his eyes, goes aft.

Mm-hm—same way in de Bay Islands, Wodie.

If I had de wings of a dove . . . Oh, yes. I can tell you something about palm tops cause dese hands have worked plenty of *dat*. Dass right. My father went away, y'know, and den my mother had to give it up since her eyes not so grand. (*shakes his head*) De thatch rope, I love doin it. Oh, I love doin dat, I can roll it fast. (*laughs*) Take three people to weave dat, y'know. Oh, yes.

He sits up, smiling, starts to speak, then stops. With Speedy, he stares at the wind banks on the evening sky. When he speaks again, his voice is somber.

Now thatch rope is de real Cayman turtlin rope: it is de best water rope you can get; you just can't beat it. Manila rope gets in water and after a while it get so slippery dat you can hardly hold it, with de moss. But dat thatch rope of Cayman, you just shake de moss right off of it, and you can pull it good as ever. Nowhere in de West Indies did dey find anything to substitute for de rope of Grand Cayman.

We gots de sisal in Roatán, but we ain't got de same thatch palm.

Well, dere is a market for thatch rope still, but it only work now for de poorer class of people. De people is had such hard times, and dey tried to profiteer off dem, grob all dey could and just pay de people little or nothin. So de people say, Well, I not gone to do *dat* no more, for I been kept down too much.

Kept down too much. Yah, mon. Dat were me.

Yah, mon. So de people say, Well, I not gone to do *dat* no more, for I been kept down too much.

Yah, mon.

The ship rolls, the ocean booms.

The ship booms, the ocean rolls.

Wodie is restless. Speedy watches him. Wodie fondles a small shard of mirror that hangs around his neck on an old string.

Speedy, dem dat accused me knowed dat it could look like I knowed something about de murder of dat child. It could look like I was an obeah worker, workin woe dere, cause dere was a basket in my house dat I always used to use for tellin what de future gone to bring. You know—just to play with and have fun, see what come to de top. Cause I didn't need no old basket to tell me things, dat was just for fun. Y'see, Speedy, I one dem people dat gets *sign* of things to come, I born with dat. Oh, dey lots of people dat gets sign, but some is more open to it den others, and I got known for it some way so dat people wanted to pay me and all dat. So it were easy to throw de blame on me.

A sound of ringing in the kettle.

What you keepin in dat basket?

Oh, lots of nothin at all—cracked bones, funny-lookin stones, old bits of wood, red beads and shiny things, sea shells, shark teeth—

He lifts the shard of mirror.

Things like dis, y'see. Keep away de Evil Eye. De Evil Eye don't like to see itself.

The mirror glints.

Evil Eye, huh?

Speedy, I see you lookin at me funny, so I tellin you now dat I never took de left-hand path, dancin widdershins, and witchin people, all of dat; I never worked obeah in my life. But de same day dat dey accused me, something tell me to turn around in de road, and dere I see one of dem take a nail and drive it down into my footprint where I left it in de white marl road dat run down past dere cabin. So y'see, it ain't de law dat made me sail from home.

Speedy is silent. Wodie lies back again, sighing.

> Oh, yes. To go up dere in dat high thicket of bush, and den cut all of dem tops in de day, and den come back out. And after all dat, you never made nothin anyways. I very hoppy I don't have to do *dat* no more. It like de old people say: I ain't gone to bother fungo with *dat*.

Speedy is silent.

> Oh, yes. I must be honest, I thought a while before I come aboard, for Copm Raib is famous in de whole length of de island for sayin his opinion just de way it come to him. But it seem like de thing for me to do was to sail down to de Cays.

The *Lillias Eden* moves off the bank into deep water. On the new course, the pitch increases, and the windlass soars and plunges on night skies.

The men crouch outside the galley, clutching their supper plates and cups, bracing hard with their legs and shoulders. The evening meal—cornbread and rice —is gulped down quickly in the weak light from the naked bulb that swings back and forth over the engine hatch.

> Bad thing we never got a fish.

> Bad sign. Not even a domn barra.

> I seen a ring around de sun

>   too rough. Water all cloudy dat way, fish can't see.

Maybe it de bait. Dat goddom lard.

Mon get sick of rice and beans. Least he could do is corry a little bacon, little cornbeef, something like dat. Mon dat don't eat meat get kind of dizzy.

Meat worth *money*, mon. Ain't like de old days. And crews ain't worth shit with so many lookin for a job.

Well, a mon dat would sign aboard of de *Eden* ought to be fed for nothin. In de insane asylum. *(laughter)* In de *insane* asylum!

Dat coffee something *bad*!

Dass cause de scuttlebutt never cleaned into de proper fashion. More oil in dere den water.

Dass right. All de food taste of dat diesel.

What say, Buddy? Got big ears dere?

Dat boy okay. He not say nothin to his doddy, dat right, Buddy?

Dat cause he scared. Raib scare'm fore he learn'm.

He back dere right now scarin poor old Vemon.

Well, Vemon deserve dat, Speedy, he such a goddom fool.

No, mon. He just *play* de fool, cause for him dass de way life go de best.

boom

The ship shudders under jolt and buffet of night seas. In the bow, legs spread, Raib keeps his balance, taking bearings on the stars.

What he up to now?

If he can figure how far we is from de point where de star is directly overhead, and den he do dat with another star, den de ship's position is at de longitude where de two lines crosses.

Shit! Dey too much weather to know where de *stars* is at, nemmine dis goddom boat!

We way out into de middle of nowhere, mon.

Athens crumples an orange cigarette package and throws it at the rail. The wind catches it and blows it back inboard, and it skids aft along the deck. He sighs, fingering his collar button.

I used to dat. Nowhere is where I been getting to all de days of my life. I like Vemon dat way—life sailin by without me.

The men move into the stern, and Speedy relieves Vemon.

. . . dis foolin round with reefs, not in de night.

We be okay. Beat out dere five, six miles off de bank, run south again till mornin.

It like Byrum say, we gone to miss a day dat way, and de season goin. We very close to May. Dem turtle gone be started south to Turtle Bogue.

Ever run south down dat way, Speedy? Costa Rica way? Limón? Ships bananas and coffee out of dere.

Cacao? Well, dat way you would pass Tortuguero.
What dey calls Turtle Bogue.

Bluefields de farthest south I sailed.

Yah, mon. I been to Bluefields.

Well, why de turtle go so far off to de southward?

Go to lay dere eggs. De she-turtle haul out on dis
long beach, black-lookin sand, y'know, with big seas
rollin in, and de he-turtle lay around dere just
behind de surf looking to coot dem as dey come
and go. Some dem big old bastard lookin to coot so
bad dat you can come up alongside and harpoon
dem, dey dat busy. You take a old board and stick
a kind of a head on it, like a turtle stickin his head
up, and by Christ he come up and try to coot *dat*.

Fall in de water, mon, you in bad trouble. You gets
grinded.

Dose he-turtle, dey like Athens dat way—dey coot
anything!

Look who talkin! I heard dat Miss Gwen gone
break her engagement to her intended dere, Mist'
Byrum Watler of Batabano, West Bay, cause he so
free with dat Canadian squints dat comes up to de
Blue Horizon.

Byrum hoots.

Now Athens, y'know, he thought he was a white
mon till he lain 'longside some dem girl come down
lately from Canada! *Dem* people is what you call
fish-belly white!

A white mon wouldn't get no Canadian squints, I
tellin you dat: dey gets plenty white up where dey
come from. Dem girls is far from home, and what
dey wants is de darker de better. (*shrugs*) It all dat
snow, dey say.

Byrum lies back with his head on his hands.

Well, anyways, about dis time of de year, de turtle have started southward to de Bogue. But de shes don't go ashore till round about de month of July, and dey some still goin ashore dere in September. Comin down to de actual deposit of de eggs, August and September is dere peaks. Course, dey goes ashore two, three times—lay maybe three, four hundred eggs by de time dey done. Likes de full moon. And de eggs hatches out two full moon after dat.

If dey makes it.

If dey makes it. Cause dem Sponnish don't let'm lay dere eggs, even, before dey turns'm. Turtle agent has de Indians rollin de she-turtle as dey comes ashore, and den when de boat come, dey send de turtles back to sea with a buoy tied to de fin, cause de seas too heavy for de boat to land dere. And de boat grob de turtle den, take dem over to Limón. Course, dey times dey *finds* her layin. Fore she comes ashore, she very coward, and she lay real quiet in de shallers; she see anything on de beach, she slip back into de sea. But once she started, mon, de ain't no stoppin: she go right on with dogs diggin out de eggs fast as she drops dem, and de goddom Indians tyin de buoy to her fin.

Got calipee poachers, too, y'know. Just grob dat turtle and spin her over and carve dat calipee right off, and leave de rest. And de turtle layin dere, still blinkin, with her belly laid wide open to de dogs and birds.

Calipatch and calipee, mon.

Oh, mon. You seen all dat, Byrum?

Copm Allie Ebanks told me dat, so I knows it good: Copm Allie knows a feller dat was dere and *seen* it.

And he tellin de manner dat dey hatchin, too, beginnin along about September-October. Dem little fellas come scromblin up out de sand, ain't one of dem big as your ear, and rummagin dere way up through four feet deep of dat black sand, and head straight for de water. Don't even look around to get dere bearins—dey just *go*. Feel dat water and head straight for de sea. Some dem nests are way up in de bushes, y'know, out of sight de sea, but ain't one of dem young turtle makes a mistake— dey *know*.

Green turtle very mysterious, mon.

Yah. But Copm Allie says he don't believe dat one thirty-second of what leaves de beach at Turtle Bogue ever makes it.

De most of dem never makes it to de water.

Dass it. All kinds birds and rats and wildcats, jaguars, y'know, and dogs, and what dey calls ringtails—all dem vermin comes out de swamps and jungles dat lays just behind dat beach, and wild hogs, too, dey say—all of dat is swarmin de beaches, and de few dat slips past de vermin got to scromble through dat big surf dere, which is one of de worst in all de world, and dem dat gets past de breakers, dey got to deal with all de sharks and fish in de deep water, and de mon-o'-war birds pickin at'm from de top when dey surfaces to get dere breath. In de mornin time when dose young ones dat come out from de night is restin in de water, dat mornin de sky is littered with birds. Mon-o'-war birds. De boobies don't grob dem so much, but de mon-o'-war do. Dey millions of birds dere. Dat mornin de sea is covered with baby turtle and de sky is black with birds, just *black* with mon-o'-war birds, swoopin down. Dey is very few dat gets away. Oh, *very* few!

Oh, I like to see dat sight! Dat is a sight dat I would like to see!

Millions of birds at Turtle Bogue dere in September. In de time of de hatchin of de green turtle, dat old empty coast is a sight to see: dat black sand and dat ugly sea, and dat sky black with big black birds in all dere millions, and de black jungle layin dere behind.

Mon, oh mon. You seen all *dat*?

I tellin you, it ain't *me* seen it; it were a fella dat were known firsthand to Copm Allie!

The men fall silent; Raib is standing at the edge of light.

Well, it a pity dat dat kind of mornin ain't *people's* first experience of dis life. I mean to say, lookin over dis crew, I think people had ought to start out with de same chance in life—one out of thirty-two. Dat take care of most of de goddom Sponnish and Jamaicans.

You be de one in *your* thirty-two, huh, Copm Raib?

Oh, *I* make it, okay! (*laughs*) It all of your*selfs* dat you got to worry about.

Byrum heaves to his feet. He goes to the leeward rail to scrape his plate, brushing the Captain closer than is necessary. When Raib half turns, gazing after him, Byrum ignores him; he speaks loudly from the rail, unbuttoning his fly.

Oh, yes! Dey very few lives to tell de tale! And dem few dat makes it disappears. Ain't *no* mon ever seen a baby turtle de first year. Disappears, mon. Vanish. De first ones dat you see, dey go five pound or better, look like a dish. (*pause*) Dat right, Copm Raib?

As the men turn one by one to watch, Raib slaps at his
sleeve where Byrum brushed him.

Mon dat know all dat much about turtle, dat is a
valuable mon. I s'prised dey let you off de
A.M. Adams.

Byrum, pissing, calls over his shoulder.

Never let me off—dey fired me! (*buttoning*) We all
gets fired now and den in life.

So you say den: I ain't had much experience of it.
De onliest time in all dis life I ever got fired off a
job was on a United Fruit vessel out of Bluefields,
and de other quartermaster were Desmond Eden.
He were smugglin arms cause we rerouted to
Colombia; he had dem hid under de deckhouse
floor. I was not into de deal, so I was innocent, but
dey grob me all de same. You call dat justice? I
mean to say, Desmond frig me *good!*

Copm Desmond Eden! After all dat fella done, all
de chances dat he took, and de money made, he
right back down here in de Cays where he begun!

Dat de most awfullest mon in Caymans. He still
owin me two hundred dollars for dat sharkskin, but
it worth dat and more just to be rid of him. He a
good worker, I say dat for him—dot mon dere ain't
afraid of work. But nobody give him a job no more;
it jail where he belong.

Well, Desmond generous, I say dat—

Generous, you said? By God, I never seen *dat.* He
had his woman shiftin along, beggin and stealin,
even when he had money. Call dat *borrowin*—done
dat to my wife. So Ardith told Desmond woman
something dat she didn't like to hear, and I was
very pleased with how she hondled *dat* part of de
motter—

If she lose Raib's money, she lucky she still alive. Raib treat dat poor woman so bad, she so scared of him, she don't know if she comin or goin. And dass de second wife, y'know—wore out de first one.

Some fellas, you got to get'm to de place where you can hondle dem. Don't do dat, you got trouble. It like Honduras (*groans*): dey beat me up! I got such a floggin down dere in dat drydock, it were terrible. I got a *floggin*! (*grins*) One good thing about it: when I left down dere, I got away owin three hundred dollars and maybe eighty from de amount dat dey had wanted to steal from me. Dey left me go with de promise dat I would pay dem, but I told'm —I sent back a message with de *Daydream*—dat dey would have to come to Grand Cayman to receive dat money. In de Court of Justice! I see dem fellas in de Court of Justice!

As Raib laughs, a wave catches the rudder, twisting the wheel from Vemon's grasp. The ship yaws around into a trench, falling broadside to the seas; she is smacked hard—*whump!*—before she rights herself, and the men bawl as a wall of spray crashes across them.

Vemon!

The ship pitches down the face of the next wave, roaring propellers hoisted clear out of the water. The old ropes that secure the boom part under the strain of the ship's labor, and before the leaping figures can secure it, the boom crashes back and forth over the deck amidships, and the block-and-tackle flying at its tip cracks the wood framing that supports the upright exhaust stack on the port engine. When the unsupported weight of the long stack breaks it loose from its elbow at the manifold, the engine room fills suddenly with smoke.

Figures surround the engine hatch. Below, Brown's form moves through the gloom, in a bad light. As the ship rolls, and the open manifold pours smoke into the hold, Brown fits and tinkers.

Dat what I call a *engineer*, mon—how he *stay* down dere?

Look like he in hell!

Byrum stares out at the ocean dark, quickly turns back again.

We could be dere, too, pretty domn quick—no goddom fire equipment. Oh, dis a *bad* trip, mon!

Dat is some hombre, dat is! Don't even shut de motor off! Hondle dat hot pipe dat way, and eat dat smoke!

Maybe it all dat diesel in de food—got so he *need* it!

Well, he finished—look at dat! Come up, den, Brownie!

Startled, the engineer looks up at the faces that ring the engine hatch. He stands there a moment, angling his sombrero, then goes slowly to the ladder and climbs out. He accompanies the men to the galley, where he accepts a plate of food and begins to eat. When his mouth is full, he looks up, smiles, and suddenly stops smiling. He has a round head and tawny eyes that search the other faces for a clue.

You from Sponnish Honduras, huh?

No, mon. Woman dere.

Where you home den?

La casa? (*shrugs*) Barranquilla?

Well, what you do down dere in Roatán? You engineer? Do any farmin like Speedy do?

I no farmer, *hombre!* (*spits*) No, mon. *Pescador.* Little bit mechanic work. Little bit common labor. Little bit everything: *chiclero.* Little bit barberin. (*pause*) Little bit soldierin. (*grins suddenly*) *La Violencia!*

Where was dat?

Brown nods toward the south.

Colombia.

Dat where your people at? Colombia? You from Old Providence or de mainland?

Brown says nothing. As he chews, a bean works its way out of his mouth and falls to the deck between his broken shoes.

You gone to go back dere to Roatán?

Es posible. Es January *ahora,* no?

April.

April?

Brown stops chewing and looks suspiciously from face to face.

Entonces—abril, mayo, julio, septiembre. Dat three month? I go back over dere three month.

A silence.

Will? Give us dat tale about de *Majestic* and Copm Steadman.

No, mon. Dat de back time now, I tryin to forget dat.

Will? You *shamed* of dat some way?

Will gazes awhile at Athens.

Well, I know *you* never be ashamed. But I thinks about de shipmates dat we left behind onto dat vessel, and dere faces lookin out at us over de rail dere. I tell you something, I gone to remember dat right to my grave. Every man of dem was silent; nobody said a word. But dere was one boy dere dat give us a kind of wave . . .

Will raises his hand vaguely, still looking at the deck, then raises his head to gaze at the men's faces.

I gone to have dat boy's wave with me on de day I die.

·4·

5 A.M.

Black waves, turning gray.

Wodie, at the wheel, stops humming and clears his throat. He pitches his voice low.

> Copm? I seein lights dere, Copm. Off de starb'd beam.

> How you know I was awake?

Raib appears in yellowed undershirt, scratching his crotch. He considers Wodie, then turns toward the dark horizon.

> Ain't no beacons in dis ocean—dem is runnin lights. Vessel must be comin out de back of Alligator. No turtle dere, nothin but sharks, so dat must be Desmond, sneakin around. (*spits over the rail*) You head west, hit de banks about daylight, we be just right.

The *Eden* turns downwind, toward the southeast edge of Gorda Bank. At sunrise she is on the banks again, running south-southwest toward the northern edge of Alargate Reef.

Raib replaces the canvas-and-lard baits with strips of flying fish. The silvery fish, attracted by the naked light over the engine hatch, have come aboard during the night. Squatting at the taffrail, he sews strips of fish to hooks with a sail needle, notching the baits to make them tail more naturally in the water. His thick hard lumpy fisherman's hands move gently, and though it is dead, he talks softly to the wild-eyed fish as if to calm it.

Fly too high, darlin, you fly too high.

He laughs his deep accumulating laugh, and his broad back quakes beneath the weathered shirt.

The *Eden* rides easily on the following wind, her jib and foresail taut. The trolling lines, hitched to the stanchions, sail out over the wake, and the baits, flashing at the surface, dart and hurry in the morning sea. Soon the fish rise; both lines go taut with a small *thump* and are hauled in hand over hand, skidding and cutting across the wake as the fish run.

Three kingfish, a Spanish mackerel, four barracuda fly up out of the sea; they slap and skitter on the deck.

A barra with black spots and a black dorsal snaps at the bare legs and Athens smacks it with a marlin spike across the head. A glaze on the gelatin eyes: the pupil dims.

The barracuda shivers and lies still.

> Blood all over de deck! Hit dat fish cross de top of de head, mon, not in de gill part! Even de boy know better den dat!

> Will, I gone get dat bastard fore he get me, dass *my* policy!

> Well, grob a bucket den and swab dat gurry off fore it get sticky!

> Listen to dis fella! Soon de Coptin out of sight, he show us who de boss!

> I de mate, mon! You don't believe dat, den wait see who get de mate's half-share!

> Nemmine, Will, you a good fella. Dem as say you so stubborn and stupid don't know you as good as we do.

> We gone eat dat barra with de spots? Dey say dem spots is poisonous.

> Me, I eats de spots, throw away de rest. Next to stripes, de thing I like de best in life is *spots*.

Laughing, Athens tosses a fresh bait to the sea.

> Well, Athens, a mon get domn sick on poison fish!

It de fishenin ground, not de fish. Dere dat famous place long by West Bay Beach, where de fish poisonous—not only de barra. De jack and de rockfish and all of dem.

No, mon. De only where dere is poison fish is on dat bank eight, nine miles west de island—*dat* is de famous place. Something dat dey eat dere turn de jack a bad-lookin black color. Dem few poison fish at West Bay Beach and over dere at Northwest Point is drifted in off de Cayman Banks. Dat right, Copm Raib?

So you say, den. But one time goin along dere I see pompano close inshore, so I toss dem a bait, pick up five, six. Dat were de worst job I ever done— near killed half of de whole family.

Mon, you should had *tested* dem. Throw a piece on de ant hill, see if de ants grob it. If ants walks away from a piece of fish, den you best walk away yourself, cause de ants *know*.

Another way, you boil de fish, den you put a piece of silver into de meat. If dat coin turn to black, *den* you know something wrong.

Mon, you know something goddom wrong *already*! Dem dass rollin on de floor, dey don't need no goddom old ants to tell dem dat dey eat poison fish!

I sayin now, if you was *suspicious* of dat fish, den you . . .

Brown squats on a blue fuel drum. His knees are level with his ears, and the tips of his rawhide chin strap dangle down over the drum rim. He is picking his gold teeth, eye rolling.

Near the scuppers, Speedy guts the kingfish. He too is squatting on his heels; the black muscles of his calves and forearms bunch and ravel. With one quick slash he splits the fish from gills to vent, then hacks the head off, chattering rapidly to himself.

Speedy can *cut*, mon! If he can't do nothin else dis boy can *cut*!

He holds up a fistful of bright guts and laughs.

Oh, Speedy a *hard* nigger, mon.

The silver fish have turned gray-white.

Speedy lops the pectoral fins with quick deft flicks. Running the knife point along under the spine, he scrapes out the air sac, then sloshes a bucket of salt water into the cavity; the water floods across the deck, carrying the gurry toward the scuppers. He rests a moment, running his hand down the long gleaming flanks of mother-of-pearl, then skins the fish, paring scales and skin together in small silver sections.

Yah, mon, Speedy-Boy can *cut*. Learned dat from school days.

The barracuda is filleted and cut in strips, which are salted and spread on the galley roof to dry.

Brown, motionless on the blue fuel drum, farts.

Starboard!

STARBOARD!

Sou'west and steady!

STEAD-DAY!

Rice and johnnycake.

I never been down Speedy way. Plenty from
Caymans dere, dey say, went down in times gone
back. All through de islands, down to Old
Providence, and all along de Sponnish Coast. Corn
Islands, Bluefields. Bragman's, dat de Sponnish
calls Puerto Cabeza. A lot dem Boddens, dey from
Coxon's Old Cay, in de Bay Islands.

Copm Steadman Bodden, dat was coptin of de
Majestic, I believe he born down dere. Copm
Steadman were a colored mon. I mean to say, he
were not real dark, but he had bad hair.

Hear dat? Some Raib own chil'ren got bad hair—

Well, I don't know dat Copm Steadman you speakin
about, but we gots black Boddens in Roatán, no
doubt about dat—I one of dem. We dere in
Roatán since 1836—learn dat from school days.

Yah, mon. We gots black Boddens in Caymans, too,
dat don't admit it. Plenty dem Boddens got bad
hair, ain't dat right, Vemon? Vemon mother dere,
she a Bodden. But he go by de name of Evers. Used
to be Avers, but in times gone back de black side
of de family took to spellin dereselves Evers, dat
right, Vemon? (*grins*) Which color *you* is, Vemon?

Goddom it, Copm Raib, you lookin at me, ain't you?

Very difficult to make you out—maybe dat just dirt I seein dere.

Shit!

You got a terrible bad mouth on you, Vemon. I very glad we not related.

Speedy bangs the rice pot hard with his wood ladle.

Well, dey ain't no two ways about Speedy, mon—I nigger to de bone. Give you some rice dere, Buddy?

No, thank you.

Dat boy seasick again, goddom it.

Well, dat wind *cuttin*, Copm Raib—it plenty rough. My first trip, I was so green—

Dis ain't his first!

He be okay. Dat right, Buddy? How you doin, boy? Nothin to say?

Westering.

Byrum relieves Will.

The *Eden* coasts the northern edge of Half Moon Reef, and the sea color changes from indigo to aquamarine to emerald.

Raib climbs to the crosstrees of the foremast, where he stands upright at the crotch of gaff and mast. He holds the mast with his right hand and the shrouds with his left, spread-eagled on the wind, hair blowing, squinting at long ridges of white surf where the wind drives seas across the coral. He points into the north, let his arm fall; a moment later he raises his palm. Will cries Raib's signals to the blind helm; the helmsman echoes them.

Port!

PORT!

Steady!

STEAD-DAY!

Steady, Byrum!

STEAD-DAY!

The ship goes down along Old Pointer Reef to the west end of Half Moon, then heads due south toward Logwood Cay. The shallow banks are roiled by days of wind, but from the crosstrees can be seen dark smudges of the coral heads below the surface. The banks near Logwood Cay are in the lee of Half Moon, and here the water clears.

Can't cross to Cape Gracias *dis* afternoon—no, mon.

Den we lost a day's fishenin.

We lost dat when he lost de longitude at Gorda Bank.

The puffs of green in the hot tropic sky to the southeast are the Savanna Reefs, called by the turtlers Serrarers.

See dere, Speedy? De *Majestic* layin out dere still.

The Captain perches in the crosstrees, bare feet swinging. When four olive-colored porpoise roll up along the hull, he skins down the rigging and runs for the bow, grabbing up a long boat pole as he goes. He bends a light line to the pole, wraps the bitter end around his wrist, and practices harpoon throws at the porpoise.

The creatures return to be tagged over and over. One glides a moment on its side; its eye regards the playing man.

Raib stops short, stops smiling: he does not throw.

The creatures go.

Coiling the line, Raib confronts the empty sea; he blinks as if awakening, then walks slowly toward the stern, where the men are resting. Eyes shadowed by their hat rims, they watch their captain come.

By God, I still pretty handy with de harpoon, I must say dat! I pretty good for an old fella!

You de best mon aboard *dis* ship, ain't dat right, Copm?

Well, dat ain't sayin so very much, aboard of here. (*laughs*) I ain't sayin but what is fair when I announce dat I is de best mon on dis ship: I mean to say, de best, and de quickest, and den de strongest, and den also de smartest, bein I know so much about green turtle and pilotin and de way of de sea!

Byrum lies back, sighing.

> We lucky to have you, Copm Raib. Dat right,
> Vemon? You a very lucky fella, Vemon, to have dat
> kind of coptin in dis life—might make a seaman
> out you yet.

> Seamanship? By Christ, when it come to seamanship
> dere ain't no mon aboard has got me beat! Maybe
> de mate dere got me when it come to turtle, but
> talk about *seamanship,* dat is something else!

> Will got you beat dere too, you goddom fool.

> Will, you got papers? I askin you, you got *papers*?

Will shifts his tobacco bulge from one cheek to the
other, but says nothing.

> You take dem papers and wipe you ass, mon—we
> talkin about *seamanship*!

> Dat what *I* talkin about, Byrum! Seamanship! Mon
> with no papers, and he calls hisself a mate!

> Green mango? Copm Raib? We gots a bag here of
> green mango. From dat big mango tree over Pedro
> way, back of Savanna—know de one? Dat old
> provision ground?

> Dat ain't de biggest tree. De biggest mango—

> Now de biggest *almond* tree, dat de one dere in
> Georgetown. Dat tree rose from de famous old-time
> seed dat were cast up on de beach at Bodden
> Town. Found dere I believe by de great great-aunt

of Osley Webster. Dat how come we gots almond
trees in Grand Cayman.

Some nice almond tree in West Bay, too, nearby
Copm Allie house. You come to de crossin and den
you go about thirty, forty fathom down dat road—

Dere he is!

What Byrum pointin at?

Green turtle, mon!

You mean hox-bill? I see two hox-bill from de
masthead soon's we come into de lee—

Green turtle! Dere he head come up again! Sixty,
seventy fathom off de bow—dere! You lookin at'm!

The turtle is inset in the green sea, and the broad bay-
colored shell, awash, glints in the sinking sun. The
ancient head blinks once, then withdraws beneath the
surface.

Wild high voices.

Well, Byrum right! Dey a few left anyway dat ain't
gone south!

By God, dat a nice turtle dere! *Big* turtle!

Call dat big? Dat one dey got on de *Cayman
Venture,* dat one went better den six hundred
pound!

How many you seen in *your* life big as dat? In de
back time, yes—dey got dem up to eight, nine
hundred pound, were not uncommon. But dese
days, dey been harassed so much, a turtle live long
enough to reach four hundred pound, *dat* is
uncommon!

Where dat black Honduran? Take a good look, boy
—you seein *turtle*! You on de only green turtle
grounds in de whole *world*!

Hear dat idiot? Why, dey turtle at Aves, over dere
toward Guadeloupe, and dey got nice turtle over
dere in Yucatán, Isla Mujeres, long dat way. And I
got de theory dat in former times, green turtle
nested out on Far Tortuga. Eitherwise, why did de
back-time coptins give dat cay dat name? Den Far
Tortuga wore away in storm, but de turtle kept
right on goin dere, circlin round dem empty reefs
for a hundred years. And when dat cay formed up
again, dey commenced to nestin dere, just like dey
done in de centuries before.

A big broad-headed shark. Byrum chunks a piece of
wood at it, and it moves off with a dull thrash; in a
moment it has turned again, flanking the boat.

Dat son-bitch waitin for me, mon. Dat tiger got my
number. (*sighs*) One voyage on de *A.M. Adams*
now, I dreamin every night about my intended
dere, Miss Gwen, and dey was turtle in de net
every last mornin.

His intended! Byrum told so many girls dat dey was
his intended dat he gettin now so he believin it
hisself. Dat last time home he got drunk dere and got
all slicked up and run down to de church. All right,
by Jesus, where in de hell is my intended! But dat day
Miss Gwen was over to Northside visitin her people,
so de nuptials never took place.

Oh, dat boy a bad drinker! Dat how come he got
fired off de *Adams*. Wouldn't take no orders—he was
givin dem!

Dass it. Byrum never gone get married! He gone end
up just like Vemon.

Oh yes, dreams is sign! If I lay down tonight and dream certain dreams, I can get up in de mornin and say, Well, Wodie, you know something, we got a cotch. And if I lay down and dream *other* dreams, I can say, All right, boys, ain't no use in goin out dere *dis* mornin. Green things—green trees, green fruit, anything green—or silver money, dat is disappointment. Dreamin bout silver money or colored folks, a black person, anything black, dat is bad luck, too.

White person, dass okay, huh?

Well, Speedy, it's been marked dat if you dream bout a white person, or white sand, white clear water, or white fruit, you can almost count on good luck de next day! Dass right! And *sign!* Dere are turtlers today dat will sit on de vessel deck and tell you when de turtle strike his net. He feel de sign. True. You go out dere at four o'clock dis evenin, and you set ten, fifteen nets. And you don't feel no sign in your hand or your feet of puttin your hand on a turtle de next day, or you don't have any nice dream: well, you can go on out dere and you find what dey calls a water set, cause dey nothin in dose nets but water.

Raib turns abruptly from the rail.

Wodie, dat is foolishness! Dat is duppy talk! (*raises voice*) De only unlucky thing about de turtle fishery is de set of de wind, and de other thing is, if you are not setting your nets where de turtle are— *dat* is bad luck. (*laughs*) Dat is de *worst* kind of luck, cause you won't get no turtle.

Copm Raib? Copm Raib? Ain't you de one believes in turtle eyesight—?

Turtle eyesight is something dat I have observed myself! Many times I seen'm do dat, from de catboat, when we was out doggin'm! Times when de water so riled up dat a mon can't see nothin, not even if he way up on de masthead. Look like a dish of milk. And de onliest way dat you find de set is by havin good bearins, dead reckonin, and den you grope de bottom to see if you come to de right place. Well, dem times, turtle pick up where dey is feedin and head straight back for dere coral head or pan shoal, straight, straight, straight! And de onliest way dey could do dis is turtle *eye*sight: dey must *see* through dat water with turtle eyesight, same as a mon would see through a hazy sun or something!

Must be divine guidance, dat is how *I* would express it, ain't dat right, Copm Raib?

Raib contemplates Vemon for a long time.

Need more den divine guidance for a job like *dat*.

Still got duppies down dere at East Wind, ain't dat right, Wodie?

Wodie smiles, eyes closed.

Y'know, I never seen a duppy, and dis is funny, for I born with a caul, and people dat haves a caul s'posed to see duppies better someway. But dey plenty in my family *has* seen duppies. My grandmother had a brother by de name of Billy, and one night he goin home in de full moon light. And when he got to a certain spot in de road, he seen a ruffly hen and chicks. So he say to hisself, Well, look, dis is some of de neighbors' chickens, so before anything destroy dem, I will corry dem home, bring dem back in de mornin. So he take up dis ruffly hen on his arm, and go walkin down de road goin home. And when he got by de cemetery, he say de hen look up in his face like dat. (*grimaces*) Hen say, You ever see teeth like dis? Say, Take me and corry me back where you took me *from*! He was so frightened he wanted to throw her down. She say, No, don't put me down; corry me back where you took me *from*! And he turn around and corry her back, and den he took off, cause dat hen had as fierce a set of teeth as he ever seen.

A silence.

Wodie opens his eyes wide, beside himself and shy. When he speaks again, his voice is high and singsong, sweet. The men stare at the stained white of his blind eye.

Course, mostways you never see de duppies, dey just got dere little ways of lettin you know dat dey are dere, like knockin something down, and things like dat. And when you *do* see something, most de time it just a kind of fireball, shape like a egg. See dat mostly over gravestones, but fireballs are common by de side de road, or under eaves, or out by de front gate—just hangin in de air. Now dat fireball might be a duppy, somebody dat is just died, or it might be de night spirit of some livin person who is out haggin—left dere body behind, y'know. Dey takes de form of a fireball or a night bird. But usually dat fireball is de spirit of someone dat is crossin over. Most de time it just kind of a glow like you can see in rotten fish, but sometimes de person's face is dere, and dey are times when de whole body is seen, like in dat famous case in de hurricane year of 1919. A fella on a ship way up in de Gulf of Mexico seen dis woman hangin in de cabin doorway, and when dey got back home to Caymans two weeks later dey found out dat on de very same night Vaney Bush had hung herself in Georgetown—

Wodie! One thing we don't need aboard of here—

Oh, Copm, you was livin in dat hurricane year, you can tell dat tale better den me—

I'member dot goddom hurricane okay, I run right out de windward side de house—

Don't 'member about Vaney Bush?

The men turn one by one to regard the Captain. He sucks his teeth.

Well, it were a MacTaggart, I believe, who seen poor Vaney in de cabin door, and I got to say dat dis case were very mysterious. But you go talkin about hens with teeth . . .

Half Moon Cay. A low cay of red mangrove, with a small beach inset in the limestone of the leeward shore. On the crest of the beach is a wind-worn lean-to and a catboat, but there is no sign of man. Sooty terns rise and settle.

At the *Eden's* rail, Will Parchment holds to his chest a package of coffee and cigarettes, canned fruit and comics.

Dat boat of Will's dere is a fine little boat. And dat boy just left her behind.

Will? Nemmine, Will—we pick up dat boat on de way home!

Copm Raib? Will tellin me dat dis port boat leakin —we could change her for dat one over dere!

Okay by me, if dass what Will want to do.

No, mon. I de pilot of dis port boat here, not dat boat on de beach.

Will returns into the deckhouse and puts the package back in its place under the small duffel that serves him as a pillow.

Dat Will's boat, okay. So his boy ain't drowned, cause Conwell too coward to go out cept in fair weather, and not always den. What dem rangers done is leave de job, abandon dat boat, and go off on some passin vessel, cause dey too shiftless to stay here and tend dere nets. Dass all it is. To see dat boy make a ass of de father dat way, dat love him for some goddom reason, I tell you dat make me sad as hell!

Oh, dey plenty like Conwell in Caymans, Copm: all de young fellas dat way now. Hang round de tourists like a bunch of barra.

Plenty like dat in Roatán, too, mon—modern time. And dey no tourists dere to hang around—dey just hang around all by dereselves.

I tellin you, he like a crab, dat boy, de way he shift along. He got a big mouth and no sense. Go from one thing to de next. He like one of dem poor egg birds flyin round dere—worse, cause at least dey tryin to get on with life. But he don't even *try*. One way or de other, I guess I got about eighteen children, and I can truthfully say dey ain't one of dem I trade for dat one Will got!

Anchored in the lee of Half Moon Cay, the ship rides steady. Between dark shapes of lime-crusted turtle grass, the moving shadow is a manta.

Rangers?

Huh? Don't know about rangin down here in Honduras? (*frowns*) What we calls *rangers*? Dat is left behind onto de cays? Well, dere is three rangers and sometimes a cook, to cook for dem. Give'm a catboat and nets, and den some water and some rice, beans, coffee, flour, things like dat. Matches. Sometimes dere two boats on de one cay. At de peak of de shark fishery, dey corried twenty boats on de *A.M. Adams* stacked up in her bows, and all of de crews and all of dere stores and gear. Course de boats pretty well nested and lashed down, or de seas could roll dem over. De *Adams* might leave fifty, sixty fellas rangin, pick dem up again on her way home.

Rangin. S'posin dey runs out of water? And den food?

De ranger knows he goin to be dere six to ten weeks, and he takes stores for dat time. He not worried about his meats—fish and all dat—he gets dat as he want it. It just dry stores and water. Got to have sufficient water. On a few of dose cays, if you starvin for water, you could scratch down in de sand and get something to save your life, but it pretty salty. You just keep diggin and tastin, and when it get to de place where you can't make it, den you stop.

Athens stands and stretches.

Oh, mon. Dey speaks about de pirates of Cayman. I took a swear dat I would never go back rangin in dis life. When dese West Bay coptins land you, dey doesn't give a domn for you after dat, especially if it wasn't dem dat paid to fit you out. Dey maroon dere grandmother if somebody paid de money down to rig her out.

Byrum nods, cracking his knuckles.

Athens tellin you de God's truth, Speedy. One time he maroon four rangers on de cays . . . who? Dis coptin here dat's always shoutin about justice! Oh, mon! Dat was what de old people likes to call a real conflaption! Sailed home to Cayman leavin four of dem fellas behind on de cays with insufficient water, and den he told dere families dat dey were doin very, very fine, and after dat he forgot about'm. Dis were nothin but hoggishness; prob'ly he smugglin, or runnin guns down to Colombia. He decide he got business at home, so he go home, not takin de time to pick dem up. Mon, dey were just lucky dat another vessel come along. But one fella from Old Bush dere, he run out of water, and den he got scared, thinkin de ship were mashed up and were never goin to come, and so he *row* all de way to some Wika village on de Sponnish coast. He row forty, fifty mile, and he arrive dere in very bad shape; he domn lucky he alive.

He all right again now, dey say. Put him away in de asylum, y'know—wavin his arms, givin orders at de crossins, all of dat. De distress of dat experience done it to him. But now he able to hondle hisself again, and he come home.

Athens coughs violently.

Oh, mon. Raib Avers is so bad and so angry and so cruel dat he don't even like his*self*! But he don't frig with *me*, I tell you *dat*! See de way he pick on Vemon and de boy dere, and even Will? Cause Will love dat mon someway, so dass what he get. But he don't pick on *me*, no mon!

Maybe he scared you beat him up.

Dat could be, mon. Dat could be.

In a sudden silence, Athens opens his eyes: Raib has come aft from the engine room and now stands over him. Relighting his bent cigarette, Athens ignores him.

Oh, yes! *Still* got pirates! Dey come by dere ways naturally, from times gone back. Dem ones dat burned de old *Clarinda* to de water line—

Raib, half smiling, nods at Athens, who will not meet his gaze for fear of laughing. The Captain reaches down and sets Athens' cap straight on his head.

How you feelin, Athens?

Okay. Pretty good. (*coughs anew*) I gone take de first train straight to hell.

Well, what Athens been sayin about pirates is correct, and he just de mon to know about it, bein dat his uncle committed de last high-sea piracy in de Cayman Islands. Oh, yes! (*grins*) Gideon Ebanks! 1931! Killed five of dem Cuban Sponnish. Den he run off into de mangroves, I b'lieve, where dey found him dead. (*shrugs*) Anyways, before de first settlements down at East End, dere was shipwreckers over dere back of West Bay. Dere at Northwest. No huts hardly—dey was just hindin in de bushes. Hidin from de world. Prob'ly dey got marooned dereselves, and dey wanted to give other folks a taste of it. False beacon fires. Right up to de turn of dis century, de island families did very well off dat: used to pray to de Good Lord to send dem a wreck, and run right out of church, dey say, when a ship struck. But de last high-sea piracy, dat was in 1931.

Raib sighs.

So de first settlers had to deal with dese wild people speakin a broken tongue. Athens here *still* speakin it: Sponnish, English, African—a little bit of everything.

Well, Copm Raib, in Georgetown dey more civilized, dey understandin me. West Bay is pirates, and de farther east you go from Georgetown, de farther into de back are de people livin. Where Wodie live, now, at East End, dey *still* livin in de bushes. Dat right, Wodie?

Oh, we be hoppy in de bushes, too.

Dem real black people out dere at East End, dey stuck out dere since de slavin days, when de slave ship *Nelly* struck upon de reef. Dem jujumen, dem obeah workers dere, dey gets dere ways from Africa. Still got cannibals out dere, ain't dat right, Wodie?

Diesel fumes on the wind eddies. Frying lard. The crew sprawls on the deck and catboat. Kingfish steaks, cooked dry and smeared with chili sauce, are dished out with the rice; on each plate, with delicate fingers, Speedy places a crude doughnut.

Will puckers his face and spits tobacco juice in a hard spurt across the rail. He takes his food from Speedy without thanks and holds it uneaten on his lap. Raib watches him.

Will? Don't bother yourself about dat catboat—we pick her up on de way home.

Will smiles mirthlessly, face cracking.

> Ain't gone to bother fungo, no mon! (*spits again*)
> What you call dis, Speedy? Dese ain't bullas?

> I hear on de radio about hot doughnuts and coffee
> makin people hoppy, Mist' Will, so dat is what you
> eatin dere, hot doughnuts. I don't know much
> about de nut part, but you got plenty dough dere,
> I tell you dat.

Wodie, singing, goes aft to relieve Vemon at the wheel.

> > *... of a dove*
> > *Fly away! Fly away!*
> > *I'd fly a-way-ay, fly a-way-ay*
> > *And be-ee-ee-ee at rest ...*

Approaching the galley, Vemon sits down on the bilge
pump, arms folded on his chest.

> Bring me my supper, Honduras!

Speedy leans out of the galley door to gaze at Vemon,
who is glaring out to sea.

> I done my day's work, and now I wants my supper!

Speedy is hooked to the galley door top by his fingertips, leaning outward between his forearms. He too
gazes out to sea. In time, he pushes himself back inside
and prepares a plate of food and a cup of coffee. He
comes out quietly and offers it to Vemon, who grabs it
with exaggerated rudeness.

Speedy squats down at Vemon's feet; his expression is calm. Vemon tries to eat, but soon stops chewing.

Speedy's finger draws a circle on the deck around Vemon's plate.

> Eat your supper, nigger. (*pause*) Dass a very nice supper dat you haves dere, nigger, so I hopes you enjoy it. And you ever talk to me dat way again, and show me dat bad face, I gone to knock you on you black ass.

Speedy looks up at Vemon for the first time.

> Dass a promise. Nigger.

Nodding gently, Speedy looks from face to face.

> I a very nice boy, but I don't take no shit. Anybody give me shit, I gone to move. I gone to travel. Fast. And any mon get in my way gone find out why dey calls me Speedy.
>
> Dass okay, mon. Best say what you got in your mind.
>
> I always say de truth—learn dat from school days. If my mother no good, I tell you. Dass right, mon. Say de truth, cause dass de way life go de best.

Raib wipes his mouth.

> Well, it time to start thinkin where we gone to set our nets. Start for Cape Gracias maybe three in de mornin we won't hit no reefs before de light, and den we is a very good way along. Maybe we get done

registerin at Cape Gracias time to run back out to Cape Bank Shoal, set a few net dere fore de evenin.

Cape Bank pretty far to de north for dis time of de year.

Well, we see dat big turtle dis evenin. Got good ground over dere.

Copm Allie say de turtle small at Cape Bank. Chicken turtle.

Copm Allie don't know everything, Byrum!

You know a coptin better'n him?

Well, dey ain't many proper coptins left. Copm Cadian dere on de *Lydia Wilson*, he was pretty good while he had a boat. Can't do much without a boat. *(begins to grin)* But I believe I as good as any as dere is today, I believe I can truthfully say dat. Dey talk about Copm Allie, but he don't sail down to de cays no more. All de coptins of dat time, dey was some very good coptins, but age is took de upper hand. Oh, yes! Dey in de downward way!

Raib laughs unabashedly while the men watch him.

Now Copm Steadman—dat were a *real* turtler. A real first-class turtler. He were a turtler dat could do everything. Hang turtle nets, which is de first step. Go out dere in de daylight and de net is bunched dere and no turtle, den you hung it wrong. Hangin de net, dat is de first thing.

Well, pilotin pretty important, Copm. Sot dat net in de wrong place, don't motter de way it hung.

I very glad you know dat, Will, you bein de pilot of de port boat.

Raib starts to laugh again, then frowns.

In pilotin, a mon must look and he must *see*. I
believe it were somewhere around '44 when Copm
Andrew made dis course with me on de *Clarinda*.
He told me to steer her west-half-north and I steered
dat course, and he went down and he sot dat place,
and give de turtle hell. And den when we come
back in '62, he say, West by north, and I say, Papa,
if you goin back to dat same set, you gone to have
to steer west-half-north or eitherwise you not goin
dere. So he say, *You* want to steer dat course, boy,
den you steer it! So I steered her west-half-north,
and even though de bottom was dark, I put her on
de point. Cause I 'membered dat dis place were full
of barracuda, and by seein barras come up around
de vessel, it give me a very good idea dat I was
over de white hole.

Raib gazes around the circle.

So I'm tellin you dat a bad memory is a disasterish
thing to a person in life. With no remembrance, a
mon cannot learn. To me—I'm not making bragado
or anything—but I know every rock out on de
banks, like my own dooryard. It were Copm
Andrew Avers dat taught me, and come to pilotin,
he were de island's best.

Come to rum-runnin, he were de island's best. Dat
Clarinda, she were swift, mon—

Athens winks at Byrum; he clears his throat.

Copm Andrew Avers! Eighty years of age, and still
sailin down here to de Cays as pilot!

A clink of tin on tin. Raib lays his fork down.

Who were de fella de other day dat were speakin out for Desmond? Dat you, Byrum? Speakin out for a fella dat would cheat an old mon out of his vessel—

De *Clarinda*?

DE CLARINDA! AND DEN TAKE DAT POOR OLD EIGHTY-YEAR-OLD MON OUT OF HIS DAUGHTER'S HOUSE DAT CAN'T STAND STURDY ANYMORE, AND DE SON OF DAT OLD MON OUT OF DE WAY DOWN IN HONDURAS—

Raib stops suddenly, gasping for breath: he tries to eat again.

Your doddy wanted to go bad, Copm Raib. Said every day of idleness was takin ten years off his life—

No! He were cheated! De *Clarinda* were a Avers vessel, and look who stole it—Desmond Eden! It a *good* thing she burned! A *very* good thing! Desmond had no business with dat vessel! Dat one he call de *Davy Jones*—dat de vessel for him! Stole *dat* one from dem poor Cuba refugees dat come in it, dem people were starvin, and he paid dem next to nothin! Put all dat crap on dere, look like a whorehouse!

A cockroach glints by the galley siding, antennae bending in the wind. Raib stamps at it and misses. The insect withdraws under the rotting wood.

Copm Desmond! A mon dat would call a vessel *Davy Jones*, funnin with de bleak ocean in dat manner, dat mon can't learn nothin from de sea!

Well, as I was sayin, Copm Allie is de best of de modern time.

Getting his breath, Raib gazes at Athens for some time. Then he nods a little, and turns back toward Byrum.

Copm Allie ain't sailed down to de cays for several years now. And dat generation of turtlin men dat come before Copm Allie, dey was also very gifted in dis fishery. Copm Andrew and Copm Steadman and Copm Millard Conally, and C. C. Bush and many of de rest was all experts on de turtle banks. But you would have to say dat Copm Steadman were as good as Cayman had, one of Cayman's best dat ever was. Oh, yes. Dey was not anybody sharper den dat old colored mon before his day and since. Will Parchment settin right dere dat sailed on de *Majestic*—Will can tell you.

Well, Steadman were a domn wonderful old mon! A very fine old mon. A *very* fine old mon. Fished turtle all de days of his life!

Dat old mon were so well gifted in dis fishery, he could sail de coast de way he wanted. Most of de pilots had to climb up to de masthead where de visibility was good for dem. But Steadman sat dere in a chair on deck and got his turtle just de same.

Yah, mon! De *Majestic*! Big boat, mon!

She were not. You old enough to remember her better den dat. But even dem dat remember de *Majestic* think today dat she were big. Will settin dere will tell you dat she were smaller den dis vessel, but she were corryin a pile of rangers, and now she so famous dat dey think she must be big. (*grunts*) Everybody think dat de twenty-seven fellas dat were lost dat year was de most ever on de Miskita Cays: dey were not. In 1876, a big hurricane den, dey was sixty-seven lost, and most of de fleet.

De *Majestic*, dat were de biggest loss in de *modern* time, and she were famous because so many fellas died dat day under a coptin dat had lost his sea wits.

●

... and dat domn half-breed dere, dat calls hisself engineer! (*spits*) Goddom it to hell—

Nigger?

A silence.

Nigger? You best not mess with Brown. No, mon.

Speedy warnin you, Vemon, so you heed him.

With Brown dere *ain't* no warnin, nigger. (*softly*) You look down and see something stickin out de ribs, dat be de first warnin dat you get.

A silence.

How come you partners with a bad fella like dat?

Brown not a bad fella and he not a good fella—he don't know de difference.

Dass it. More and more like dat dese days, don't care about nothin cept de next meal, no more den vermin. No ambition. Dey just livin along.

Dass it. Dey just livin along ...

Brown's head, yellow-eyed, has appeared out of the engine hatch. His narrow mustachio hooks down sharply at the corners of his mouth, which hangs half open. He does not climb out. As if sensing danger, he withdraws to listen, descending two steps on the ladder, but the peak of his sombrero is still visible. Hearing the silence, he disappears entirely.

Byrum's belch makes the others laugh.

Speakin about de *Wilson,* and den also remembrance—dey is *turtle* remembrance. Copm Allie always tell dat tale about dat turtle come home from Caymans to de cays here, to de same rock at Dead Man Bar. Very mysterious.

Dat ain't so much. Dere was another dat escape from Key West and come home to de cays here and got caught again—had to come all de way round Cuba and down de Yucatán Channel, seem like.

Yah. Well, de way Copm Allie tell it, Copm Raib—

Byrum, I not talkin about Allie! I talkin about C. C. Bush! Dis turtle *I* speakin about were caught twice by Copm C. C. Bush, White Charley Bush! On de old *Annie Greenlaw!* (*more quietly*) I were a boy den. Turtle washed out of de crawls dere in Key West. In a hurricane. Had all dese fish bites on de fins so dey remembered, and dey look on de calipee and found de brand of Charley Bush, cut in dat same season. Now Allie's turtle come back south from Caymans, but *dis* green turtle come all of de way from Key West, mon, cross de bleak ocean. To de same rock! All de way round Cabo San Antonio dere in Cuba. To de same *rock!* Now dat is a fact, mon, dat has been seen many's de time, dat when it come to navigation, dey ain't no bird in de world is in de class with de green turtle!

Byrum, who has been whistling, stops to clear his throat.

Yah. (*pause*) So, y'see, de crew was all upset dere, dat de *Lydia Wilson* had been lost, but Allie arrived at de conclusion right away. It was Harley Rivers caught dis turtle and brought him down to Miskita Cay, and he advised Allie dat dis same turtle dat he caught dere at Dead Man Bar in de week before had been caught again, and he asked if de *Wilson* had gone down, cause de *Wilson* was corryin dat turtle home.

Byrum glances at the Captain, who is silent.

Dat day gone a week, Allie had told him to mark some turtle and put dem in de *Wilson* crawl, cause she goin home. One of dem was a he-turtle, a pretty turtle, well-shaped, with a very yellow calipee dat looked like gold. So de *Lydia Wilson* left, bound for Cayman, and a norther come down just after she got home and wash dis gold turtle out de crawl. And de second week after de *Wilson* had left, Harley come down from Dead Man Bar with dis same gold turtle, askin if de *Wilson* had sunk. Allie said, No, if de vessel had sunk we wouldn't have de turtle, cause I don't think dere was anybody on board would had thought to go and cut de turtle loose, which would had meant dat de turtle would drown bein dat dere fins was tied.

You finished, Byrum?

Dass de conclusion he arrived at, see. In a tight place, de vessel sinkin, everybody would be scufflin for dereselves. So Allie told Harley dat in his opinion de turtle had escaped out de crawl. Took dat gold turtle just a week to come back across two three hundred mile of ocean from Cayman to his own rock dere at Dead Man Bar.

Gold turtle, mon.

You finished, Byrum? (*pause*) Now dat were *White* Charley Bush, de first coptin of de *Noonan*, dat I talkin about, not Black Charley Bush, dat were prob'ly some relation to Wodie dere. Call dem White Charley Bush and Black Charley Bush. (*laughs*) Dat were de distinction between *dem* two fellas. White Charley Bush, he de grandson, I believe, of dat Copm Carl Bush dat learned navigation from de British Navy and brought it back to de Old Rock, long about 1870. In de fifty years before dat, dey was sailin down here to Nicaragua and home again just by dead reckonin.

Copm? You wrong about de *Noonan*, brother. De *Noonan* never come until 1932, and de master were not C. C. Bush—it were Copm Allie.

Will? Goddom it, Will, you and Byrum—

Den Elroy copied dat design and went to work and built de *Lydia Ebanks Wilson*, with frames of Cayman mahogany in de place of oak. Den he went to work and built—

Will? You think you have de knowledge to instruct me on dis motter?

I only sayin—

I got to say, Will, dat you very quiet compared to some dese fellas, and dat is best, darlin, cause you makes de most sense when you haves your mouth shut.

Athens lights a cigarette from the one he is throwing away. He crumples the empty orange pack and flings it at the rail, and again the wind carries it back onto the deck.

So Vemon say to de woman, Goddom it, Vemon say, Goddom it to hell, he say, *Talk* to me! He slap her, y'know. And she just proceedin to walk along dere like he were some kind of a miskita. So he say,

Talk to me! He say, You goddom old bitch, you *fuckin* on me! (*laughter*) Now his woman dere, she hadn't wanted to acknowledge it, y'see? So she just kept on easin along, easin along, like she was walkin over dere to Boilers to cut palm tops. Make him a nice hat or something. And he still runnin alongside of her, in de sun. So he say, *Talk* to me. He don't say, Talk to me; he say, *Talk* to me! He say, You goddom old whore, you *fuckin* on me! And she kept walkin. When he slap her, she kept right on walkin.

Dat woman not talkin, mon. She walkin.

Yah. (*laughs*) She sayin to herself, Woman! Woman, you best hold your speech!

Look at Buddy! First time I see him grin!

Raib grabs at the blowing orange pack and misses.

Dommit, Athens, throw your mess downwind—

·5·

A cool night wind, and stars.

In the bows, a clank of chain and shriek of ratchet; a
storm lamp shudders in the galley.

Silhouettes on the night sky.

Over the engine hatch, the yellow bulb rolls with the
ship, shifting the shadows. Raib is crouched over the
hole, hands on knees, peering below; his voice is
muted, in respect for darkness.

> Last night you hear me say we sailin at three dis
> mornin, and you wait till I wakes you to oil dem
> engines? *No*, mon! Dass no good!

A silence. In the darkness of the hold, Brown's eyes
gleam in the reflected light.

> Nothin to say?

A wisp of cigarette smoke on the wind. Low, heavy coughing.

Raib straightens, turning toward the galley.

Who in dere? Athens? You de cook now? Why ain't you forward with dem on de windlass?

Athens coughs, pointing at his chest.

Dat engineer doin okay de other night with dat busted manifold.

Okay? Okay, you said? Sot dat port engine wrong so dat de shaft still vibratin, and we miss a day's fishenin on account of dat—call *dat* okay? Put a Stillson wrench on de pipe threads? Corry all de nuts and parts in a wet carton with holes in it, so dey all over de deck and bilge—dat okay too? He call de manifold "mon-fool," he such a fuckin idiot, and after dat he call hisself "engineer"! I believe "mon-fool" be a better name for him!

Athens dumps coffee into water brought already to a boil.

Raib bellows at the night:

MON-FOOL!

Now Brown is on deck, in the swaying light. In the shadow of his sombrero, his eyes are hidden. He says nothing.

Wind blowing. The rawhide chin straps dance on the ragged shirt.

Underway.

Coming aft from the windlass, Vemon salutes the Captain; he takes coffee from Athens.

Copm Raib! Copm Raib! We headin for Cape Gracias, Copm Raib?

The Captain acts as if he has heard nothing. Then he turns so swiftly that Vemon slops his cup.

What de hell you ask dat question for? You *know* we goin dere!

I didn't think you go so far west as Cape Gracias, Copm Raib!

You domn fool, dey ain't nothin tween here and dere on de course we headed! What you know about it anyway? What you *care*? I don't mind answerin a serious question, but when a mon ask a question just cause he got a mouth to ask it, dat is something else!

Vemon mutters, nursing his coffee. It has a bad burnt smell and a faint stink of petroleum.

Hear dat? He blast two of dem already dis mornin.

One of dese days de *Eden* gone to rot dere at de barcadere, cause no mon go crew with him, he be dat disagreeable. Every day de mon blast you de way he do, den one day you say, Kiss my ass!

Mind you don't say it too loud, mon—he might throw you to de sharks.

The *Eden* beats across the Main Cape Channel toward the coast. Over her wake, stars fail; the horizon swells. The men take their coffee to the stern and watch the sky fill with pale light. A rim of fire, a great fire flow where the corona clings to the horizon. Then a livid sun escapes into the sky.

Domn wind again today. Y'see de sky color?

Dis wind got no business with us in de fair-weather months; dis be de wind of June!

We ain't gone to set no net *dis* evenin, I tell you dat. And de season gettin away from us. Prob'ly de *Adams* at Miskita Cay, gettin set to clear for home.

Dat Brown should had dat engine oiled, dass right enough.

Dat ain't no reason, Will! De reason is, we set sail in dis half-ass fashion, with no cook, no proper engineer, no rangers—

Dere weren't time. (*sighs*) Copm Raib say de world gainin on him.

Dass it, so now we hurryin, only we runnin de engines at half speed!

He breakin dem in.

You come all de way up from Honduras—dey ain't broken in?

Well, dere's dat shaft on de port engine.

Mon, dat vibration mostly in his head! He don't know nothin about engines! You see de way we work like donkeys on dat windlass dere, and dat wind blowin? With dem engines, he could had ride forward over de hook, and slack dat chain—save ten minutes when de wind blowin!

I don't know, mon. As a coptin, he okay. Got to give de mon dat much; he know de sea. It only de way he treat de men—dat de back-time way.

He a wind coptin, dass de trouble. He a sailin mon, and he used to de old-time way. All his life he been ziggin and zaggin, he don't know how to go straight.

With sunrise, the wind freshens. Iron seas rise in the *Eden's* wake, picking up her stern so high that her propellers churn the surface, then sliding her down the sea's back, to wallow in the trough. The swells pass on beneath the bow, unrolling in broad ranks toward the mainland.

How de boy doin, Doddy? He kind of quiet.

He seasick, dat de motter with *him*. I should had left him home into de school, but he like to hang around with me some way.

Raib opens his jackknife and shuts it again, using one hand.

He a good child, never give me trouble. (*laughs*) Maybe *dass* what de motter is—lack of spirit.

Buddy very nice. He got nice manners.

Oh, I seen to *dat*! De manners dat dey is dese days
. . . well, some things he do very good. De way he
prog dem lobster, dat is very clever. Rum Point
Channel. Swim right among de reef, mon.

Well, dass very fine.

Speedy, I believe dat he lack nerve. You remember
de other day when de ocean was so high, he look
kind of coward dere.

He only seventeen, mon.

When I were seventeen, I were sailin to de cays as
pilot!

Well, dass fine too.

Went rangin when I was fourteen! Den I sail one
trip in de crew, and I spent dat trip up on de
masthead *lookin*, and *seein*, and *rememberin*! And
de next voyage, dey had no choice but to put me
dere in de port boat as pilot!

De boy somebody else, got to remember dat.

De manner dat he stand dere lookin at me . . .

Maybe he stand dere lookin at you cause he hopin
dat one day you look at *him*.

Foreign vessels intending to engage in the turtle fishery on the Miskito Banks must register with the customs officials of the Republic of Nicaragua, and go to port to clear again upon departure from these waters. In addition to port fees, foreign vessels must pay a tax on every head of turtle to be transported from the territorial waters of the Republic of Nicaragua.

Toward noon, the *Eden* comes in under Cape Gracias. Because of the heavy surge, the ship drops anchor well offshore.

A coast of giant mangrove backed by low hills, heavy sky: there is no smoke nor sign of human presence. A low bar where dirty waves break in a fringe is the outer delta of the Coco River, which carries so much silt from inland jungles that even here, a mile at sea, the water is the color of dead mud.

The *Eden* swings heavily on her chain. Now her bow heads up into the wind, and from the pulley on the mast her port boat is swung over the rails. When the ship rolls, the catboat bangs against the hull, and the sound brings the Captain from the deckhouse. He is wearing clean shirt and pants, mostly unbuttoned, and street shoes and a bent Panama hat.

Papa? It say here in my book dat Cape Gracias a Dios got dat name from Christopher Columbus—

Hold her off dere! Hold dat boat off!

Dem short masts, Copm Raib! Can't swing her clear!

Can't use an oar to hold her off while she goin down? Never heard about dat?

With dat short swing—

Nemmine! Men dat know dere job—

You sayin—

Nemmine, I said!

Copm Raib? Copm Raib? You all dressed up! You lookin like you plannin on gettin married!

Dis how *you* looked when *you* got married? Wouldn't s'prise me. (*shouts*) Buddy! Run get dat shoe box with de ship's documents! Who goin ashore?

I willin, Papa.

Go get dat box, I said! (*grunts*) Okay dere, Speedy. Nobody else? Don't like rowin? Well, c'mon den, Vemon, I get some work out of you yet!

How about Athens? Athens never—

He sick! Dass what dey tell me about *dat* one! Dat one too *sick* to work!

Dat ain't justice!

I say, get in de boat! I take care of de justice around here! Hold her off dere, Speedy! Speedy, you row in de middle till I see how you do!

Copm? Know de channel? What you do is dis—

You sayin I don't know my way on de Miskita Coast? By God, Byrum, I never thought I hear *dat*!

Nemmine, den. But I was here on de *A.M. Adams* since you was last here—

Shove off dere! Let go dat line!

The blue catboat falls downwind from the *Eden*. Raib stands upright in the stern, holding a short blunt Miskito paddle. Speedy and Vemon step the mast, a spruce pole with a piece of dirty canvas wrapped around it;

the mast is hand-adzed, with flat facets, like rail fence. The sail is gaff-rigged, and there is a small jib which Vemon secures to the bow: in place of a tiller, there are rudder lines, secured to both ends of a yoke fixed to the head of the rudder, like the top of a T.

Now the wind thumps in the sail, and the catboat scuds away toward the coast.

Copm Raib? Which gang you got me in, Copm Raib?

You be with Will in dis port boat. You and Athens; you got your partner dere to pull for you. (*laughs*) I take Byrum in de starboard gang with Speedy here, cause Speedy green, ain't dat right, Speedy? Green but willin!

I do my domnedest, Doddy.

Den dere's Buddy ...

Nemmine about Buddy—dat is *my* business.

Copm Raib? Buddy gettin a full share, ain't he? I mean to say, seem like dere an extra man aboard— don't need but eight.

Goddom it, with dis lot, I *need* an extra mon! And maybe de extra one is *you*, ever think of dat? Goddom drunken—

What I mean is, Copm Raib, I think I like to change into *your* catboat, so I *learn* more. Dat fella you got dere for mate, he just got too much mouth for me.

Raib laughs quietly for a long time.

Now I heard plenty said about Will, but dat is one thing dat I never heard about. Will pretty quiet when he ain't got something to say. Ain't like his boy. Neither one of dem got sense, but Will got sense enough to keep his mouth shut when his brain ain't workin.

Dass right! You recall dat time you told him he were wrong? And den he—

Raib starts to laugh again; he wipes his eyes, looking shy.

Well, I guess you ain't de only one dat got faults, Vemon, it just *seem* dat way. But Will a pretty good sailor, I got to say dat. Dey don't come no better den dat in days like dis. I mean to say, you couldn't hardly expect a first-class turtler; ain't many of *dem* no more. Will can pretty well take care of de job on de vessel deck, and set de nets too, he can set de nets. But de important part dere dat he don't know much about, and dat is where to *put* de nets. He not a first-class pilot.

Dass right. Dass—

But come to seamanship, he as good as you will find today. Him and Byrum, dey as good as you will find today.

Well, seamanship, dat is one place dat I got Will beat.

A silence.

I bet you thought dat Will had seaman's papers, dat right, Copm Raib?

Raib cocks his head.

How soon after we gets home you gone have your
money spent on rum? Can you drink it all up in one
week?

Huh! Maybe I won't drink at all!

Dat would be de best thing, darlin. Dat would be
de best.

Vemon struggles to look injured.

Once I went two, three months without touchin no
rum! I was *workin*! My own provision ground.
Over dere north of Salt Creek, between Salt Creek
and Batabano. Yams. Papaws. Had a grass piece
with a cow in it! Dat time I was workin for myself,
de provision ground of Vemon Evers—

Vemon *Dilbert* Evers.

Vemon Dilbert Evers. And during de time dat I
was workin for myself, I never touch it once. Not
even *once*.

Dass very fine. Have your own ground. Man dat got
a cow, he got it made. I plont some young trees
now, small plonts. Later on, Speedy got fruit. You
know? On my own ground. In de Bay Islands.

Vemon sets his striped cap hard upon his head.

In dem days, over dere north of Salt Creek, I were
feelin good. Dat were my chance in dis life, and I
lost it.

Buddy, Byrum and Athens are dozing in the stern. Will is mending net, and Wodie sits on the galley roof, bare black legs swinging. Brown is perched on his blue fuel drum, staring at nothing and singing with no expression.

> *I can't help* (voice cracks) shit!
> *I can't help it*
> *If I still in love with you*

Delta. A circle of dark birds over the trees.

Oh, yes. I work a little on de turtlin boat, learn
how dey do; den I go home. I givin up de sea, work
on de land. I workin my plontation. I can *hoe*,
mon.

I tellin you, Speedy, some dese young fellas dat dey
got dese days, dey can't even work a hoe. Dat
Conwell dat is son to Will, he one of dem. It like
Old Copm Jim dere, what I heard him say to de
Tailor from Jamaica. (*laughs*) Copm Jim, he must
be close to ninety years of age, and dis day he fightin
mad dat de Tailor from Jamaica made so much
money from just settin dere and tailorin.

In Jamaica?

No, mon. Tailor *from* Jamaica. He tryin to establish
hisself. Come from Jamaica about twenty-five years
ago. Dey calls him de Tailor from Jamaica for dat
reason.

Got no name, huh?

In Jamaica, prob'ly, dey give him some kind of a
name. Anyways, Copm Jim say, You ever tote wood?
Mend net? Work a hoe? Copm say, How many
grandchildren you got? (*laughs*) Cause dat is de one
thing, and de *only* thing dat Copm Jim has got,
and dat is grandchildren. And great-grandchildren.

Copm Raib? Copm Jim got grandchildren he don't
even know about!

Dass it. Poor old fella, dass about all he *do* got, and
dat ain't much, in *dat* family. So he say to de Tailor
from Jamaica, How many grandchildren you got?
And den he say it couple times again, just so he
could hear de words.

Brown? Like singin? Cause dere was an old song dat
we had down at East End, it were a song we called
de Hox-bill Song. Calvert Conally and a guy by de
name of Garwin Rankin used a catboat, used a trap
net, to cotch turtle, and dey were around on de
northeastern part of de island, called Bluff Bay,
fishenin and trappin. And dere was dis hox-bill
dat were not in de nets, dey claim; dey hook
him up with a fish hook from de bottom. But
Bonnie Dixon had a net sot, and he claimed de net
were tangled, and when he examined de turtle, de
turtle had line marks on it. So he took de turtle
from dese boys, and Calvert grandmother, she gave
Bonnie Dixon de name of Black Cat, and dey
made a song off of it. I would have to set back
a little to remember all de words, but I remember
it because we used to use it as a dance tune.

It was a holiday in de month of May
Calvert and Garwin went Bluff Bay
Caught one hox-bill, so dey say
But Old Black Cat went and took it away . . .

Lord, what a miser-y
Took away dat cash mo-ney
People, people will be sorry to see
De graveyard for Bonnie and de gallows for me!

Slowly Brown opens his eyes and mouth.

Bailar? Dance? To *dat?*

Grandmother say, Dat Old Black Cat
I hope to God it will make him fat
And he mother say, I will cut he throat
If your Uncle Hedley don't take de case to court . . .

Wodie wears his red-black-white checkered vest cut from flour sacking, and seat-patched dungaree shorts. Heedless of Brown's stare, he laughs, keeping time with his bare heels against the cabin side.

Dere was a boy name Bertram say:

> *If Old Black Cat don't give me some*
> *I gone to drink Uncle Willoughby Rum*
> *Den I go out on a spree*
> *And kick Old Bonnie right in three!*

Oh, dat were a *big* song, mon!

Dat no fuckin *song*, mon! No fuckin love in it! (*outraged*) *Amor!*

Well, Brownie, I just tellin you a little bit about Cayman, y'know. Pass de time dat way.

Shit! No *amor!*

Coco River.

Banging in over the bar, the boat ships water and the shoe box of ship's documents is soaked. Raib curses brutally, staring about him; in the stillness, the distant jungle waits at the far bank of the river.

The shallow delta is a mile across, scarred with stumps of twisted trees. To the west is the wall of mangrove, silent, under yellowing gray cumulus; to the east a barrier islet of low scrub. On the tip of the islet, against a thickened sea sky, figures run and wave.

Ain't gone to help dem?

The Captain squints at the far figures.

Prob'ly dey refugees from some goddom place. (*pause*) Prob'ly dey desperate for a boat. You want to go in dere? (*pause*) In times gone back, a mon would go to help people, but in dese days dey too many dat needs help.

Make me feel funny, Doddy. S'posin it were us in trouble—

De Coptin *tellin* you, Honduras, we go in dere, it *could* be us and pretty domn quick!

Modern time, mon.

Lord, what a miser-y
Took away dat cash mo-ney
People, people will be sorry to see
De graveyard for Bonnie and de gallows for me!

Wodie lies back on the galley roof, sits up again. Brown remains motionless on the blue oil drum.

Oh yes, Brownie, it gone to be dry weather. When de risin sun throws out rays at de horizon, it gone to be good weather, good times, and when she go down, and de rays comin dis way (*gestures*) shinin back on you, you gone to have plenty rain. (*sighs*) Today all de rays left her; she just a pure ball of light. And dat means dry, dry weather.

All dat old kind shit no use to me in life.

Well, dose are de things we studies at East End, not havin radios to tell us when de hurricanes is comin. Now in Caymans we ain't lost anybody to hurricane since 1932. Dat were de heavy storm dat struck down Prospect.

Brown spits toward the Miskito Coast.

Dat old mon no pay me. No *dinero*.

Anyways, all along East End de storm had washed de sand away, and fill de channels. Dese are real channels, not de flats in de coral reef where ships goin aground in hurricane break de coral down so small boats can come and go. Where one old wreck struck on de reef was de flat we called Old Anchor Flat, but dat growin up again long years ahead of me.

When dis voyage finish, I be naked.

Oh, yes! De corals is fillin it in.

Brown, picking at his rags, suddenly sings.

> *I can't help* (voice cracks) shit! Help *it* . . .
> *If I still in love with you!*

Oh, yes! De corals is fillin it in.

The two fall silent. Wodie gazes westward.

In the delta, the wind dies. The men lower the mast, and the boat drifts back on the brown flood. They run the oars through thatch-rope thongs bent to the gunwales.

Raib takes up his Miskito paddle, which is heavy and short, with heart-shaped blade. Vemon is at the bow oars, Speedy amidships. Vemon bends with the long pull of a fisherman; Speedy has the choppy stroke of a man used to a paddle.

> Dey calls you Speedy, dat right? Well, speedy ain't no way to row. You gone to row a *catboat*, you gots to *row*!

> Vemon right dis one time, darlin. I don't think you got de theory into it yet.

> You learn me, Doddy. I willin.

> Don't use your arms, den—use your back.

Dass right, put your domn *back* into it, mon—I sick of corryin you!

Vemon, it a very poor thing to shout at other people in dat manner when dey is learnin. You gots to figure dat each and every person got dere faults, and dat while you is thinkin dat you yourself is faultless, you may be de wrong one into de case. So what I try to do—

Copm Raib? I knowed you figure dat ever mon got his fault, Copm Raib, but I never knowed dat you was so much against speakin *out* about dat fault!

Speedy's laugh is a squeal of pleased surprise. Vemon sinks low at his oars, so that his striped railroad cap is barely visible to the Captain over the tattered shoulder of Speedy's T-shirt. The crown of the striped cap has a rusted button.

Vemon frowns at his own shoes, clearing his throat.

Oh yes, dat were it. (*gruffly*) Dat provision ground north of Salt Creek were my chance in life and den I lost it.

Raib makes three quick powerful strokes, using the paddle like an extension of his heavy arm. Then he gives a little cough and begins to laugh, a soft sweet laugh that collapses his broad face. The mirth rolls up slowly from his belly, until his body quakes with it, and his eyes weep; he stamps his foot in the bilges of the boat.

Speedy squeals anew; he cannot row. Vemon, too, dares a little sniffing laugh; resting his oars, looking innocent, he scratches.

Vemon Dilbert Evers! You okay, Vemon! You not such a poor fella as I always thought!

The *Eden*. Noon. Wodie is washing his flour-sacking shirt.

... wreck at de lower end of East End, dat was de old *Storborn Head*: dat wreck struck dere when my grandmother was a little girl, an old coffee wreck, and she say dass when de rats came to Cayman. She say de rats came ashore off dat ship in rafts and infested all de land.

Brown knocks his sombrero back to look at Wodie.

Por qué you t'row dis old-time shit on me?

Well, y'see, Brownie, dem other fellas *knows* about Caymans—

I *Sponnish*, mon! I *travel*, mon, see de big towns! I ain't no Cayman nigger!

Wodie's good eye comes to rest on Brown's dark arms and bare dark knees: he wrings out his shirt as Brown curses him.

We ain't shamed of color in de Cayman Islands, Brownie.

The engineer, still hunched on the fuel drum rim, turns his ragged back to Wodie.

I mind my business, *entiende*?

Black trees, gray clouds, gray sky.

The catboat moves slowly up the estuary. A bigua surfaces, dives forward, surfaces again and flies.

Dat bird more like a seal, de way it duck under dere!

I seen seals in a pitcher show one time. Dat were de year dat I sailed up de Delaware, and I went to dat pitcher show in Chester, Pennsylvania.

Dey had seals in Chester, huh?

In de back-time now, dey had seals here in de cays.

No, brother. Seals is *north*—

I tellin you, Vemon, dey had seals. Call dem *monk* seals. I *read* about'm.

Read? Dat don't mean nothin. I can read a little bit myself, and some of de things it said dere—

Seals! One of de fellas saw one, I don't believe it were thirty years ago, over dere at de Coxcones! Reginal Barney, dat went down on de *Majestic.* And den dere is Seal Cay—why you think dey calls it dat? *(more quietly)* Dey killed off de seals just like dey killin off green turtle, and de crocodiles before dem. De snipes is gone now. Ain't no iguana left up at Northwest. Mahogany, logwood, fustic— all dat gone now! Dey cuttin it all away!

A waste of mud bars and stranded trees, set against the silence of the jungle.

The water freshens; the river margins turn a livid green. High on the banks are huge trunks of mahogany from the inland forest.

    fish ripples

         a white egret, transfixed

             slow circling hawks, inland

    passing rain

At a fork in the river Raib chooses the west branch, which dies eventually in a slough choked with blue hyacinth.

The still birds deepen the silence.

Talk about hell, dis a hell of a place, dass all I sayin. A *hell* of a place. In a civilized country now, you don't got to be a explorer to go through de customs. (*angrily*) Seem to me I been up dis Godforsaken river all my life, and every time it changin, it never look de same!

Byrum sayin—

Dis river *changin*, dass all! A mon can't count on it. Ever' domn time you try to go up dis river, you gots to hunt out a new channel, or you die dere in de mud, like one dem old stumps.

I glad I not here in de night, with all dem stumps. All dat hair and arms on dem—

It de domn Sponnish! Dey don't put markers out, not even a stick! Every place you go in de lands of de Sponnish, it de same! And when finally you finds de channel, it lead to nothin. One hut dere, and a couple Indians! Boy, you know dat you come to de end of de world! Cape Gracias a Dios! De end of de world is Gracias a Dios!

The tide is falling in the estuary, and soon the boat is grounding on soft bars.

I were six days away from marryin dat woman when she start foolin round.

Who she fool with?

Oh, she not fool much, just a little bit, but Speedy don't like dat shit: you is or you isn't. Den I find Miss Pansy.

So you marryin Miss Pansy.

What dey calls common-law. De old kind of marriage, dat is disappearin fast. Least in de poor people. Don't get around to dat.

Too busy cootin. (*shouts*) Can't cross dere, Vemon—don't see dem birds wadin in de shallers?

De one thing dat I thankful for, we ain't got rivers in Caymans. Dat right, Copm Raib?

Dommit to hell, I never see it bad as dis in forty years!

The Captain jumps overboard in his shoes and sinks up to his knees in mud; his curse hangs in the air. Vemon and Speedy ship oars and climb out of the boat, which is careened onto her side and hauled across the shallows; the mud is so soft that the men must lean on the boat to extricate their knees after each step.

Heat and mosquitoes. In the humid air, their shirts suck at their backs.

Stop leanin on de gunwales while Speedy pullin!

Leanin?

Afternoon half gone and we not even found de channel yet! We gone miss another day's fishenin!

It ain't *me* was leanin—

We lucky for dis little wind, Doddy—hear dem miskita? I can hear dem all de way over dere in de mongrove. If dat wind quit, we finish.

Shit! Miskita on de one side, and over on de other side, we get too close to dat little cay, de sand flies! Out here we okay—all we got is snakes and leeches, maybe a stingaree!

And dey got fresh-water shark here. Nicaragua. Dat right, mon.

Oh, I believe dat! Anything bad dat dey ain't got in Honduras, dey bound to have it in Nicaragua!

On the far shore, two Indians in a dugout cayuca slip along under the buttonwood.

Talkin about miskitas now: Miskita Cay dere, Copm Raib—dey name dat for de Indians? Or de miskitas?

Miskita Cay name for de Indians dat used to live dere in de former time, but de Indians might be named for dis stinkin coast dat got de name *Mosquitia,* and dat name come from de sand flies, which de domn Sponnish calls *mosquitia* out of dere ignorance.

You speak Sponnish, Copm?

No! I be shamed to speak it!

I tellin you, dis pullin ain't no sailor's work, dat right, Copm Raib?

Dis donkey work! It take a donkey to work like dis! And dis port boat leakin, see dat? She a new boat and she leakin—dass de way dey make boats in dese goddom days!

Dat mate you got, he say dis port boat leak cause you never put flowers on de bow—

Flowers? Will say dat?

Boy? You got dis kind rivers over dere in Honduras, boy?

You speakin to me?

De colored dere, dey *used* to what we calls donkey work, I guess.

Speedy stops pulling long enough to spit.

Dass right, nigger. We ain't like you. We ain't afraid of work.

Don't get discourage about Vemon; he can't help hisself, poor fella.

I not discourage. I never been discourage in my life. I just walk ahead every day. I got four suits aboard de vessel, and my family got plenty clothes. I a hard-workin mon, work hard all de days of my life.

Ain't like your partner, den.

When Brown done with dis voyage, he gone be naked. Dat what he say every night when he lie down: When dat old coptin done with me I gone be naked.

The Captain's thick toenails are caked with river mud.

He were naked when he come aboard! I give dat fella his first chance! I bought him dem shoes he wearin, and now he think he somebody! But he don't know nothin, and he don't want to learn!

Brown ain't got a willin mind—

Top of dat, he stupid! He so stupid dat he—

Dass what *I* think, Copm Raib!

You think? Dat don't mean nothin!

Don't mean nothin?

Stop leanin on dat gunwale, I tellin you!

Brown say he were with Che in Guatemala—
maybe he mean he were down dere at de same time
with Che. Or maybe havin Brownie with him were
de reason dat Che lost! (*hoots*) And after he got
done with Che, he went over to de Yankees.

Che?

Don't know about Che Guevara in Grand Cayman?
(*grins*) Oh, dey too much water between Cayman
and de world, don't know about *Che*!

How de hell Brown find his way to Guatemala? Dat
fella call de manifold mon-fool, he such a fuckin
idiot. So what he doin for de Yankees? Spy? Fella
stupid as dat, now, dey ain't *nobody* would suspect
him—

Oh, dey had a camp in Guatemala for de ones was
goin to de Bay of Pigs. Lot of food dere and no
work, mostly fellas like Brown dat called dereselves
Cubans and went over dere to eat de food.

He say he done some soldierin—dat where he done
it?

Soldierin! (*pause*) *No*, mon. Dat were Colombia,
back up in de country. "La Violencia," mon. Oh,
dat were very uncomely, what de *banditos* done
down dere. Killed people by de thousands.

You were runnin guns down dere, ain't dat right,
Copm Raib? Makin good money?

Raib smacks his paddle on the river, sending a dash of
water over Vemon. The water drips untended from
the bill of Vemon's cap, and from his chin; he
squinches his small face, but does not wipe it.

You gettin smart with me again?

Me?

And after dat he went to de Bay of Pigs?

No, mon. But de Yankees thought Brown must be some kind of a Cuba nigger, so dey sent him up dere to Miami. Den dey found out he never *heard* of Cuba. So while dey was tryin to figure what country to send him back to, he run off and wandered around on de Gulf Coast a while, living in de woods, stealin off de land.

Stealin? Didn't look for no job?

Mon, he say dey so many niggers in de woods it hard to find a place to piss. Jamaicans. Haiti. People starvin, and dey goin to de States. De woods dere are full of strangers, lookin into de houses in de night. Dey no record of dese wild niggers but where Brown was, dey was raidin de houses, so de police come out into de woods with dogs. Brown sneak down to de coast and dis coptin say, Okay, nigger, you can work your passage, and Brown say, *Donde va?* De *Desirade*. She bound for Ceiba, but she got caught in de hurricane, put in dere to French Harbour. When Brown jump ship, all dat he had were a pair of pants and a black T-shirt, I remember dat. Didn't speak hardly no English till he come to Roatán.

Who give him de name of Brown?

Mon, I don't know. Pick dat up in de States, I guess, long with de name of Smith.

Midafternoon. The tide still falling. A mosquito whines.

The catboat is barely a mile above the delta, and the customs post is far away upriver. Vemon, exhausted, mutters to himself. Speedy tastes the water, spits it out. Raib reviles the thick blind flood and aimless winds.

A broken sky.

Strings of ibis and egrets, bone white, turn pale pink as they cross a broken sunset.

De last time I come down dis river, Copm Raib, we corried a drum of water and de crew; dis time we be lucky—

Turn dis domn boat around. TURN HER AROUND!

Copm Raib? We come back at sunrise, Copm Raib, and try again!

You domn fool! It be low tide at sunrise, just like now! I ain't gone to lose another day! No, mon! We sailin for Bobel dis very evenin!

The boat drifts down the river in soft rain.

A school of mullet, parted, sprays the surface; a heron squawks once, passing over, under a hidden moon.

At the delta, the catboat is hauled across salt wavelets on the bar and launched into the surf. There are no stars; the sea and shore are dark. Raib has taken a range on the way in, using the islet point and a great stump; adjusting his heading, he glances back every few moments down the straight line of his wake.

Rain pocks on the night sea.

A masthead light, blurred by the rain.

Well, I glad to see dat *one* of dem got sense.

Still see de light? I lost it.

Dey got a squall dere now. But I got a bearin.

Raib shakes his head. He sighs.

I got a bearin.

· 6 ·

Night wind

the moon comes
the moon goes

night clouds

Underway. The *Eden*, bound offshore, buffets the wind.

4 A.M. Wodie relieves Byrum.

The rusting schooner bangs and lurches: white crests pour down the faces of black waves, in a loud wash. Crouched, leaning, braced, the men gulp at their coffee, squinting out over their cups at the toiling dark.

Byrum, pants down, is perched on the rail behind the catboat on the starboard side. Across the pile of stove wood stacked just forward of the galley, he can see the iron hair of the master of the vessel, seated on the rail to port. Over the wind, both shout at once.

fish a few days, den crawl dem turtle   Miskita Cay   register at Bragman's   stinkin river stinkin country   don't believe dat   if dey believe we corryin turtle   search   Señores, ain't no green turtle aboard dis vessel, only dis green turtle shit. Put *dat* in your fuckin customs house and welcome!

                    tell you, Copm Raib   you never listened! You

                    follered de calm of de stream comin down along, y'know?   little kind of calm streak side de shallers   big piece of mahogany   went and we went and we went

                    dat main channel down to de deep river   stick further to de south

                                        de south?

                                                  river domn long river,   hundreds of miles   tide comin out strong

                    Adams boat draw quite a bit less water den dat port boat of mine   Christ A'mighty   boat layin right on her broadside   pullin her and pullin her and pullin her   leakin   God A'mighty   fore de evenin!

                                        you got tangled in de water lilies

At the edge of darkness, Wodie's checkered shirt flies on the shrouds.

The men crouch down out of the wind.

> We got a old wild tree, y'know, grows wild and big, with little bells dat dey call a fig. And de old folks claim dat dese trees are haunted, dat dey used to see ghosts around dese trees. So dat is what dey callin duppy trees.

> Duppy trees! My, my!

> Course, any place dat is uninhabited is where de duppies likes to be, and places dat is lonesome. Dat is why folks doesn't stay alone in dere houses in de night. And duppies will foller you if you go corryin rum and johnnycake. De old people sayin dat dey been bothered in de bushes, and certain times dey been hearin de sweetest music and all of dat. So one day I was out in de bush nearby to where dey call de Shadow Pond, way out in de bushes by myself, where I know dere was no other person dere, cause nobody s'posed to go dere but myself. And I hearin sweet music dat couldn't be nothin else but ghosts.

Raib shouts at Wodie from the wheelhouse.

> DAT IS NONSENSE DAT YOU TELLIN, WODIE!

Wodie grins shyly at the other men, who signal him to keep talking. He lowers his voice.

> Now dis was told me by my own grandmother's brother by de name of Wilson. Wilson was courtin

de woman dat became his wife, and was goin home about one o'clock de night. And down de road, here comes a strange black dog, and de dog was not standin on de ground but kind of leapin from one side to the other. Now dis were a night black as de grave, but dis dog had a kind of glow, like you see in bad fish dere, or punky wood, so he knew right away it was a ghost. So instead of takin de road, he took de seashore. And de dog follered. So he went into de sea and started to go down until he come abreast of where he wanted to go ashore, which was a goodly distance because he lived in de *west* end of East End and he was comin from de *east* end of East End. But when he come ashore, here comes de dog again, and dere is something 'longside de dog, look like a woman. And he took to de sea and swam back to where his girl friend lived and in de mornin time dere came de news dat my grandmother had died.

I very glad to hear about dem old-time things, y'know. Dey dyin away on de west end.

Oh yes, Mist' Will! I was just a boy dat loved to keep old people company! I loved to know something about de old people and de old ways. I loved—

TELL ABOUT DEM OBEAH WORKERS, WODIE! TELL ABOUT DE MURDER OF DAT CHILD!

First light.

A black hump on the black horizon.

Athens! ATHENS! Buddy, run back dere and tell de helm to head her off de wind another point. If he were not asleep, he could had seen dat landfall for hisself!

One day dat Athens gone wake up in de grave.

Bobel Cay.

Look dere! A vessel!

Against the cay a white shape rises. Raib turns from the rail as Buddy reappears.

Athens! ATHENS! (*to Buddy*) Run back and tell de helm we changin course! Sout'-sou'east!

Copm Raib? Copm Raib? Must be Desmond's vessel! Your own doddy aboard of dere—don't want to speak him?

Raib turns a mean stare on Vemon, who steps backward and salutes. The crewmen laugh. Raib's chin juts and he starts to speak, then stops. He gazes at his men.

You want to lose another day? All right, den. BUDDY!

In the gray light, a yacht, decrepit. Her varnished cabin sides are patchy and her white hull is stained with rust; her afterdeck, under a torn flapping canopy, is littered with cartons and refuse. A few turtles, unprotected from the sun, are scattered on the main deck, forward. Old auto tire fenders from her last port hang along her sides, and rust, barnacles and algae crust her water line. On her bows, large eyes are crudely painted, and on her stern is the name

DAVY JONES

Yawning and scratching, her men drift to the rail. One pisses into the gray water.

Call *dat* a turtle boat, in dese domned days!

The *Eden*, coming alongside, settles heavily against her fenders; her crewmen take the *Eden*'s lines. The two crews nod in greeting but do not call out; all watch the *Eden*'s captain.

Raib stands, feet spread, at his own rail, which lies below that of the *Davy Jones*.

What dem eyes for? Desmond need dat to find turtle?

What say dere, Copm Raib? Come up, mon! Come aboard de yacht!

Call dat a yacht, huh? Copm Andrew dere?

Yah, mon! Come up!

A silence as the *Eden*'s engines are shut down. Wind, and a wash of sea along the hull. From Bobel comes bird shriek and the thud of surf on the shore to windward; the daybreak sky takes on a silver shine. On the north point of the cay, a fire darts and shudders in the wind. There figures gather in one mass and break apart again.

Raib remains standing at the rail, feet wide apart.

He can't come to de rail? Copm ANDREW!
(*pause*) Can't hear me, den?

Yah, mon. He hearin you good. Settin right dere.
But he ain't talkin.

Goddom it—

Hurt his heart, jumpin out de catboat. Rough
weather, y'know, and de rails is high. Must be
he shamed of hurtin hisself, cause he won't talk no
more.

Raib swings onto the deck of the *Davy Jones*.

Andrew Avers, dressed in clean, sun-worn khakis and
high black shoes and a round-topped thatch hat, is
seated in a rough chair knocked together out of boards
which stick up behind his head. In his lap is a sun-
whitened conch shell, cupped ceremonially in both
spotted hands.

Under the clear gaze of his father, Raib starts to speak,
then stops, and makes no move toward him.

Catboat? Goddom it, to bring a man dat is eighty
years of age—DESMOND!

Ain't aboard, Copm Raib. Desmond spend de night
dere on de cay with dem Jamaicans. (*winks*) Dey
got rum and pussy over dere, but Desmond say
he go dere to talk *business.*

Raib points at Will.

Throw dat boat overboard! I goin ashore!

Bobel.

Speedy and Buddy stand beside the boat.

In a ruined copse on the high ground of the cay, a litter of tin and broken glass gives off a weak reflection of the distant fire. Here and there on the spears and stumps a sea bird poises, wings held high over its back; the shrieking birds lift away on the dawn wind which blows through the broken sea wood unimpeded. Striking the first sun rays, overhead, the sharp wings turn from gray to white: the terns beat forward, stroking hard against the wind to remain above the head of the intruder.

The dry smell of bird guano floats lightly on a pall of human excrement. Placing his bare feet carefully, Raib spits out his breath in bursts. The smooth track of a hawksbill turtle leads up above the tide line, where the turtle has pushed aside torn purslane and trash to dig her nest.

The sand spit on the north end of the cay: a dead fire, and flimsy wind breaks built from the killed trees. Here dark forms lie in a ragged pile.

On the open beach, two figures copulate and a third sits hunched up like a fetus. His ragged shorts are tangled at his knees, and his hands are bloody; he is cradling his stomach. He croons slowly in bewilderment. Noticing Raib, he blinks, then scowls, but the scowl gives way to a yip of pain. In an effort to spit toward the copulating man he fails; the weak spit bubbles.

Boog son-bitch cut me. Oh, I dyin now, mon. Oh, I dyin.

The copulating man and the man dying wear small street hats.

On hands and knees a black, thick-bodied girl stares at the sand. Her ragged shift is up around her waist. Because of her big belly, the man has mounted her from behind; except for his street hat and a pair of ragged shorts hung on one ankle, he is naked. A knife glints by his hand. His ear is pressed to the girl's back, as if he were listening for the life in her. One hand clutches her right breast, the other a bottle of *aguardiente* that is stuck into the sand at her left side. Heavily he fucks her, stops a while, then fucks again.

The girl lowers her right arm to the sand while keeping her buttocks high. With her left hand, she reaches back and wrenches at the bottle and drags it forward, but before she can drink, she loses interest. Slowly the bottle falls.

The fluid leaks onto the sand.

Raib rights the bottle. The girl raises her hand as if to brush sand from her eyes but does not complete the gesture; the hand falls back. She lowers both forearms to the sand and rests her cheek upon her hands, her mouth forced into odd disfigurement.

On the lee side, in stained shallows, wavelets lift melted labels, floating feces, a pale plastic bottle. In the offal is the bobbing head of a green turtle; its shell and guts are scattered on the sand. Another turtle lies upright on the beach, facing inland. Its flippers are bound, and its great weight, unsupported, slowly smothers it. When Raib turns it on its back, it blinks, gasping its ancient sea sound, and sand grains falling from its lids stick in the fluids from its eye.

Leaves and twigs on the broken bushes do not bend downwind, but twist and fly in tumult. The dawn sky is swelling with the light, but at the horizon the sun is hidden by a squall line of black clouds moving fast toward the south. The squalls emerge from a dark place in a towering mass of gray. With rising light, the bird shriek mounts, piercing the sea boom to the eastward.

In the new sea, a sliver of light flips back and forth over a round green leaf of sea grape. The playing fish arcs out of the water, flashing its silver side, its eye a bright black spot.

Raib stands transfixed. On a coral rock protruding from the sand, a bleeding-tooth snail budges, and a ghost crab, half hidden, extends dry eyes on stalks.

White feather, blowing.

In the beach vine, illuminated leaves spin, dark and pale and dark. Leaf shadows turn in the early light. A floret of purple morning-glory, blowing.

The sea, breathing. The fish leaps into the air.

the fish leaps into the air

the fish leaps into the air

the fish leaps into the air

On the corner of the beach a man sits alone, facing the east. Raib's bare feet are silent on the sand.

The man's legs are crossed, and a cigarette hangs from the center of his mouth. The big head bent over the rum bottle is balding and the neck is scarred and tight whorls of sweated hair mat the swart back. Heavy legs are stuck into black rubber boots splashed with red paint, and from ragged shorts a penis hangs out in a tatter.

The black clouds are afire; at the spine of the beach the broken bushes glow and blacken. On the windward shore, the ocean pours across a wave-washed bench of coral, lashing the islet with white dragon tails.

Desmond!

In silhouette against the sun Raib stands motionless, wind curling the frayed edges of his hat.

Desmond Eden nods a little, struggles to rise, sits back again, off balance. He grins, shaking his head; he offers rum to Raib's silhouette, shielding his black glasses from the sun.

Raib does not move. By his feet, a ghost crab glides away on knife toes, stalked eyes taut, making delicate thin curved slashes in the sand.

Slowly Desmond removes his glasses. His gritty face is poor in color, not bearded but unshaven, with broken eyebrows and a heavy mouth. His left eye seems to protrude; he looks lopsided. He gazes at Raib, bloodshot, then returns the dark glasses to his face.

Oh, dat sun wild, mon.

Raib is silent.

Oh, dat sun *wild*, mon. Hurt my eye.

The men aboard ship watch the two figures on the beach. Will clears his throat.

You fellas seen Conwell anyplace?

A boy with kinky red hair and pale freckled skin steps from the cabin door of the *Davy Jones*.

What you wantin with me?

Why you hidin? Cause you left my catboat rottin at Half Moon Cay? Cause you walked off de job?

Call *dat* a job? Rangin? You livin in de back time, Papa!

Will runs into the deckhouse and returns with Conwell's packet. He shies the packet toward his son, but the wind catches it; it hangs a moment like a kite, then skitters down into the water. Cigarette packs bob, and spreading comic books in leaking colors.

Don't come home no more, Conwell!

Cursing, the boy strips his shirt and dives over the side. He grabs at the packs and papers, which shred in his hands. Treading water, he holds the remnants in the air.

You fucked me good, old mon! I *need* dem smokes!

Noon.

Raib and Desmond face each other at the rails.

A cigarette butt stirs, shifts, blows across the deck, coming to rest against the shoe of the old man in the chair.

Desmond points.

Byrum Watler standin dere dat heard de talk dat mornin in West Bay, right under dem big grape trees by de church.

Dass right. I was—

Goddom it, I talkin to *you*, not Byrum—

Well, best let Byrum tell it, Copm Raib, so's you believe it.

Well, we was settin on de boats under de grape trees, lookin out over de West Bay beach and down toward de sout'ward. And Desmond were settin sail dat mornin time, bound for de Cays. And Copm Andrew look kind of sorrowful dere, and he say to us, Dommit, boys, every day I settin idle is costin me ten years off my life! So den I told him dat he was lookin very well in his appearance, and dat prob'ly he could sail again as pilot, bein dat he was so well instructed about de sets. And Copm Andrew noddin away dere.

Goddom it, Byrum, you just de mon to stir de pot!

Byrum ignores him.

Well, Copm Andrew say, Dey many things dat I
have learned dat now has left me, but not what
I learned out dere in de Miskita Cays. In de fifty-five
years dat I was at it, my memory is just as fresh on
dat today. Says, I can still do what people knew dat
I was capable of doin, cause I can lay down dere
in my daughter's house at any moment dat I want
and picture dose sets just as natural as if I had used
dem yesterday, and all de courses, too, and if I went
out at it today, I would be no stranger.

Desmond winks at Byrum.

Dass it! De very words! And den he say, I couldn't
be as active in de boat as what I was!

Pity he didn't think of dat before he sailed!

Copm Raib, he were willin to go for nothin, but I
signed him up for a half-share. He needed to go, and
I needed a pilot—

Raib spins in a complete circle, stamping a foot hard
on the deck.

Half-share! Copm Andrew Avers! *Dat* be your little
way! Wait till I gone away down to Honduras, and
den to sneak in dere—God DOMN it! NEVER
HEARD ABOUT A STROKE? *(points at the chair)*
MAYBE YOU GOT HIM CRIPPLED UP FOR
GOOD! MAYBE NOW HE SOME KIND OF
A IDIOT!

Panting, he stops short. The men stare at the still
figure in the chair, who seems to smile.

No, mon! Copm Andrew say, I ain't dyin in no hospital, I gone die here on de turtle banks. And dem were de last words dat he spoke.

Thin tern cries over wind and water. To the east, in the white haze of the horizon, squall shadows towarding.

You got no business with him, Desmond.

Licking his teeth, Desmond spreads his hands and gazes at soiled fingernails. He checks the wind, the sky; he sighs.

Maybe you right dere, Copm Raib. I think you best take Copm Andrew on de *Eden,* so he be with his rightful son.

He grins ferociously at Athens, who suppresses a hoot. When Desmond speaks again, his voice is hard.

Rig dat chair to de block and fall and swing it over.

Desmond's men rig a sling under the chair seat and hook it to a pulley. They remove the old man's palm hat and tuck it beneath the old white conch. The chair is hoisted high over their heads, and Andrew Avers, swung outboard by the boom, rides back and forth between the vessels. Over his head, the blue sky fades in a film of white, with tints of green.

Raib makes a thick ugly sound, stops, clears his throat and speaks.

So dass de way you sneakin out of what you done, and knowin we just commenced dis turtle voyage, with no bunk for dat poor old fella, and no stores sufficient—

Raib stops speaking. Desmond's hand has stayed the boom. Over their heads, the old man sways with the rise and fall.

Don't want your doddy, Copm Raib? Dat what you sayin?

The ships lurch and the chair spins and unwinds again on the rope bridle. Captain Andrew, hands upon his conch, turns west, south, and north. In the wind, old white shank glistens between faded cuffs and a pair of high black shoes warped upward at the toes. As its arc increases, the chair gains momentum; the white hair flies. Unblinking, the old man circles on the clouds that are moving up behind black skeins of rigging.

Raib grabs for the whirling chair but cannot hold it; he is dragged against the rail. Desmond takes the guy line from a crewman and eases the chair down to the *Eden*'s deck.

Raib is panting. Desmond laughs.

Keep de chair, den, Copm Raib! No charge for dat!

We settle dis motter another day, Desmond!

I be waitin on your convenience, Copm Raib!

BROWN! START DEM ENGINES!

Desmond winks at Byrum.

Where you bound for, Desmond?

Can't go turtlin without a pilot, Byrum. Get a few
shark maybe, some salt fish. Bird eggs. Maybe I pick
up some dese Jamaica boys (*points toward beach*)
down around de cays, corry dem over to de land
of opportunity.

You still in dat game, huh?

Know something better? (*shrugs*) I guess I be goin
on dis way forever so.

HOW ABOUT HIS GEAR? HIS KNIFE
DERE? AND HIS SHARE OF DE CATCH?
YOU KEEPIN DAT?

I like to, Copm Raib, but you too smart for me.

An old duffel is slung down to the *Eden*, and three
turtle are transferred. Desmond tosses a big old-fashioned knife to Raib, blade first; Raib dodges it, and
the heavy blade gouges the deck.

CAST OFF DERE, WILL!

You kind to speak us, Copm Raib! Bye, Copm
Andrew! Hear me dere? Goodbye, old mon!

DUE SOUTH AND STEADY!

STEAD-DAY!

LASH DAT DOMN CHAIR TO DE MAST,
FORE HE ROLL OVER!

The *Eden* falls off toward the south. As Bobel sinks astern, two long dark skiffs appear, bursting free of broad sheets of spray, then vanishing in the smoky chop. Though they look too small for the open sea, the boats are driven at full speed, banging across the wind in white explosions.

Now they veer toward the *Eden.*

Dere some of Desmond's pan-heads!

Reapin bird eggs! It dat time of year

de crazy way
dey go!

de way dey go! I venture dey spoilt de turtlin ground all de way south to Dead Man Cay!

Three silhouettes in each skiff are standing. On the green sea the figures rise and fall; black arms gesticulate.

We gone to speak dem?

Speak *Jamaicans*? NO!

Slowly the skiffs gain on the *Eden;* they slam violently into the seas, flanking her wake. In the skiff to starboard, a naked figure in street hat and dark glasses sways and careens as he points at his mouth, points at his belly; he brandishes a bottle, points at it, then at the *Eden.*

Must be dey hungry, mon! Want to give us rum!

Smell dat rum, Vemon? Dey know you here!

The skiff comes grinding alongside, sliding and skidding in the wash. A line is tossed, and Speedy grabs it. Snatching the line from Speedy, Raib slings it free.

PAN-HEAD NIGGERS! GET DE HELL AWAY!

The black man in the street hat shouts: his violent mouth looks square. When he slams his hat into the bilges, his hair shoots out in spikes all over his head.

RAS CLOT!

A hurled bottle smashes on the *Eden*'s hull. The figure in street hat and dark glasses, upright, shrieking, slashes at the sky with a machete. The others make obscene signs; they screech. Over the motors of the *Eden*, in the cross wind, torn voices rise and are blown away.

BUMBO!

BUMBO CLOT!

AI-EE KANAKEE TUTTLE-FUCKAHS

The skiff to starboard falls astern, and the other comes up beside it, tossing in the wake. The six figures gaze after the *Eden*, burnt black on the white sky.

They rise and fall.

·7·

Due south and steady.

From the chair lashed to the mast, the old man can
observe his son's approach.

Raib whispers.

Copm Andrew? Can't talk to me, Papa? (*pause*)
Can't ye hondle yourself, den?

Beneath the thatch hat, the eyes in the brown skull
are round and bright, and the mouth is firm. The old
man is not absent and not present; he seems intent on
a voice in the far distance.

You had too much ambition, Papa. To sail with dat
domn mongrel fella—

The old hands twitch on the white conch.

You waitin to hear me say I never burned her? You waitin to hear dat?

Raib falls silent. He turns his back upon his father, gazing all around the empty sky.

Wodie sits on the galley roof, picking his feet. Hanging from his fingertips in the galley door, Speedy stares astern.

Don't like dose Jamaica fellas, den.

Well, out to East End, we don't bother so much about dem, cause mostly dey hangs around in de big towns. Georgetown. Jamaicans come as poor as what de old people call Job's turkey dat only has one feather, but when dey gets around with de girls and what not, dey gets high-minded: dey finds dereselves better den what is in Cayman. Den you hear de Caymanian call de Jamaican pan-head sonofabitch, something like dat. (*laughs*) And dey calls us kanakees, cause we not s'posed to be so civilized as on dat island.

You blacker den dem or what?

No, mon! We ain't so black as dey are!

Speedy wipes Wodie's black ankle with one finger, then inspects the fingertip.

Color don't matter in Caymans! No, mon! We a democracy!

Well, dass very fine. **Only** how come *you* de one dat sleepin in de sail locker stead of de deckhouse?

Cause I a East Ender!

Cause you a East Ender.

Speedy?

Speedy returns into the galley shadows.

Speedy? Y'see, Speedy, in de days of de old sailin boats, de schooners used to go to Lucea and Port Antonio, Sav-la-Mar, Kingston Town and all dat to sell turtle. So de Jamaicans dere had a way of teasin de Caymanians, dey called all Caymanians Uncle John-John. Hey, Uncle John-John, Johnny-Whyna, Johnny-Tuttle! Johnny-Whyna, dat how dey say Johnny-*Cake*. So dem old wind coptins, dey didn't want nothin to do with dese Jamaican boys around de dock: dey say, Look, mon, ye goddom pee-can Jamaican wharf-rat bastard, ye better get home! And de Jamaican say, Uncle John-John, ye kanakee ras, ye cocksure as dat, I gone break your ass out!

On hands and knees on the galley roof, squealing with laughter, Wodie lowers his head into the doorway to see Speedy's face. Sitting immobile on the ware chest, Speedy regards Wodie's one-eyed inverted head without expression. The face hangs in the blue sky. Then Wodie straightens, his grin uncertain, and lies back on the galley roof. Soon his heels thump soft on the gray siding; he is singing.

East-southeast to Edinburgh Reef, across the beam seas of the trades.

Spray, flying clouds, a glint of brine in the hard wood of the decks.

Under the roof of the port companionway, Will and Byrum construct a bunk for Captain Andrew out of the boards used to build cargo racks in the turtle hold.

Speedy is laboring his pots, using the sea spray to help rinse; he works with such style that Buddy, handing him each pot, is an impediment.

At the helm, Athens is coughing. Behind him, Byrum and Vemon work on the broken taffrail.

Wodie, on the galley roof, turns the salt fish.

Raib is in his unfinished wheelhouse, gazing down at the new engines.

Brown is perched on his blue fuel drum, hugging his knees; he stares away to sea, unseeing.

Sharks, mon! See dat cobber knife? Off de port bow
—wait, dey down behind de wave—dere! Up again!
See something white? *Big* sharks, mon!

                                        something
white! Run tell de helm to head her south a little
till we see

        manta?

Raib climbs the masthead as the engines slow.

Copm Raib?

You see it, Copm Raib?

Copm Raib?

Beneath the surface, off to port, a pale shape seems to
grow, gathering and unfolding, lifting and falling on
the sparkling swells. Sharks circle at a little distance,
the dark fins mute in shining seas. As the ship nears,
the fins withdraw beneath the surface. The shape
turns as the ship passes, and long shark shadows loom
and fade.

Because the *Eden* is broadside to the seas, she is riding
heavily, and Raib's figure, high in the rigging, is black
on the veering sun.

Raib? Copm Raib?

                —still see it?

Copm Raib—!

—dead whale, I said!

Dead whale? Ten fathoms long? How come dem
sharks goin round and round, and never touchin it!

Was *you* up on de masthead, Byrum? You see it
better den me? DEAD WHALE, I SAID!

horizon

Ocean rainbow.

... the name of your vessel? Please repeat your position ... latitude 15'30 north, longitude 85'21 west, is that correct? Over.

Vemon lays his chisel down.

Somebody in trouble, Byrum.

Ain't surprise. Dis goddom wind.

Dat over by Cape Cimarron, along dat way—dey goin aground.

Bad thing to go aground along dis coast—ain't no help in two hundred mile.

Athens shouts at them from the helm.

Rob you and kill you—*dass* de kind of help you gone receive on de Sponnish coast. Dey all thieves and smugglers!

Look who talkin! Didn't you sail one time with Copm Desmond?

Immigrants, mon. (*laughs*) Now *dat* is a good business. We corry dem up to Tampa. Desmond charge dem a fat fee, you can b'lieve dat. Copm Desmond *Eden*. He say, Dis is de land of de free and de home of de brave—now get de hell off my vessel!

Tampa? Dat is where my papers is at, in de Union Hall!

Oh, Desmond very clever, mon. He used to corry a bunch of turtle on de deck, bought dem cheap out de bottom somebody's crawl dere in North

Sound—de half of'm was dead when he bought'm.
And den he take dese nineteen fellas dat wanted
to go to de U.S.A. to seek dere fortune. So
Immigration say, Tell me, Copm, what you do
with all dem men on a vessel only fifty-three ton
and fifty-five foot in length? And Desmond say,
Why, dey help unload de turtle. Take four mens to
each turtle. (*laughs*) And a couple days after dat,
when he went to clear, Immigration say, Where in
de fuck is de crew? And Desmond look at me and
de cook, which was about all dey was remained.
Look puzzled dere a minute. *Goodness*, he say,
Couple fellas must got drunk or something.

Fingering his one button, Athens sniggers.

Well, Immigration didn't know whether to swaller
dat or not—he look pretty vexed dere. So Desmond
say, I hopes dere be no hard feelins. And
Immigration say, We see about *dat*. So Desmond
slip out of dere dat night, and de next time he lease
a different vessel and corry dem over to Texas. Dat
time he had a little bit everything—Cubans,
Jamaicans, Haiti, everything—dey all look raggedy
as Brown dere. And he say, Dis is de land of
opportunity—now get de hell off my vessel! And
he land dem on de coast dere. In de night time.

Copm Desmond Eden!

Domn good thing it was de land of opportunity,
cause Desmond took every last centavo dat dey had
fore he let'm off of de boat.

I remember one time—Copm Bennie, I b'lieve it
was—he wanted to lease dat old shark scow dat
Desmond had, and Desmond demanded three
hundred pounds for ten days. I told Bennie, I say,
Mon, if dat vessel worth thirty pounds a day after
all de crewin paid, why in de hell ain't Desmond
out dere fishin sharks three hundred and sixty-five
days in de year?

Well, dere is one thing Desmond know and dat is
sharks. I told you why—cause he a shark his*self*!

Hear dat? Come to Desmond Eden, Raib can hear you
in a goddom hurricane.

You been in dat sharkskin game dere, ain't you,
Copm? On de Sponnish shore? I heard you was
runnin guns dere, bringin back sharkskin.

Raib comes down into the stern.

Dass what de Administrator say, but he didn't have
de facts to face me with. I told de Administrator
dat if he did not proceed in a more proper fashion,
I take him outside and *lynch* him. (*laughs*) And he
took dat very well, cause he a very polite little
fella. (*with contempt*) De mon still green, and scared
to flap his wing. Don't have de guts to perform
his duty. Dat time all de liquor from Cuba were
found in de North Sound, only a few fathoms from de
shore? And de so-called Member of de Legislature
dat *owned* dat cargo, he run on de ticket dat forbid
liquor in de islands, he tell de people of Caymans
dat liquor *bad* for dem—

Keep de price up dat way.

Dass it. And de people of Caymans, dey so simple,
dey so far into de back, dat dey b'lieve dat mon got
dere interests in his heart, and dass where he got
de big part of his votes—

He weren't convicted, and dass what counts.

Dass what counts, you said, Byrum?

I find Desmond all right.

You find him "all right," you said? (*incredulous*)
Well, I tellin you dey didn't always think dat way in

de Cayman Islands! A mon had to be better den "all right," or nobody foller him!

All I said—

De people of Caymans should have de sense to know dat dat mon never followed de truth! He go around yellin about progress, about bringin in oil bunkerin stations and gamblin, to make poor people rich; but it dose Yankees dat pay him off—*dey* de ones dat gone get rich! And de home people gone get frigged! And we don't like dat, de Yankees gone find out we all commonists, and dey gone take over, mon—dat be dere little way! Oh, mon. I done a couple hitches on a United Fruit vessel, and I seen just how dey done in de small countries!

Home of de brave, mon.

Loud and clear, Cap, loud and clear. Come back, Sue Ann.

—the Sue Ann, the Sue Ann. How do you read me? Over.

You're comin in good, Sue Ann. Loud and clear, Cap. Over.

Well, that's very fine, Cap, very fine, and thanks for the radio check. We're under way now, everything A-O.K. and don't expect no more trouble. You hittin any over that way?

Just pickin, Cappie, just pickin. Somebody must have give 'em hell down here.

Well, it ain't like other years, Cap, I never seen it so poor as this. Gettin to be a desert around here.

Roger. Well, that's right, Cap, and so we will be clearin with you now, this is the Two Brothers, WG 6428—41, over and out.

Roger. This is the Sue Ann, WG 6835—48, over and out.

I knew a fella went by dat name, dey call him Roger
Powery, cause his doddy give him de name of
Roger.

We got numbers like dem vessels, Copm Raib?

Yah, mon. We de Number One.

Dem is a couple dem big Yankee shrimp boats—
I worked a hitch on dem. Dey crewed in Roatán.
In de Bay Islands. Dey suckin de last shrimp out of
de sea.

De little vessels cotch big turtle and de big vessels
cotchin shrimp.

Dey wastes more den dey cotch. All de small shrimps
get packed into de trawls, and by de time dey sort
dem away, dey dead. No market for dat small
shrimp, mon, so dey dump dat over by de tons. So I
tell de coptin, Dass a bad thing, Copm, wastin food
dat way—why not give it to de poor people? And
he show me a bad face. He say, *Where*? And I say,
Just put in any port along de Caribbean shore. So
he tell me not to go agitatin amongst de crew or he
get me arrested. (*hoots*) Call Speedy-Boy a
*com*monist!

Thought you was one of dem commonist spies, most
likely.

Spyin on de shrimp, mon, dat were me.

Vemon throws his chisel down with a show of fury.

Goddom commonists! (*spits*) One thing I ain't gone
to stand for and dat is a *com*monist! (*voice rises*)
Why, dese goddom godless sonofabitches, dey come
in dere to a democracy and *com*monize ever'thing
dat way! I heard dat myself, right on de radio!

(spits) SHIT! *(triumphant pause)* Y'hear me? I tellin you, I don't *go* for dat shit, no mon! *(fierce)* I tellin you right here and now—if *I* was de President of de United States of America, I'd give de order to bomb out every last one of dem goddom Cubans—

Vemon?

make de world safe for democracy, goddom it! And *God!* Y'hear me! *God!*

Vemon? You ever *see* a commonist? What de hell you know about it anyway, ceptin what dey give out on de Yankee radio?

and safe for *freedom!* Dass right, *freedom!* And de *forces* of freedom! Dey know about freedom down dere in Honduras? Cause *dat* what we got in a de*moc*racy! And justice! And God! Y'hear me? GOD! And dem dirty goddom commonists comin in dere and tellin me what I must do! *No*, mon! Tellin a *free* mon what he must do? NO, mon!

Free mon! Listen to dat idiot! He ain't even free to drink hisself to death without workin like a donkey first to pay his rum! Ain't had a shillin in his life dat some politician yellin about progress didn't steal off'm, but he free, okay! He one free nigger, mon! He free to drown hisself or blow his brains out, either one he want! *(shouts Vemon down)* You a *stupid* mon, Vemon! You just de kind dem people need! Squawkin out everything dey tell you on de Yankee radio like some kind of a goddom parrot! Now pick dat chisel up and finish— ATHENS! DON'T LET HER FALL OFF IN DAT MANNER!

Raib, contemplating Vemon, shakes his head, begins to laugh.

Dat time in Honduras I checked on you, Vemon, to make certain you didn't sneak ashore and go adrift on de Sponnish Coast—

You checked on me? Nossir, Copm Raib, cause you *knew* I wasn't goin ashore!

I knew you wasn't goin, dass right, darlin, but *you* didn't know it yet. (*laughs*) Like de time dat woman you had dere, you told her you had no money. Yah, mon! (*joyfully*) Vemon Dilbert Evers! You could hear dat a goodly distance when dat woman slap poor old Vemon; flogged him with a double length of rope, dass what she done to dis poor old fella, and took all his money away from him. Ain't dat right, Vemon? Went through his pockets while he layin on de ground!

Well, she had a hell of a time gettin it. I told her, I say, Hon—

I *know* you got money, she say, and you ain't gone to drink it all away on me, not *dis* time! He say, No, Hon, I ain't gots none! She say, I know you lyin— (*with feeling*) you goddom worthless—

Mon! It Vemon woman where de woman's-tongue tree gots de bad name!

I had some of it spent behind her back already, y'know. I don't let *no* domn bitch like dat—

Oh, you a hard mon, Vemon! You one hard nigger, boy!

At Edinburgh Reef, no land is visible, only broken patterns of white surf; even to leeward of the reefs, where the *Eden* anchors, the water is roiled and rough. Raib has no need of a chart to find good holding ground. From the masthead he finds the range where the reefs lie in accordance with his memory, then makes a downward chop with his hand; the windlass rattles and the chain rumbles overboard. Engines idling, the *Eden* drifts downward to the full length of her anchor line, then comes up taut as the chain snubs her.

THROW DEM BOATS OVERBOARD!

The deck vibration dies, and the sea slop on the hull is loud. A shriek of pulleys: a catboat smacks onto the sea. The catboats are a faded water blue.

Raib goes down into the starboard boat, and Will into the port; their crews pass down the gear. The Captain is shouting as he works, bashing the kellecks down.

Green turtle like wild animals, mon! De more you harass dem, de fewer dey gets! Dey likes de quiet of de deep, you gots to come up on dem like a shadder. Dey hear dem Jamaica motors tearin up de water, dey gone to move on!

The kellecks, each fastened to a length of rope with a long buoy at the other end, are stowed in the bilges aft and under the middle seat; the lines are run forward to the stack of buoys in the bow, to avoid tangling. The nets are passed down last and stacked astern.

Out on dese cays, de Jamaicans growin ganja, y'know.

Rascally-lookin people—dey no good, mon. See dat fella in dat skiff with de spiky hair? He one dem Niyamen.

Mean-lookin guys. Smokes ganja out dere. Dey smokin weed. Some of dem very nice, but a few of dem gets hostile and want to do anything. Dey just walk in and want to take things from you just to get involved. And if you say nay for an instant, den dey grudgeful. And you're out dere, and you're unprotected so far away, and dey do as dey like. Dey nasty guys to deal with.

Raib stands up straight.

Dem ones I seen on Bobel Cay ain't people any more—dey animals. And Desmond Eden right dere with'm—dass where he belong.

Dey ain't no nice Jamaica fellas, huh?

Oh, dey some nice Jamaicans, Speedy, but you got some dat comes to Caymans, come in dere teared pants and twisted shoes, and after dey finds a job dey can put on a wrist watch and a pretty shirt, and den dey think dere is no guy in de world like dem. No good, mon. Cause Caymans people, we always got something to eat, something nice to wear, so we don't have to worry, and dey don't like dat cause dey poor over dere. Oh, dey *poor*, mon. Dass why dey spreadin out like rats, to dis place and all over.

When the oars and masts are passed down to the pilots and stacked on top of the fishing gear, the men come back aboard. Wodie serves large white tin plates of rice and johnnycake, with coffee, and a platter of salt barracuda on the side.

Let's hustle, now! We got to set net right after we eat! Buddy? Dat food ready? Den give his plate to Copm Andrew!

He won't eat, Papa! Just takes a little water!

Dat his business! But you got to give de mon de choice!

The men stop talking. Buddy carries a tin plate from the galley and extends it to the motionless old man. In the noon sun, as the chair rolls, the shadow of the foremast boom crosses the freckled hands, which make no move. Buddy sets the plate on the shrunken lap.

Mon, I hopes we pick up one dem hox-bill; my gut cryin for fresh meat.

Maybe we get a chicken green: green turtle something *good*.

Hox-bill bad for my asthma. (*laughs*) Gets my courage up so I can't sleep. Dere was dis fella went to de doctor, he say, Doc, can you give me something to get my courage up? I havin trouble lately gettin my courage up.

Courage! (*laughs*) Dat pretty good, boy, dat pretty good!

Joke ain't finish, Copm Raib!

Ain't finish? Well finish it up, den!

Old Doc give him cascarilla tonic from over dere in de Bahamas, something like dat, I reckon.

What hoppen to de *joke*?

Well, someway I forgot de way it finish. I got to laughin over de courage part and forgot de joke part. I was in a bar, y'know, over dere at de Blue Horizon, and time I got done laughin dis fella dat were tellin me de joke had turn aside and were talkin to somebody else.

Buddy loiters at the rails, seeking his father's eye; Raib is watching the old man, and the untouched plate on his lap.

Papa?

His father regards him briefly without answering, then turns to Will.

You begin on de south side of de white hole dere, and work back up into de north. Don't bring none dem net back here; you just set'm all along dat reef out dere!

Papa?

And reef dem sails! Can't corry sail like dat out dere, not *dis* afternoon, darlin!

Mon, dat wind really cuttin now!

Can I go in de boat, Papa?

You think you can pull dat oar out dere? (*shakes his head*) Boy, I know you try, but tryin ain't de same as doin. You keep de fire burnin in de stove and see to de wants of Copm Andrew—dat be your portion.

Will leads Athens and Vemon into the port boat; Raib, Byrum and Speedy jump into the starboard boat. Brown squats upon his fuel drum, toes curled over the rim, and Wodie climbs to the galley roof.

We see you later, Buddy!

Let go de line, boy!

Rudders are rigged, and the starboard boat drifts
astern. Byrum and Speedy step the mast as the boat
tosses; the sail canvas snaps and ripples. The port
boat, already free, beats cross wind on a northerly
tack. In the glittering green troughs, its gaff-rigged
sail rises and falls.

Now the starboard boat heels away downwind. Warm
spray flies over the bow, and the crew leans outboard;
she comes about and heads up toward the reef, close
to the wind. Raib is shouting.

Dass de way you know a fine sailin boat, boys—de
way she beat to windward when you slack off on de
sheet!

A mile away, well short of the reef, the port boat has
dropped her sail.

What de hell Will doin, Copm Raib?

Raib jumps up in the flying boat.

What? Goddom! God*dom* it! I never think he be as
poor as dat!

         settin at shadders, way
out dere!

        sailin to dese reefs
all de days of his life, and den he go and set his net
out dere—dat mon can't learn nothin from de sea.
Dat mon

       what Copm Andrew used to say: Old

Bush people can't learn nothin
from de sea

        put de old mon in dat boat as pilot.
JESUS! If he deaf and dumb, he *still* do a better
job den Will, he *still* do it!

The brown sail flutters aloft again; the port catboat
has seen Raib's signals. She gathers speed, bending
away toward the reefs.

He ain't pickin up dem net! Dem five, six nets is
wasted!

I make a bad mistake when I call dat mon a pilot. I
done a bad job *dere*.

No turtle out dat way, huh?

Well, he might have de luck to snag one comin and
goin, cause green turtle out dere in de *day*. Dey out
dere grazin on de sponges and de sea grass. But
in de twilight dey go up under de reef. Ain't no
turtle in de world gone to spend de night out
dere amongst de grasses.

The blue boat drifts in the green sea, in twenty feet of
water. In the lee of the reef, the water clears. Dark
coral heads gather; they loom and sink away.

Green turtle, mon! See dem two dere? Dem two big
bastard dere lookin to coot! Dey gettin set to go
down to de Bogue!

Ain't no chicken turtle on *dis* reef, dass what Copm
Allie say!

Strike dat sail, Byrum, take de bow oar! Stay dere
amidships, Speedy!

The catboat is rowed against the wind, from set to set —lone coral heads, narrow reef channels, round wells of white sand ringed by coral, called "white holes." Between sets, Raib rigs the next net to its buoy and clears the kelleck and the buoy line, so that it is ready to heave. With hands, toes and teeth, he spreads the whole length of the net to be sure it is hung properly and will not tangle, then heaves the kelleck on its line and throws the net out after it, using an overarm motion that casts the mesh wide in the air. One end of each net is secured to the log buoy of light wood, and this end is anchored by the kelleck. The net floats down the current like an underwater flag, shifting position with the change in tides: it is borne up by small floats along the surface line, and since the bottom is not weighted it hangs in the current at an angle. With its wide mesh, the light net encourages tangling, yet permits the turtle to haul it to the surface when it has to breathe.

De onliest thing, Speedy, when a small turtle hang up too close to de kelleck and got to drag *dat* to de top every time he breathe, why den you go out dere in de mornin time and find dat turtle drownded.

The boat works north along the reef, setting the channels and the edges of the jagged pan shoals that hide just below the surface; the coral walls of the shoals and channels descend steeply to white coral sand.

Easy on de bow oar, Byrum! Pull best, Speedy!

Speedy chatters to himself.

Hear dat, Speedy? You too, Speedy! Pull best, Speedy-Boy, you doin fine!

In the western light, the coral glows, afire. A shark glides outward from the dark wall, then accelerates with a stroke of its huge caudal. Farther on, bonita crisscross, chasing bait fish; where the bonita chop the surface, the minnows spray into the air in silver showers, all across the sunlit coral.

Byrum, grunting, rests a moment on his oars.

> Dis de onliest place I ever see bonita on de inside of de reef. And dey jack dere—jack crevalle!

> Keep her head up, Byrum. Pull best, darlin. You take a rest in dis wind, mon, she walk away from you right back down to de vessel.

The sprays of bait fish, catching the sun, have drawn the hunting terns, which beat along against the wind, just overhead. Fish and birds chase back and forth across the catboat's bow, the tern shriek lost in the cavernous booming on the reef.

> Where dem birds *come* from, way out here? How dey know dat bait was dere?

> Dat what dey call *mystery*, Byrum. Dat is *mystery*. Many's de time I seen dem noddies on de Cayman Banks, not ten mile west of de island, and egg birds with'm, and boobies. And not one of dem thousands of birds ever comes in sight of Grand Cayman.

The ship swings on her anchor. The catboats are drifted aft on lines of different lengths so that they will not collide or bang the hull.

Vemon! Get your ass out of dat deckhouse! Don't you see dese other mens workin—day ain't none of dem dat is drier den you! When de work is finish and de deck secure, *den* you tend to your own self!

Hear dat? Now come out dere, Vemon!

Huh! Call yourself mate, and den you—

I say, Come *out* dere, Vemon!

I *comin*, goddom it, Will!

When de Coptin change he clothes, den we know dat our day's work be done, and we change too! Dat be de rule of de sea!

Both gangs are wet, and at twilight the wind is cool; they change their pants while Wodie and Buddy cook their supper.

I said, Move his chair in under de roof dere, case it rains!

Twilight.

The wind relents a little, but thick waves rumble on the reef, and the sea gnaws the hull.

See dat silver light? Make me sad, someway.

Gloomy, mon. What de old people calls de Mouth of de Night. Cause de night hungry, mon.

boom

The sea expires.

boom

Feel like dat reef *waitin*, someway. Watchin and waitin.

Athens, mon, you gettin worse den Wodie here.

How about yourself? Always talkin about dat big old shark out dere—how you know he de same one, Byrum? How you *know* dat?

Cause I *seen*'m! Got a big notch in de fin!

Dey some things a mon don't have to see, but he know it all de same, cause he feelin sign.

Hush up, Wodie.

Darkness.

Copm? We seen dat same dead mess again! Risin and fallin on de far side of de reef!

Raib glares at Will in warning.

Dat old dead whale?

Copm Raib? Copm Raib? Dat thing must be alive! Eitherwise by now it would have fetched up on de coast. Wouldn't be foller'n us around out here.

Dem sharks still with it?

HE TOLD YOU, COPM RAIB, ON DE WINDWARD SIDE! HOW IN DE HELL COULD WE SEE FINS IN DAT MESS OUT DERE!

Vemon, why you answer me in dat big voice? I ask a mon if he see sharks, and he—

NO, brother! All we seen was dat same awful-lookin thing, risin and fallin in de seas!

Must be alive. Or else de currents—

Maybe dey *two* of dem—

Silence.

Maybe it got business with us.

Now nemmine dat, Wodie! Nemmine dat duppy talk! We ain't gone to speak no more about dis motter!

A heavy slosh along the hull. Spars creaking. The men retreat into the cabin.

twenty-five, dis goddom wind

                                        east wind

                                                east wind

de wind of June

                in April

                                worse on dis same reef. By
Jesus Christ it had blowed   not less den sixty-
knot wind   blowed de hairs of out ye   pick
up dat anchor and chain, dat   small anchor
and thirty-five, forty fathoms of chain   picked
dat up and she got broadside   go to de
westward   fouled or something hooked back
into de bottom, brought her head back to de
wind   a press of wind like dat. God
A'mighty   not ridin half as hard as she were
ridin den. If she had dem tall masts now, she be
pitchin her jib boom out of sight   masts cut
down   Honduras   don't hold de wind so
much

        chop dem masts out, sometimes

                                with sails,

ye can't do much in de night   domn thing you
can do is stop and take a floggin. Dangerous just
to *tack* under sail in de night. In de night especially.
De day be just as bad, but dere is light, and dere
is hope someway.

Hope, mon. Learn dat from school days.

Where you think dat white mess got to now?

Oh, it out dere someplace, waitin on us.

Good thing it ain't black or green, ain't dat right,
Wodie? Bring us bad luck.

One time with Copm Andrew dere at Verrellas, in
de same time of de year, and de wind blowed in
pretty domn fresh, same as it is now. So we left dere
in de *Clarinda* and brought dat weather up around
Coxcones, nineteen mile further east, but de further
we went to de northeast, de better it were. And
we just sailed along and sailed along, and it
increased to be better all de time. And by de time
we got out I would say seventy, eighty mile, just off
de edge of de bank, oh mon, it were de prettiest
weather in de world. And we corried dat pretty
weather right straight home.

Weather can change. Any time, mon.

Best change pretty quick, we gone get turtle.

Dey pretty good holdin ground where I am here. De
onliest way we would get in de rocks is if de vessel
drag quite a distance and get down to de edge of
de deep. Course I was not lookin for dis weather.
To tell ye de God's truth, I was not lookin for it,
not in dis time of de year. It must be dat atomic
trash and shit de Yankees puttin in de sky; mon
can't even count on de way of de wind no more.

Domn wind, y'know. Plays with de nerves.

I mean, dis is de worst April I remember, and I
been fishenin on de cays for forty year!

Now de best thing for de nerves, dat is conch salad.

Raib points at the crosstrees and the rolling stars.

Blowin my *life* away, dass what it doin! Dis goddom wind is blowin my life away!

Oh, yes. Conch salad, mon. And cocos.

·8·

Edinburgh Reef.

In the gray light, the leaky boats are half submerged in wave water and rain. Wind blowing hard, and wind banks to the eastward.

The turtles grow restless with the coming of the light and struggle to reach the open sea: because sometimes they escape, or tear the nets as they drag them across the coral, the catboats are off before the dawn.

Gray sea, gray sunrise: a cold silver light.

... not *dis* mornin!

Will sot dis reef with me and another time with Copm Teddy! A mon dat has worked turtle all de days of his life, and still he sot way out here stead of goin up into de reef! And de goddom fool tellin me he fishin *spots*!

He settin at shadders, like I said ...

Dis is an *hombre*, dis is! Sign him on as mate, and den he go ...

Near the reef, the catboat heads up into the wind, sail snapping. Byrum lashes the sail around the mast, then lowers the mast into the boat.

See dat one flouncin on de weather side? And dere and dere—dey two in dat other net!

Green turtle, Speedy-Boy! Green turtle!

Speedy, dass a goddom log'red you pointin at, but dat one a turtle over dere.

Log'red ain't turtle?

Log'red ain't no kind of turtle at all! I guess you might say it in de turtle family, dass about all— dommit, take dat oar into de boat once you got hold of de net! Can't hondle turtle with no oar stickin out like dat!

No use gettin excited, Copm Raib! Dis boy doin okay for a new fella.

I not excited! I just likes to hustle!

Sometimes a mon hustle too much, lose more time dat way.

Now dass enough, Byrum! I never come out on dese reefs dis mornin to take lessons about turtlin from *you*!

The nets trail downwind from the reef, the float lines bunched up here and there in a rude tangle; the turtles thrash and sigh. As the catboat comes up on the net, the creatures sound, dragging the floats beneath the sea, but they are tired and soon surface.

Raib hooks the net with a small grapnel and hauls it in. Each crewman seizes a fore flipper of the turtle. They hoist it upright, facing away from the boat, then haul it on its back over the gunwales. It rests on the thwart until freed of the net, then is lowered, still upside down, into the bilges.

Look like Will got turtle after all! Green turtle! See de pale belly comin up over de side?

Nemmine Will's turtle, mind your job! Can't corry no turtle in dis boat, you don't stow dem better den dat! Don't take two men to do what you doin dere, just take one dat knows his job!

Raib jams the turtle under the thwart.

You sayin I don't know my job?

If you was on de *A.M. Adams*, you had ought to knowed dat de Coptin never come up into de bow dis way if de two men know dere job!

You right dere. But—

All right, *I* de Coptin *dis* mornin! Dey ain't nothin in de world you can teach me about turtles! (*more quietly*) If de men know dere duty, dey see de motter through dereselves.

You sayin I don't know my duty?

Now dass enough, I said!

There are five green turtle in the nets, each one two hundred pounds or more, and the broad calipees of bamboo yellow cover the bottom of the catboat. When first taken aboard, the turtles slap their flippers on their bellies; soon they lie still.

> Where dat easternmost net? I sot it right off de edge of dat pan shoal!

> Goddom log'red bearin it away, dass what it is! Look where he got it!

The catboat drifts down on the last net, which floats on the surface in a snarl. The huge loggerhead is wound inside it, wound so tightly that it cannot sound as the catboat nears; its small eye glowers through the netting. It is dragged into the catboat to be disentangled, and soon the massive head is freed, but the taut net and the beast's great weight make the job difficult in the small boat. The men move gingerly around the head, with its pink warty neck.

> Goddom it, we best take dis sonofabitch back to de vessel, h'ist'm up, work on him dere! We be all mornin out here, and dere Will back down to de ship already!

Byrum slings the boat painter to Buddy and draws the catboat alongside; it heaves and bangs. Raib swings onto the deck.

> Buddy? Did Copm Andrew eat?

Buddy shakes his head.

One by one, the turtles are hoisted from the catboats by means of a bridle secured to the bases of the fore flippers. Suspended from the tackle at the tip of the foremast boom, they are swung inboard over the rails. Athens grabs the heavy tail of a hanging male, to steady it, then pierces its flippers with a red poker brought from the fire in the galley stove: a hissing sound and a quick sweet stink of flesh. The turtle blinks. Then it is lowered to the deck, where palm thongs are run through the flipper holes, and the flippers are lashed tight across the belly.

... big fella here hatched from de egg and come up out of de sand dere at Turtle Bogue and feel dat water and run for de sea fore something get'm; after dat, he disappear. And in all de years since, ain't nobody knows where dat old turtle been until de time we seen him flouncin out dere off dat pan shoal.

Green turtle very mysterious, mon.

Green turtle, mon.

Wodie slides the turtles aft, into the shade of the starboard companionway. Since they will be transferred to a crawl at Miskito Cay, they are left abovedecks. To keep them from sliding in rough seas, Wodie kicks wedges under the shells and a wood pillow is placed beneath each head, which would otherwise hang back unsupported.

The starboard boat has landed five green turtle, the port boat four green and a hawksbill. Will's shy smile is warped by his tobacco plug.

You done as good as we done, mate, settin at shadders!

I fishin spots, Byrum, like I said.

Byrum, dere was another green we lost to sharks! Still layin on de bottom with no head on'm and fins off. And dere were dat many sharks goin around dere, and big ones!—I tellin you, it made my blood run cold!

Byrum looks angry, glaring toward the reef.

You funnin with me, Athens?

No, mon! Jesus Christ, Byrum, dere was some black sharks dere, some tigers, dat I knowed never went less den fourteen feet! Dey was as big around as here to dat binnacle, and every one of dem goin right round and round dat turtle, and not a one touchin him. Turtle layin down dere, calipee up, look like a face!

Look like a face?

GODDOM IT, GET DEM BOATS ABOARD OF HERE! WE GOIN TO CAPE BANK!

Cape Bank? Dat *north* of here! De turtles is headed *south*!

I tellin you, *Cape Bank*! Goddom Jamaicans tearin up de sea round here, dass why we done so poor. But dey ain't no shelter for dem up dere at Cape Bank, we have dat high-sea fishery to ourselves.

We have it, but who want it.

Yah, mon—no shelter for dis vessel, neither.

Mon, we runnin all over de goddom ocean—

STOP DAT MUTTERIN AND H'IST DEM BOATS ABOARD!

The wind is unrelenting, and the sea is rough. Since the angle of swing is much increased by the shortened masts, it is difficult and dangerous to bring the heavy boats across the rails. Will takes a turn of the stern rope around the shrouds as he eases the catboat down, to keep her from crashing inboard as the ship rolls.

Call yourself a mate? After all dese years at sea, you still so green you don't know better den dat? S'pose dat stern line part? S'pose dat turnbuckle rust out, or de cable frayed?

Now listen, Copm, listen—

With de vessel rollin de way she doin, you could kill half dese men against de galley side!

All de years I been to sea I never done no different den dat way! Dat way is de way it *done!* Dat de rule of de sea!

Not aboard de *Eden!* No, mon! Not aboard of *here!*

H-ss-t! Nemmine, Will!

All de years I been to sea I never done no different den dat way! Dat de rule of de sea!

8:00 A.M.

The men have eaten, and the *Eden* is underway.

Raib and Brown are in the wheelhouse; Buddy is at the helm. Wodie lies on the galley roof, singing the

Hawksbill Song. By the port catboat, Will is mending net, his arrowhead needle darting in and out of the salt-caked twine; his face is taut and he mutters as he works, yanking the mesh. Speedy and Byrum, disentangling the loggerhead, are counseled by Vemon and Athens, who drink coffee.

Watch dat hox-bill dere with dat bare foot, mon. You so busy keepin your eye on dis log'red, you gone lose your big toe to dat hox-bill. Hox-bill *bite*, mon—ain't like green turtle.

Dass it. Green turtle very nice, mon. Keep dere mouth shut. Ain't like some.

He crazy, mon. Dass why I say he crazy. One minute he laughin like he crazy and de next minute he crazy with anger. Fuckin *wild* mon!

Dere ain't no need for him to corry on de way he do; dere ain't no need for dat. Dey ain't a steady mon he can call he crew from one voyage to de next.

No, mon. Nobody gone work like dat, dey gone move on. One day dis boat just be rottin in de sun—ain't gone go *nowhere*, mon.

Boat rotten already, mon. Turnbuckles all froze up, and de cables kinked. You seen de riggin at de masthead?

Well, he vexed dat Will got turtle, dass de trouble; mad if he did and mad if he didn't. Just plain *mad*, dass him.

Well, Will were lucky, but Old Raib don't know we know dat—he think Will made a ass out of'm.

A-purpose. (*laughs*) He figure Will done it a-purpose.

Dass it—dass got'm.

The loggerhead lies twitching on its back. The heavy reptilian folds of skin are a dirty pink color, and its head and jaw look too big for its body. The upper jaw is beaked. Upside down, it gapes and stretches, hunting something to snap at.

Lookit de barnacles on'm. Green turtles don't corry all dat barnacle and shit—green turtle *clean*, mon.

Dat a bad sign, all dem log'red. Will hit three in de port boat. And dem big shark.

What we do with him?

Nothin to do with him. Dey good for nothin.

Maybe we do what Desmond do. (*laughs*) Where Desmond used to set, dere was plenty log'reds, y'know, and de log'reds used to humbug his nets, like dis one here. So he went to work and he rigged a block-and-tackle up along his boat mast. Den he got one of dose big shark hooks and he hook dat in de log'red's chin—

In de chin, huh?

All four men are laughing now.

Yah. Took him half de mornin riggin it. I sick of fuckin with him, Desmond say. So he hook de block to dat and h'ist de log'red by his chin. Den he runs him up de boat mast, and old log'red's neck runs out about a fathom—

Athens whoops, scarcely able to continue.

—and den he take a knife and cut his throat! Pulls dat neck out straight, and cut his throat!

The men laugh for a long time; they sigh.

Dass Desmond Eden! Took half de mornin riggin up a log'red to cut his throat!

Copm Desmond! *Every*body got stories about *dat* fella!

Shot a mon, y'know, dat were his enemy. Shot a fella down around Honduras.

Dat mon were *not* his enemy. See, Desmond were in trouble and were livin in de woods. And dis fella were his *friend*, who used to feed him, used to take care of him—

Moggs?

Moggs, dass it. Moggs' wife, now, dey owed money. And she want to get clear of Moggs. And she knew dat Moggs knew all about Desmond smugglin through de cays, and she tell Desmond dat Moggs were gone report him. So Desmond kill him in de woods fore he found out she were tellin lies. Den he heard dat Moggs' son were sayin dat whenever he sees Desmond he would get'm. So he got two guns and he handed Moggs' boy one, and he say, I Desmond, boy, you lookin for me?

What hoppen den?

Well, first place, de boy knowed Desmond were a dead-eye shot. And second thing, he not so sure dat Desmond give him de best gun dere.

So what hoppen?

Nothin, mon. Nothin hoppen. Dat boy forgot what he had wanted.

Desmond! I 'member de time he were always swingin dat domn machete around, just missin people, y'know. Dere were some woman had him all riled up. He say, Athens, he say, I gone to cut dat woman in two. Oh, yes! I gone to get my piece of dat if I got to cut her clean in two!

Athens straightens, singing, as the Captain nears.

> Now I can say, dear, you de worst of your kind
> De gold rush is over and de bum rush is on ...

Everybody grob a fin, we throw him over.

The great turtle strikes the surface and disappears in the wave washing astern.

Maybe de screws get him—dat would be best.

Why you didn't cut de throat den, Copm?

Don't like de way it lookin at me, darlin. Don't like foolin with dem log'reds—dey looks too scornful.

Athens walks away, still singing.

> Yes, de gold rush is over and de bum rush is on ...

Hear dat, Vemon? Your partner gettin so weak he can't hardly talk, but he can *sing*.

Copm Raib? Dat disease burn'm out quick, Copm Raib!

He all burnt out already. I three times his age and I *still* a better mon.

Well, he sick, Copm.

Ain't too sick to steal. No, mon. He ain't too sick to
steal.

> Siempre las palabras que ma mujer ...

Copm Raib? Copm Raib? *Other* one singin now!
Dat one calls hisself Brown! Can't talk but he can
sing!

Talk enough to tell me dis mornin dat de
tachometer can be used for de oil gauge! Dat de
kind of engineer you get in *dese* domn kind of days!

> *Siempre las palabras que ma mujer ...*
> *Bum bum bum-bum, bum bum bum-bum*
> *corazón ...*
> *Whispers ... whispers* (voice breaks)
> Aw shit!
> *When you whispers dat you love me so*
> *sincere*
> *Love must always, love must always be*
> *unkind ...*

Dat pretty good, Brownie! Best come over here, sing
us a song!

Brown comes slowly toward the men, who sit upon the
starboard catboat and around the galley door. He tries
to look careless, but he is pleased. Shyly he takes off
his sombrero and, holding it at his navel, rolls it
round and round.

Maybe I sing in a club. I sing *muy bien, entiende?*
Pero, I drinkin and smokin. I lost it. *Perdido.*
(*pause*) You ready?

> *Last night was de worst of my life, oh darlin*
> *I stayed up home, someone else in your arms*

I cry cause I love you in all of my mind
I miss me, oh I miss me, at your house last
night . . .

Brown's dog eyes are soft and golden brown. He offers a smile: his gold tooth glitters.

I miss holdin hands walkin down de lane
I miss dat sweet kiss dat was mine for so long
When you hug me with your arms wrap
around me so tight
I miss me, oh I miss me, at your house last
night . . .

Buddy has been relieved by Athens; he comes up behind Brown and leans against the mast, legs crossed, as if he had to urinate.

I got a nice voice, too, dey say, but I don't know no pretty songs.

Buddy speaks so rarely that when he is finished, the men only nod politely; they do not know how to encourage him.

Brown is still smiling.

My *chico* dere in Barranquilla—*dat* little bitch can sing! Oh! Go to dat juke and he sing! De juke and him! *Hay no diferencia!*

Raib winks at the crew.

Boy like dat, now, Brownie, you can train him to get a job singin, make good money, support you in your old age.

Si, si! Go right dere to dat juke! Oh, *le gusta! Si!* Miguelito!

Miguelito, huh? I s'pose dey calls him Brown.

Turning to stare at Raib, Brown looks puzzled. When he gulps, the rawhide chin strap of his sombrero, hung on the stubble of his gullet, rises and falls. He decides to smile again.

Everywhere I go dey calls me Brown. I am Miguel Moreno Smith, but everywhere I go dey calls me Brown.

He glances at Speedy, who is wringing out white T-shirts.

Moreno. Dat is "brown." So dey call me Brown. Sometime Brown, sometime Brownie. (*confused*) I got a future as a singer! *Avenir!*

He got a future all right, but not much. Dis engineer say dat de oil gauge can be used for de tachometer— dass what he say. Ain't much of a future waitin for a fella like dat.

I sing another song!

> *Tonight I find you in de street*
> *And my heart lay at your feet*
> *I can't help it* aw shit, help *it*
> *If I still in love with you.*
>
> *Dis other guy is by your side*
> *And he look so satisfied*
> *I can't help it . . .*

Land o'er!

Cape Bank Reef is submerged except for one flat-topped pan shoal, barely visible at low tide; it lies north of Cape Gracias, off the remote Caribbean elbow of Central America. Spurts of white water, exploding into a white misty sky, signal the presence of the reef from miles away.

The men stand on the taffrail, clinging one-armed to the deckhouse roof; they roll and swing with the ship's motion.

See dat, Speedy? Reefs dat break dat way, we calls dem blowers!

Copm Raib? I think you got to get up right *next* dat reef, you gone to cotch *turtle*, Copm Raib!

You think? Dat don't mean nothin.

You sayin dat don't *mean* nothin?

Not much. (*looks up*) You ain't a bad fella, Vemon. You ain't nearly so bad as I always b'lieved. But you don't know nothin.

No, I don't know nothin! And if I did, I wouldn't *say* nothin aboard dis fuckin ship, cause it wouldn't do no good!

Raib's look of astonishment changes rapidly to mirth; he pitches up and down the deck in tears.

See dat? He laughin! Dass why I say he crazy! I speak him back de way Vemon done, I be walkin de plank!

Byrum? I gone put you in Will's boat place of Athens dis evenin; him and Vemon ain't strong enough to pull it. Athens shot. (*still laughing*) Dat boy finish. All wore out, poor fella. (*laughs anew*) He so tired he can't hardly talk, he sound like a goddom Jamaican, dass how bad he is—can't hardly understand what he sayin. All he can do is sing— him and de engineer dere. (*hoots*) Dey a pair of birds, okay! Pair of *black*birds, singin dere life away!

Raib's laugh is so wholehearted that, grudgingly, the men grin. Then Athens, leaning back against the mast, laughs in harsh imitation, and there is silence. The men stare expectantly at Raib, who squints at Athens but says nothing.

In the ocean distance, white birds lift and fall.

Best come with me in place of Byrum, Brownie—
we see de way dey do.

No, mon. Dis shit ain't no use to me in life.

Best come with me. After dat we corry a few nets
back to Roatán, cotch a few turtle.

Okay, Speedy.

The boats are launched. In the mounting wind, they
bang at the ship's hull, and the men curse as they load
the nets and kellecks. In the starboard catboat, the
wind tears the rotten sail almost as soon as it is
hoisted.

Wodie? You come in my starboard gang in de place
of Byrum.

No, mon, Copm—*Brown* goin! Him and Speedy!

Brown?

Rowing upwind from set to set in the rough water, Brown hurls his weight into his stroke in rage and snaps his oar off at the blade.

Dass it! Dass all I need! Come out here in a wind like dis with two greenhorns for a crew! Now h'ist dat sail, we go back to de ship!

Look dere, Doddy! Turtle shit! Dey *turtle* here!

I seen it, too! But we can't set without no oar!

Gim dat poddle.

What?

Brown say give him dat Indian paddle; he use de paddle for a oar.

He do dat in dis goddom wind, he break his back—dat paddle *short*, mon! Got no pull in it!

We greenhorns, Doddy—we too stupid to know dat. So just give dat boy de poddle, and let's see can we get us some dem net sot fore de night fall.

Speedy rigs the paddle to Brown's oar thong.

In the heavy chop, the catboat pounds from set to set. Grunt by grunt, his mouth wide, speechless, Brown must stroke twice for every pull of Speedy's oar.

By God, Byrum, dat greenhorn crew is de best crew
dat I got! Dey strong and willin! To row all
afternoon in dat mess out dere with a *paddle*—dat
is *willin*! Brownie? Brownie, I got to hand it to you,
boy, you done a job for me today!

Brown has raised broad blisters on his hands and broken
them, then blistered the new skin beneath. He sits
sullen with his pain, the hands limp in his lap.

Athens? What you and Wodie do dis afternoon?
Lay in your bunk? I thought you was gone to
butcher dat hox-bill, give us stew to eat!

Dat hox-bill be all over de deck! Can't butcher
turtle when de sea like dis!

So you say, den.

In the port companionway, the old man sits upright
in the shadows. Behind him lie the turtles. Their
mouths are closed and their breath infrequent, as in
the sea, and the expiration, when it comes, is a hollow
gasping.

A turtle sips air and subsides again. Its weary sigh,
and the tears of lubricating fluid that squeeze regu-
larly from its eye, go unnoticed except by Wodie, who
pauses now and then to adjust the headrests; the other
men step on and over the bound, silent creatures as if
they were part of the ship's gear.

Weather changin, look like.

Weather changin, but not de wind. If dis were not de month of April, I tellin you I would be lookin for sign of hurricane. (*shakes his head*) When de stars shootin straight down into de wind, to de horizon—dass okay. But last night I seen stars shootin *across*—y'know? Cutting right across de horizon. And dat makes me scared.

What do dat mean?

Raib bangs the wheel housing.

Wind, mon, WIND!

In Roatán, we lookin for a ring around de sun. In de Bay Islands. Ring around de sun and ring around de moon.

The Captain nods.

One telltale thing for a hurricane, you feel de wind pullin toward de north or de northwest. Course dere are regular northwest storms, but dat is in de winter time. Usually from July, August, September, October, anytime dat wind goes to de north, dere trouble comin.

Yah, mon. A north wind in September, mon, you better not stop dere askin questions, cause dat is *hurricane.*

Sometimes you can see a half-circle, cloudy—

Raib draws his arm in a half-circle over the horizon.

Yah. De old people call it a hard sky. My grandmother

squally
and blusterous black clouds, and behind dat blackness is a tropical storm a-blowin. De squall from a hurricane will not be long fore it will sort of break up in its pass over. But fore it gets cleared up good, you will see another squall formin, and each time it blowin a little harder. (*sighs*) I never forgot dat hurricane in 1926, how de people was standing by dere door dere lookin to windward. I never forgot how dem people looked when dat hurricane come down—dey looked like *children*. De people stood dere in dere door lookin to windward at dat awful sky, and dere *faces*—dey looked like *children*.

A long silence.

Will's voice comes from the deckhouse.

Dass de way dem fellas was lookin down at us from de rails of de *Majestic*. Dey just stood dere watchin in dat wind till de boats was out of sight. (*pause*) Dey looked like children.

Will? Come out and tell dat tale to Speedy while we eatin.

No, mon. I done with dat.

Whole gale.

At twilight the wind jumps and buffets. A heavy chop batters the ship, which labors on her moorings. Over the wind men have to shout, and when dark comes, they avoid looking out to sea. Soon they stop talking and lie still in their berths.

The wind rises through the night to fifty knots or better. Intermittently the sky is clear, and the masts of the rolling vessel carve great circles in the stars. The hull squeaks and bangs with strain. Where the ocean crashes on the reef, wind and waves are lost; there is no time, no space, but only the chaotic rush of the dark universe.

Raib prowls the ship most of the night, watching to see if the anchor drags, checking the water in the bilges, taking soundings. Periodically he goes to the port companionway, where his father sits staring straight away into the storm. Then he returns aft and sits against the wheel housing to rest. Sometime after midnight, Byrum comes out of the deckhouse and sinks down near him: then Speedy comes aft from his own bunk in the engine room. The three sit close by the doorway of the deckhouse, which vents a sad stale smell.

Won't come in out of de wind, den.

No, mon. He won't sleep.

Ain't got time to sleep, no, mon. Not when you dyin.

In his bunk, Athens stops snoring long enough to cough, a long string of dry coughs and a wet one. He sits up in order to spit, sees the three men watching him, and swallows. Even in his bunk, his cap sticks out to one side of his head. Mouth slack, he listens to the wind a moment, then curls down around the cardboard suitcase that is still lying on his bunk.

... a sundog—gale-wind bird, some of de old people calls it—cause it a sign dat a hurricane is approachin. What? Well, sundog is a little color, little piece of cloud look more like a rainbow, on one side of de sun or de other. You don't see it cept when de sun is goin down and at de time of de sunrise. From July on, mostly August, September, October, you must watch for de sundog, in de mornin and in de evenin. By dat you can always tell in what direction dat hurricane is travelin. In days gone by, before dere was any wireless and all to tell'm things, de people used to use de gale-wind bird as sign dat bad times was ahead.

A cigarette glows and dies. In the night shadow of the port companionway, a heavy rat sniffs the old man's high black shoe.

Wind southeast, it seem like.

Yah. (*sighs*) I seen plenty of bad nights. You go out to de edges of dem high-sea bars, and a night like dis cotch you out dere, I want to tell you, it is not agreeable. De first year dat I sailed as pilot for dat old man settin out dere, it were de prettiest weather in de world, and dat afternoon before I got done settin, I saw de turtle comin in towards de nets. Goddom it, dat wind come down, and dat vessel started to drag her anchors. Dragged and hooked, every now and den she hooked into de rock, and she would keep on buckin and pitchin till she tore it away. Anyway (*groans*) de two boats was up alongside and she was gone mash dem up. And we never had no crew, I mean to say, de crew was not experienced fellas. Experienced fellas don't sleep very much after bad weather sets down. You take dis weather dat we got now, you fellas knows enough to get a little bit uneasy.

Yah. Goddom wind plays with de nerves.

Anyways, de next mornin, she pulled de anchor out de rock, and it come up short of a clew. So we went into Miskita Cay, dat was Tuesday night, and we never got back till Sat'day mornin. I found five turtle, but out of my gang of nets I lost sixteen, and de other boat lost seven.

Wind is de enemy of mon. Learn dat from school days.

Well, you got to have trouble if a east wind like dis cotch you out dere on de high-sea reefs. But what I do I take my boats up on deck before night. Dat way your men mightn't get damaged, cause fellas dat is green, y'know, messin around in de night with boats, de vessel draggin or ye got bad weather to take in dem boats, you can't fool too much before you get in trouble. It take real good men, good experienced men aboard of a vessel, to hondle boats like dat in rough weather. (*pause*) Course it very hard to find good men today. You two fellas is very good, and den Will—I speakin about de work on deck now. You fellas is about as good as you will find today. But it not like it used to be in de old days.

Modern time, Doddy. We de best dey is, we got to be good enough, ain't dat so, Byrum?

Dass it. You lucky to get us, Copm Raib. You a very lucky fella.

Raib squints, looking at Byrum.

Well, I mean to say, a mon in de crew could take an order den, and keep his head. Now dey answer back—I don't go for dat, mon. I don't go for dat.

Time is changin, mon. De old days a mon burn de johnnycake, he walk de plank. Dese days we got unions and all of dat. A mon got rights.

A long silence. Then Raib speaks quietly.

You hear dat rushin out dere, Byrum? De wind and de sea comin together? Dat de sound of *hell*, boy, dat de sound of *hell*! You way out on de edge, boy, you out on de edge of de world. No mon! Ain't no unions on de turtle banks, I tellin you dat! Ain't no rights out here! Ain't nothin out here but de reefs and de wind and de sea, and de mon who know de bleak ocean de best has got to be de coptin, and de men don't listen to de coptin, dey stand a very good chance of losin dere lifes!

Raib gives an unwilling whimper, then begins to laugh.

Course Copm Steadman Bodden dere, he were an exception to de case. He told dem men dat were abondonin de *Majestic* dat dey had no business tellin him how to do de job. De day he drowned dere at Serrarers, Copm Steadman told dose men dat dey best stay with him on de vessel, bein dat he had fifty-four years of sea experience! Dat right, Will?

The deckhouse lies still: Will does not answer.

And just de day before, dem dat were drowned was
settin dere just like you fellas, just settin dere
thinkin about dere belly and scrotchin dere balls.
Never had no idea at all what was comin down on
dem. No idea at all.

Raib laughs for a long time, staring outboard. The
two men watch him wipe the tears out of his eyes.

·9·

Daybreak.

Clean black clouds of fair weather chase the gray wind banks of the day before, but still the wind increases, and short waves rush westward in disorderly ranks. The port boat is awash.

The men crouch at the galley door.

Will, I got to keep crew enough aboard to raise dat anchor if need be. So one boat got to do de job.

Dat port boat leakin pretty bad, dass all.

Take my boat, den. Pick de two men dat you want.

I want de two with de most experience of catboats and nets.

Dat Byrum and Vemon. You want Vemon?

Don't much want'm but I got to take'm.

Shit! What de motter with Speedy?

Well, dass right, Vemon, Speedy de better mon, but he didn't got de theory of pullin oars and hondlin turtle in no sea like dis. Mon don't do just right, capsize de boat.

Byrum bangs the *Eden*'s deck with the flat of his big hand.

Well, let's go den, Vemon. Anybody see my knife?

Speedy and Buddy haul the catboat alongside. It is leaping so that Will and Byrum time their jump to the catboat's rise. Bailing the boat with a half-shell of coconut, Will is silent and his face is tight. Byrum is noisier than usual; stepping the mast, he nearly capsizes the boat. Vemon has gone into the deckhouse, but when Byrum bellows at him, reappears and perches on the rails, awaiting his chance to jump. His striped cap is pulled down tight against the wind, spreading his ears.

You find your knife, Byrum?

Fuck my goddom knife! Get in here and let's go!

Almost affectionate, Raib grasps Vemon by the back of the neck.

Get in de boat, Vemon! What you scared of? You lost your life, you still ain't lost nothin!

Vemon hops neatly into the boat. As Buddy lets go the line and the catboat falls astern, Vemon, gazing upward, answers Raib with a kind of smile.

Will takes the tiller as Byrum and Vemon hoist the sail: the three brown faces gaze back toward the *Eden*. Wind strikes the canvas—*whamp!*—and the blue boat heels over. Then she is gone on gray-green waves. In the early light, the men's bent silhouettes are high on the catboat's weather side. The wind buffets her, and she falls off to leeward, then heads up again, moving fast, spray flying.

The men on deck watch their shipmates disappear. They do not speak for a long time. Raib picks up a torn net and begins to mend it, but soon his hands stop; he gazes out to sea.

Dat ocean look so *old* in de mornin time.

He frowns at the uneasy faces.

You see de way Vemon smile dere, Speedy? What de hell he *smilin* at? (*shakes his head*) Dat one thing I got to say about old Vemon—dat fool surprise you. I knowed him since we was children, and every time I think I know de kind of a fool he is, he turn around and give me a surprise.

Vemon ain't no fool. No, mon. He just *play* de fool, cause for him, dass de way life go de best.

Speedy is restless. He hauls the port boat up under the stern, and jumps down into it. The boat fills with leak and slop almost as fast as he can bail, yet he works furiously, water flying. Like Raib, he keeps one eye out to sea, but from the water line he cannot see the catboat sail; the ocean is too high.

Still seein dem?

I seein dem, darlin.

Okay den, dass very fine. (*stoops and bails*) Pull *best*, Speedy! Dass *you*, Speedy! You okay, Speedy-Boy! You doin fine!

Two miles to the east, where the surf lunges at the reef, the boat sail flutters, disappears. When the mast rises once again, the sail has disappeared.

Athens? Fix dem men a good meal, boy, dey gone be hungry!

Yah, mon, dass what I doin. I gone to give dem dis nice lumpy rice—

What?

some dis old barra dat ain't got too hard yet in de sun—

You gettin smart with me? If you had butchered dat hox-bill—

Copm Raib, if I was smart I wouldn't be on dis vessel in de first place.

If you wasn't on dis vessel, you would be in jail! Cause you a thief!

Athens grins at him.

Dey all kind of thieves, Copm Raib. I only de one kind.

You de worst kind! You steal dis whole domn boat if you could do it!

Dat might be, Copm. Dat might be. (*pause*) Less I had de insurance. Den I might burn her to de water line.

Raib glances at Buddy.

What do dat mean, Athens?

I don't know, mon. What do dat mean to you?

A glint of oars.

Dey drawin now.

Vemon know he done some work *dis* mornin. Pullin dat boat into dat wind, den losin all dat ground every time dey draw de net—no, mon. Dey get back here by noon, dey doin good.

Wodie is tending to the turtles. He wets them down by splashing buckets of sea water over them, and fixes the wood rests beneath their heads. Over those exposed to the open sky he throws old nets and canvas and dead rope.

Dass de first thing dat one-eye obeah worker done
aboard dis ship without bein told to do it. De first
thing. *(whistles)* Dey *all* surprisin me *dis* mornin.

One turtle dyin, Papa. Dat one. *(points)* I been
watchin him. He keep kind of gaspin; he kept me
awake last night, gaspin.

The turtle's calipee looks sunken in, and a sick squirt
of green manure lies lumped over its tail. Still gazing
eastward, Raib probes his fingers into the folds of its
neck, then under the hind flippers, gauging the turtle's
fat.

It were not dis turtle kept you awake—dat were de
wind. I ain't slept all night.

He straightens, forgetting the turtle, and contemplates the boy.

I bet you glad you ain't out dere in dat boat dis
mornin. *(squints)* Don't be shamed of it. I glad dat
I ain't dere dis mornin, and I domn sorry dat I
glad: must be gettin old.

Raib takes up his net again; he cocks his head.

Why you standin dere? Nothin to do? You know
dat de bilges ain't been pumped dis mornin, and
you ain't took Copm Andrew to de rails so he might
ease hisself, and you know dere is ropes to splice
and ends to whip up and down de ship *(his voice
rises)* and you standin dere starin at *me*! *(points)*
DEY MEN OUT DERE RISKIN DERE LIVES!
You gettin a share of dis voyage just like dey are,
and you not a experienced mon; dass why you got
to work twice as hard! You got to *jump,* boy! How
many times you got to be told: in dis life you got

to *jump!* (*quietly*) Should have left you home in school stead of makin a ass of yourself out in de cays, seasick all de time!

The boat returns at midday. Four turtles are hoisted aboard, and the men follow. Five nets have been lost. Will and Vemon do not talk; they go straight to the galley and sit there side by side looking down at their hands as they wait for coffee. At the rail, Byrum, still breathing hard, is pissing. Raib speaks to him politely.

De wind's moderatin, Byrum. Ain't blowin fresh as what it was.

Byrum spits toward the reef.

Don't feel dat way out dere. Rough, mon. Ain't got no wrists left.

Dass turtlin, boy.

Think so? (*turns toward galley*) I like turtlin as well as any mon, but I don't like dat mess out dere.

The *Eden* moves west along the reef, toward the *Maggie* white hole.

De *Maggie*? I don't know, mon. She was long years ahead of me. Edinburgh Reef, dat is another one. I venture some ship by dat name struck on dat reef, and dey named de reef after. But several fishenin places named after vessels dat found dem, like de *Ginevra* Bar, and de *Thane* Bar, and de *Sisters*— dere was an old turtlin vessel named de *Sisters*. Dey was de vessels found dese places, and dey still good turtle places today.

The *Maggie* white hole is a drowned amphitheater of white sand surrounded by steep walls of coral. Because it lies in the lee of the reef and the wind is dying, the nets are set in a near calm. Toward twilight, an egret appears out of the western sun, alighting on the submerged pan shoal and stalking with care across the silver water.

Don't like a lonely bird like dat. No, mon.

Sailing back on a light breeze, the starboard boat flies her small jib; she crosses the darkening water with a hiss. Raib brings her about at the last minute, stopping her alongside the schooner in a swirl of spray and snapping sail. Byrum and Speedy lower the mast and jump aboard the *Eden,* but Raib yells at Buddy to throw down a line, sail needle and a flour sack; he remains in the catboat, patching the rotten sail.

Turtle dead, Papa!

Course he is! Y'see de way dat goddom Desmond had dem? On de open deck?

Raib stands up on the catboat thwart to stare at the dead turtle. Its plastron is depressed and its mouth slack but its open eye regards him.

Why de hell dat goddom Athens didn't butcher it straight off?

Buddy resumes work at the bilge pump when his father finds him staring.

Well, you were right, boy. I be very sorry to lose Copm Andrew's turtle, owin to de fact dat he have so few, but I glad dat you usin your eyes not only to *look* but to *see*.

Dat were not de old mon's turtle. Dat de *Eden*'s turtle. He cheatin his very own father.

As Raib jumps back down into the boat, Buddy calls after him.

No, Papa, it were Wodie seen it. It were Wodie dat told me about dat turtle dyin.

Byrum turns to look at Wodie, who stands in the port companionway, holding the conch shell to the old man's ear.

Know something, Speedy? Dat Wodie some kind of a Jonah. One eye, and dat crazy shirt—

No, mon. He just wanderin a little. Wanderin and wonderin.

Athens butchers the live hawksbill and the dead green turtle.

whack!

With a hatchet, he chops the hawksbill's throat, then lops the flippers, and hard jets of dark blood shoot across the deck.

The dead green bleeds slowly.

whack!

Best show me how you doin dat, mon. Cause I gone corry a few net back to Roatán. In de Bay Islands.

Have to pay me to learn you dat. Come down to butcherin, you watchin de island's best.

Oh, mon! Hear dat?

Come down to thievin, he de island's best. Speakin fair now, he just about de best.

Athens hacks off the last flipper.

whack!

Yah, mon. De island's best.

With a machete, Athens cuts free the calipee, then trims the edges off the belly plate, saving the central strips of unossified cartilage; similar strips, darker in color, are cut from the outer edges of the carapace. Vemon puts the strips into a pot to boil; later, they will be dried on the galley roof.

Calipatch and calipee. See dat, Speedy? Sell dat for green turtle soup.

Calipatch? Dat from de back?

Yah, mon. In de old turtle, now, de calipatch turn to bone, but de calipee stay very very nice.

Athens carves fat from the gleaming pieces, then tosses them into the turtle shell, which is used as a tray. Speedy, Byrum and Vemon squat on their heels around him. Brown sits on his fuel drum in the shadows, and Wodie lies on the galley roof, watching the sky.

Copm Andrew ain't eat yet, y'know—don't want to eat.

Maybe he eat a bit of turtle.

No, mon. He stubborn. He just like de son. All dem Avers, dey belongs in de back time, y'know—

Gone to salt dis fella here, cause he died by hisself.

Corned turtle, Speedy—dey's dem dat prefers dat to fresh.

Course Caymanians people don't like turtle meat less dey kill it dereselves with its own fat. Turtle is like beef—a leany cow ain't tender.

Wodie, smiling, rolls over on his belly.

Oh, yes! Dat put me in mind of dat old song—
y'know de one? It was a cow died in where dey call
Cane Piece, back of Georgetown, and a whole
crowd of dose fellas went up dere and butchered it,
cut it up, and hauled it out—dey made a song
of dat:

Sharpen your butcher knife, sharpen your
butcher knife,
Beef in de Cane Piece, beef in de Cane Piece,
Sharpen your butcher knife!

Went something like dat!

Dat is quite a song now, Wodie. Don't hear songs
like *dat* no more!

It tell about how one got de head, one got de hide,
and all of dat! Oh, it were a *big* song, mon!
Oh, yes!

Athens winks at Speedy as Wodie descends from the
galley roof.

How dey hear about dat Georgetown song way out
dere at East End? Take Wodie to know dem
back-time songs. Dem East Enders still got hip-roof
cottages down dere, thatch roofs, like de school
learn us in pictures of de olden times, up England-
side. People at East End still ridin donkeys. Lot
of dem still got dirt floors dere, and sleepin on trash
beds. De only modern convenience dat dey got is
dem old strips of auto tire dat dey wears for shoes
when dey comes up to Georgetown, what dey calls
"whompers." Dat right, Wodie?

Well, we comin along. But in my boyhood days dere
was no road to Georgetown; had to go by boat. De

road came through in 1935, and it were around about '38 dat I first went walkin up to town.

Old Wodie come whompin down de road, yah mon.

Athens cuts turtle steak from the hawksbill's quarters, back of the fore flippers; all the rest is put aside for stew. In the sinking sun, the purple reptile flesh is twitching.

Calipatch and calipee, mon.

Wodie, motionless, studies the guts: one by one, the men turn to watch. Then the Captain stands before him.

Wodie? How you *know* dat turtle was gone to die?

On the Captain's foot is a dark blood crust, and on the deck beside his foot there is a fly. Wodie murmurs: the men strain to hear.

I feelin it when he come aboard. I got de sign.

Dese guts givin you some kind of sign?

Raib flings the guts over the side. They float away downwind toward the coast, a blob of cruel colors in the sea.

Speedy goes to the rail and watches the guts until they disappear.

Don't eat de guts?

We don't. In Jamaica dey eat it. In Jamaica, dey so poor down dere dat dey eat everything.

We eats guts in Honduras, too. It okay to eat it. Hungry people ain't too picky. Modern time, mon.

Anything okay, I guess, if it don't kill you.

In Jamaica dey eat dem bird eggs dat dey rob at Bobel Cay. Taste like bad fish. And dey eats dem dragons.

Eats dem in Caymans too, down to East End. Never eat iguana? Something *good*, mon.

Don't like dragons, mon—dey looks too scornful.

Eatin *hox-bill*, now, you know you eat something. Put lead in your pencil, mon.

Don't need dat! (*laughing*) Ain't like de old days.

Yah, mon. All dat Indian squints. Y'see, Speedy, every turtler had he woman at home, and den he had he Indian at Miskita Cay. Copm Steadman kept dis Miskita woman—

Raib is working on the catboat sail; his head appears over the rail.

Never had no Miskita woman.

Copm Steadman?

No, mon. Copm Steadman had one dese Creoles, what we calls Wika. What is actually de Indians, with a very long bow nose, all dem fellers died out over dere. De ones dere at Miskita Cay, dey call dem Miskitas but dey Wika. Lot of colored blood.

Dey talk English, and dey talk dere own language, too.

Raib mumbles his idea of Indian language.

Sound like dat—I never could cotch it. But dey born with it.

Raib hoists the catboat sail, which he has patched with checkered sacking that reads GOLD RING FLOUR.

Throw down a knife, till I trim dis patch!

Let de mon borrow your knife dere, Vemon. Ain't you de one so proud about his knife?

Proud? De hilt of dat knife come from de famous pirate knife dat were found guardin de treasure dere by Meagre Bay! And de blade better'n any goddom knife aboard dis vessel!

Will raises his eyebrows, then speaks mildly.

You seen dat knife stuck above my bunk? You take a look at *dat*!

You de mate? Well, you go fuck yourself!

Throw de pirate knife down, den, or any goddom knife!

Look above Vemon bunk, you find an old rum bottle, most likely.

Athens passes down a big hickory-handled knife. Raib gazes at him.

Dat is Copm Andrew's knife.

Dass right. Used it for butcherin.

Raib climbs up out of the catboat; the men make a place for him by the galley.

Course in dem days when Copm Steadman kept him a Wika woman at Miskita Cay, de old mon never cared a bit about goin home. Once he got his turtle crawled dere, and everything handy, he just as soon lay around dere a little while. But his son Autway, he a young feller at dat time, and he got anxious about goin home. Den a nice southeast wind come up, a fair slant for home, but de old mon say he wouldn't go. So Autway look at de father and he look at de Wika woman, and den he say, Dis be a *pussy* wind, Autway say. (*laughs*) So Steadman sit straight up at dat and he say, What you said? And Autway say, Dis be a *pussy* wind, Autway say, I be a mon now and I say anything I want. Den he say dat last part again just so he can hear de words; I be a mon now, Autway say. But de poor fella got lost in de storm dere at Serrarers, long with de father. And dat were de end of a first-class turtler. Steadman Bodden were a first-class turtler.

Wash of seas along the hull.

Will? You gone to give us dat tale dis evenin?

No, mon. Everybody know dat story, Copm Raib.

No, Will, I ain't heard it good in many long years gone, and dey's men sittin dere dat *never* heard it—Buddy, and den Speedy and dat engineer, and maybe Wodie. De news take quite a while to travel down to East End, ain't dat so, Wodie? So you best tell it, just so's we know you can talk good when you know what you talkin about.

Will, seated on the deck, squirts a jet of tobacco juice between the rails. He wraps his arms around his knees and squeezes hard, rocking a little, so that his bare toes dangle, and as the ship swings, the twilight shadows play on his lumpy face.

Well, we left Cayman on de thirteenth of June on de schooner *Rembro*. 1941. And we went to de northern cays, de high-sea cays. And a crowd of us rangers was put off on Coxcones. De boat put off rangers at de Hobbies, den from dere to Seal Cay, and from dere to Verellas; den she put us off at Coxcones, den from dere she went on to Logwood Cay, and from dere on to Alligator Cay. Now de other turtlin boat, de *Majestic*, were her sister ship, and she went down to Miskita Cay. And she corried *her* rangers out around Diamond Spot, Dead Man Mahagan, Dead Man Bar, and all dem places. But we stayed on de northern cays and fished for nurse and hox-bill and green turtle.

What Will speakin about, Speedy, in de beginnin of de shark fishery, de nurse shark was de most valuable, but now dey found de tiger shark has a better skin. If you could get a hundred tigers, well done up, you'd have some money, mon! De hide is thicker. De white-tip and dem, dey is all right, too, but in de sand shark, de hammerhead shark, de hide is thin; de hammerhead, regardless of his size, de hide ain't worth much. Desmond say—

Let de mon tell his story, Byrum!

Well, we was supposin to sail home around de twenty-second of September, round about de nineteenth to twenty-second of September. But de

Rembro never come to us. She never left Cayman
till about de twenty-second. So Copm Steadman
went down to de Hobbies, picked up de rangers
dere, and he went to Seal Cay and picked up de
rangers dere, and he went to Verellas and picked
up de rangers dere, and den he came on to
Coxcones. Picked us up on a Thursday, which
would have been de twenty-fifth of September, and
we went on to Logwood Cay. On Friday, in de early
evenin, we sailed for Alligator Cay to pick up de
balance of de rangers, which were de last men we
would have to pick up, and den we would sail for
home. But unfortunately we had to make a stop
at Serrarers to pick up some nets and so on, and by
den we didn't have enough sunlight to see
anchorage in Alligator Cay, so Copm Steadman say,
Well boys, we will abide here till de mornin.

Now, when we had left Logwood Cay, de wind was
to de northwest, eighteen to twenty, twenty-five
knots of wind. Well, dat evenin round about six
o'clock, it come up squally, and de wind pulled up
to de north-northwest. Copm Steadman claim dat it
was ordinary weather, and we gave him de benefit
of de doubt because, y'know, he were an old sea
coptin and well-experienced, and we put our trust
in him; we figured everything must be all right.
So Copm Steadman say, Go below and sleep, you
ain't got nothin to worry about—ain't nothin
but a common norther.

Dat were near October! Every mon dat know
something about de sea know about north wind
in October!

Byrum! Hush, mon.

So all dat night it were squally weather. So we say,
Copm, what you think about de weather; and he
say, Well, he had knowed worse weather den dat,
so he didn't pay dis weather any mind. (*sighs*)
Copm Steadman were de world's best turtler, a
goddom wonderful old mon. A very good old man.

(*nodding*) A very good old mon. But long toward daybreak his son Autway tell him, Father, I gone tell you something: we best get to Miskita Cay, or we gone *drown* right here today. And he tell Autway, Dat north wind don't mean nothin, boy, dat ain't no hurricane.

On Sat'day mornin which was de twenty-seventh, I mean to tell you de schooner *Majestic* couldn't corry a *kerchief* on her, much more a sail; it was *bad*. And we was anchored ... well, by dat time she had dragged her moorins prob'ly fifty fathoms from where she was anchored. And de weather keep on gettin worse and worse and worse all of de time. Every time it come up squally, de weather got a little worse. So round about I would say ten-thirty, one de sailors by de name Edilue Dixon say to de Coptin: Copm, what about de weather? De weather looks *bad*! And de Coptin tell him, You know what? De barometer has gone crazy. He say, De barometer has gone crazy. I can see now dat it's a hurricane approachin, and it's down on us. Den Edilue Dixon say, Well, what you gone do about it? In my opinion, Copm, we best try to go ashore, get on dat cay.

Well, Copm Steadman say we not to leave de vessel, we must ride it out. So Edilue say, Very well, den, Copm, I ain't stayin aboard de boat, I goin ashore. And Copm say, No, mon, you ain't throwin no boat overboard off dis vessel! And Edilue say, Copm, I throwin dat boat overboard, and you stand in my way, I gone throw *you* overboard along with de boat, cause I goin *ashore*!

So den Edilue Dixon look at Autway and dem other fellas in de crew. Dey all lookin pale dere, starin at one another, y'know, and den at Copm Steadman, watchin dem from dat chair dat he had settin dere on de deck. And not one of dem fellas would go up against him. So den Edilue look at us rangers, and for a moment dere, nobody moved, nobody said a word, dere was nothin but de wind tearin de

riggin and de rush of sea and things bangin up
and down de ship. And den it seem like a whole
crowd of us young rangers jump forward at de
same time. I was right dere in de front, like I was
picked up by dat wind, cause I knew dat Edilue
Dixon was de last chance dat we had. But I was in
friendship with Autway Bodden, so I cross de deck
again and grab his arm, and I yell into his ear,
Come on, den, Autway! Cause it were Autway dat
advised dat old sea coptin dat all dese men would
drown dat very day dere at Serrarers. But Autway
Bodden just look at me kind of sad, and shook my
hand, and never said one word. De old mon yelled
at me, Stay, den, Will Parchment! You belongs
with us! But I shook my head and yelled, Goodbye,
den, Copm Steadman! And I crossed dat deck
again. So we took two boats and threw dem
overboard into de sea.

Now Copm Steadman say he gone report dat we
had deserted his vessel on de high seas, he called it,
dat he would call us deserters, which would mean
a charge against us. Course de most of us dat
wanted to go was rangers, but dere was one mon
was a crew member, and dat was Edilue Dixon. And
had it not been for him, dere wouldn't been one
soul saved dat day. He de only mon dat ever
thought about goin ashore on Port Royal Cay.

Well, den, dis young crewman by de name of Asher
put his suitcase in de boat, and jumped in de boat.
And Copm Steadman say, You put dat suitcase
back on de deck, boy, cause dem dass goin ain't
gettin nothin out dis voyage. So Asher went back
aboard. He was in de boat but he jumped back
aboard at de Coptin's orders. He were young, like
de rest of us. He didn't know nothin about sea
rules, and he got frightened from de Coptin. His
suitcase come home, but de boy got drowned.

It were Asher and Autway dat cast us off, and stood
dere together at de rail, and watched us go.
Autway were wearin a red shirt dat he was proud

about, I seein dat red now in my mind's eye. And
Asher, he wavin to us like a little boy: I carry dat
wave with me to de grave. I were not at de oars, and
I try to wave back, but Asher never saw dat, cause
just den his cap blowed away aft. De poor fella had
dat cap set down so tight dat his ears stuck out, but
de wind took it all of de same, and he runned after
it. And by dat time we were fallin away fast, and
dat were de last I ever saw of him.

Now we had to pull de catboats into de wind, cause
we was around in de lee of de cay, and I tellin
you it were terrible, cause I don't think we had
less den a sixty- sixty-five-knot wind. When we first
leave dat vessel, at de end of de first four, five
strokes of de oars, we had fell five fathoms *astern* of
de *Majestic*, dass de way it were blowin, and I
thought we were gone. And den dat wind (*whispers*)
she died right down, just long enough, and we
pulled and we pulled and we pulled and we pulled
and we got ashore. We got ashore onto dat cay.
Two boats. Den a sea caught us, we were on de
south side of de cay, near a hell of a pile of rocks,
and when dat sea hit us, it shoved de boats right up
into de middle of dat cay.

So dat is how we quit de boat; took two big boats
and went ashore. We waited for de rest of de boys,
but dey never come. Cause when de first sea hit us
dat fling de boat into de bush, we was watchin de
Majestic; we seen when she swung off. She parted
her moorin and she fell to port. She swung her head
right off—at dat time dey were choppin de masts
out, and de masts fell. She didn't go very far from
where she were, she went down only about a
quarter-mile from where she were anchored. All de
Majestic ever did was turn around and go about de
distance of her moorin. When she went out over de
reef, dat anchor hook in behind de reef. Every
time she rise and fall, de sea chuck her back into de
reef, and punch her bottom out. And she lay right
down on de lee side of de reef. She struck in dat
piece of coral reef, and knock out her bottom, and

dat is where dem fellas met dere fate. De wind and de sea covered her up, and we didn't see her any more.

Well, by Sat'day evenin de weather got so bad dat de cay started to overflow. We got de boats up dere between de mangroves, and when de rush of water come through from de outside of de cay, our boat stayed steady. We put de sail over de boat to cover us, but we was in water, sittin in water in de boat. De next day mornin, after dat hurricane had broke with us and de water had all gone out de cay, our boats were way up de mangrove roots, not less den six to eight feet above de ground. We had to cut sticks for skids and launch dem, to get dem down on de sand again.

Well, den, dere weren't much to do but look around us. Dere were still wind, but some way it were very very quiet. It were Sunday. One fella taken three breads along with him, and it come out round about one slice a man. We wanted water, and we knew we had left three drums of water at Logwood Cay. With a two-inch knife blade we cut mangrove trees for masts, and we went down to Logwood Cay. But when we got dere, all we see was some old turtle nets out in de sea, hook up in de pan shoal, and we find de bung for one drum, and no water. Nothin. All dere was left of Logwood Cay was reef: de land was gone.

Dis was what hoppen in times gone back to Far Tortuga—

Well, while we was talkin and thinkin and decidin, we saw a little object between de two cays at Serrarers. And dat were a ranger from West Bay, remember? Wee-Wee. Dey had saw de *Majestic* anchored, but Friday was so bad dat dey couldn't get down to us. Well, Wee-Wee brought a little bit of water and a bread in case if he found some men alive. We had to mix dat little fresh water with salt water, and dat went around one little thimble a man—sot you cravin water.

Well, Wee-Wee had water on Alligator Cay. So we put back out den for Serrarers dat Sunday afternoon, and slept dere till mornin, and we reach Alligator Cay about eleven, twelve on Monday. And he had dere about five, six gallons of flour—dass what twenty-eight men was eatin out of for four days. One meal a day.

Dat day we saw a airplane pass, but dey didn't see us, and dey reported to de people back home dat dere weren't any sign of any life out on de cays.

All dat day we lay quiet, hopin and hopin. And on Tuesday afternoon we sighted de *Rembro*, Copm McNeil Conally, who took us back down to Bobel. At Serrarers, we saw de *Majestic*'s spars out dere, but we never saw no sign of life—everything gone.

Den dere came another boat, de *Lydia Wilson*, Copm Robert Ebanks, who had lost five rangers at Dead Man Mahagan and Dead Man Bar. So Copm Robert say he were goin home and would take all de men dat wanted to come. So we all went aboard de *Wilson* and left for home on Wednesday mornin, and Friday mornin we was bright and early in Cayman.

It were twenty-two went down with de *Majestic*, and nineteen was saved. Oh, it were *something*! (*laughs happily*) People's joy at de ones comin back home, and people sighin; you could hear de screamin way out in de harbor. When we landed at Georgetown, dey had to keep people from talkin to us, dey had to corry us away quietly—it were just we couldn't stand it. We were too upset, and we were weak and everything. (*licks his lips*) One fella dere, he had took a swear, told de blessed Lord if He grant him one privilege of puttin his foot back on Grand Cayman, de only way dat he would ever go back turtlin in de cays would be if he couldn't find anything else to make a penny to get on. Dat were one experience he got enough of dat one time and for all.

Oh, mon! I guess he meant *dat*, okay.

Oh, he meant dat *den*, but he went back—been sailin down here to dese reefs all de days of his life.

Were dat a fella dat dey calls Will Parchment?

Will laughs, embarrassed. He is very excited.

Copm Steadman tell us on dat trip dat he was seventy-seven years of age and old enough to die. And Edilue Dixon, sailor, were de only crewman saved. De remainder of de crew was Autway Bodden, sailor; Steadman was master; Copm Dilmore Conally from Gun Bay went as mate; a guy from Georgetown by de name of Woodly MacField was cook; another guy's little brother by de name of Asher—his first trip out dere—he was lost on de boat as well. And all dem rangers too.

Well, you fellas sayin how news takes so long to travel out to de east part of de island, but we knowed about Dilmore Conally dyin in de cays before dey knowed in Georgetown. Oh, yes! We got our own way of learnin about things.

Dat so, Wodie?

Y'see, Dilmore Conally of Gun Bay dat went down on de *Majestic*, he were a East Ender, but his uncle were old Tom McCoy, up at Old Man Bay. And on de day of dat storm, Tom McCoy were settin in his door watchin dem black clouds rushin by, and his daughter hear him say, I can't go with you. You can go, but I am staying. Dere were no person dere. And later Tom McCoy informed his daughter dat he were speakin in dat manner to de ghost of Dilmore Conally. And by dat dey knew dat Dilmore had died down in de cays, and dey will tell you de same today.

The men glance at Raib, who sits expressionless, eyes closed.

How come dem fellas stayed onto de boat with dat old mon?

Well, owin to Copm Steadman's experience, all de days dat he had sailed de sea, dey listened to him. And he sat right down dere in his chair and let a hurricane come down on him, after knowin dat de barometer had fallen from Thursday; and knowin dat when you see de wind goin around to de northwest in de month of September . . .

Oh, mon! Anytime you see de wind go to de northwest in de month of September anywheres out around de tropics, you doesn't stop to ask if a hurricane is approachin!

If he had left Friday evenin instead of stayin at Serrarers, even if the weather had got bad Friday night, he would have made it into Miskita Cay Sat'day mornin early, and been in safety. And every mon would have been saved. But if we had reached Alligator Cay on Friday, and had pick up dose last rangers, and gone on, we would had been at sea when dat hurricane come down upon us, and I would not be here right now tellin de tale.

Athens stretches his arms over his head and yawns.

Maybe if *all* dose men stood by him, Copm Steadman could have saved his vessel.

Raib opens his eyes to study Will's expression.

Nemmine, Will. (*in a different voice*) Yah, mon! (*laughs*) Copm Steadman told de men dat mornin dat he had fifty-four years of sea experience. And by noon he had had a sea experience dat were not much use to him, cause he were dead.

·10·

The sun has not yet risen, and the reef is dark.

Raib's voice is quiet: he is pointing at the sky.

Any mon see dat star? Buddy, you never seen it?
After all de times I tellin you to watch de weather?
(*voice rising*) Dat star went straight cross de
horizon. Now dat is *true* sign! Sign of *wind!*
(*gasps*) I tellin you fellas now, if dis were not de
month of April, I would be lookin for sign of
hurricane!

April Fool Day, mon.

Dis de worst April dat I remember! De worst one!
I never *see* such a April, with dis wind gone crazy
every day. Take a fool to be a turtler!

April Fool Day, mon.

Dass exactly how I would express it—Fool Day!
Every goddom day is Fool Day!

April Fool, mon.

Brown and Speedy go with Raib in the starboard catboat. Brown's hands are still swollen, and he sits sullen, half asleep, sombrero tilted low over his eyes.
Careless, he drops a kelleck close to Raib's bare foot.

You fella Brown! Don't lay dat kelleck dere!

When Brown mutters, the Captain, who has turned
away, whirls back. Speedy stops whistling.

How dat go? Speak out, mon!

Brown say dis be no use to him in life.

So he say, den. But no mon gone to come into dis
boat dat ain't willin to learn!

We got to be willin in our mind, Brownie. Maybe
we come turtlin again and maybe not, but now we
can go home to Roatán and pick up a few turtle
if we lucky.

I no pick up shit! I a engineer and den a singer!

So you say, den.

The catboat slides from net to net. There are few
turtles. In the gray dawn, the oars thump dully on the
gunwales, and the new turtles sigh.

You ain't got de theory into it yet! Turn dat oar
over—you can't row like dat!

Dass de way *you* understand it, Doddy, but my
hand don't understand it dat way.

Okay, den, Speedy, I agree—do as your hand say in
dis motter.

A wash of sea as the boat rolls; hard flippers on wood
and calipee. The slap of bare feet on the thwarts.

We comin up, now—you, Brown, grob de net!

Aw, shit—I miss it.

Okay, Doddy, Speedy got it! You a nice boy, Speedy!
Just like school days, Speedy!

Goddom it, Speedy, lay dem oars right in de boat!

Okay, Doddy!

Easy, Brownie! Pull best, Speedy!

Pull best, Speedy! Dass *you*, Speedy! Speedy-Boy,
you doin fine!

Sunrise: stars rising in the day. A sudden sweet whiff of the tropics from the coast thirty miles away.

Mon! Smell de land! Gone to give up de sea, go back to de land! Go back to dat sweet land of Roatán!

I no work more in dis fuckin boat.

You can say *dat* again, darlin. No mon gone to come—

Copm? Let Buddy come into dis boat, place of Brownie.

Buddy? He can't pull dat oar when dere is wind.

I pull strong enough for two. I *strong*, mon, I one strong nigger. And dis way dat boy gone learn something about turtlin; he won't learn nothin settin by de galley.

The Captain grunts.

Ever since he were a frock-tail boy, Buddy want be a turtler, cause he daddy and he gran'daddy and he uncles, every one of dem, all de way back, dey turtlers; he want be a turtler so he can hang around with me. But he *ain't* a turtler, no more'n de rest of dem boys I got; dey like de big ships better. I brought dem down to de cays and trained dem good, and now dey ain't one of dem turtlin, not one: dey all abondonin dere home, dey livin up dere in Tampa and Miami. Can't work with me, dey said! (*quietly*) I tellin you now, Speedy, cause you a good mon, you de onliest one of all dese fellas dat might amount to anything, I tellin you now, boy,

dat I bitter. Dere are days when I very, very
bitter. Cause I wore myself out to get to de place
where I de best dey is in de main fishery of de
island, and now dat fishery don't mean nothin.
No, mon. De schooners all gone and de green turtle
goin. I got to set back and watch dem ones grow
big on de Yankee tourist trade dat would not have
amounted to a pile of hen shit in times gone back.
I got to swaller dat.

Modern time, mon.

Buddy dere, he stubborn, y'know: he take after
Copm Andrew dat way. Except he no domn good,
and he not strong, and he get seasick every day he
on de water, and still he say, Let me go in de boat.
Dat be a very mysterious thing. Sometimes I think he
must be some kind of idiot, but in de school he
very clever, so it can't be dat. Dey *some* way he an
idiot, okay, but I can't figure out which way it is.

Old-fashion boy, mon. He love his doddy. Ain't
many today dat knows which one dere doddy is,
but dis one know.

Dass it. (*laughs*) He love his doddy, dat were *his*
mistake in life!

Raib stops laughing. As if listening, he looks all
around the skyline. The wavelets slap the hull. Then
he speaks quietly, avoiding Speedy's gaze.

Dis mornin sea tryin to tell me something, Speedy.
It so *old*, mon. Make me wonder what I doin way
out here on dese reefs, all de days of my life. (*sighs*)
Life has got away from me, some way—I just goin
through de motions.

Get dem boats aboard! We take advantage of dis wind to go to Miskita Cay, crawl dese few turtle, den go dere to Bragman's to register. After dat, full moon be nearly past, and we gets fair weather, we go offshore dere to Misteriosa and cotch dem on dere way south to de Bogue.

Hear dat? You hear me tellin him de other day dat comin to Cape Bank were de wrong direction? Now he tellin *us*!

Well, where in de hell is Misteriosa?

Way out dere. Out Queena way.

Never been dere, mon.

Nobody know dat place. Dat why dey calls it Misteriosa.

Just so long's de *turtle* know about it, dass de main thing.

The ship weighs anchor; the crew come to the galley for their breakfast.

Eighteen turtle altogether. By Jesus, dat is *poor*!

Seventeen, Copm. Cause one died.

In de sailin days, I were afraid of de full moon in May time, cause after de full you would have a calm. For maybe a week, wherever de current carried you, you went. But since I got motors into her, de goddom wind never stop blowin!

Oh, mon! I know something about wind myself. One time comin from Swan Island we dismasted in

de *Jemsons*, right in sight of de island. In a
hurricane. And we drift from dere and we went
back over to de Hobbies. Dat is how many hundred
mile? And from de Hobbies Cays we come back
pretty near to Cayman, and den we got corried
down again pretty near over to Sennillas. And den
de hurricane swung from de south and landed us
right back on de east side of de Old Rock.
Wherever de breeze took us, we went, and dat where
she left us, right back in Cayman! Seven days in
a hurricane! Dismasted seven days!

Raib contemplates Will, amused.

Hear dis fella? Since he told us dat tale of de
Majestic, he can't stop talkin! (*shakes his head*)
Dey many's de times you go to dismast de vessel
yourself—

Oh, yes! One time dere on de—

Well, de story about *dat*: I left home in 1939, on de
nineteenth day of October, nineteenth day of
October in 1939. And I sailed out here to de cays
to get some guano, to fertilize—

Bird shit.

Bird shit. Dass good enough. So I went out to de
cays and loaded up dis bird shit manure, got de
vessel about two-thirds loaded. De crew wanted to
take some more, but—

You had more bird shit den you know what to do
with.

Yah. (*laughter*) Didn't want to overload de vessel,
cause it were in de hurricane time of de year.
Anyway, I left dis place in de mornin, and I seen a
real horrible roll of sea, a *ugly*-lookin roll of sea.

Nice weather, y'know, but a heavy roll of sea, and down around sout'-sou'west was awful coward overcast, all from de horizon, a very heavy-lookin mass of sky. So I told de fellas dat could be was a hurricane approachin, cause de barometer was fallin in de time of her risin, and we would try to scud along to de northward, Cuba way—

Give me some more dat gray stuff, Athens, just so I fill my gut.

Gray stuff? Know what *dat* is?

Nemmine tellin me. I just tryin to keep it down

standin up to de wheel, and he sung out, Land o'er! Yes! We was all de way northward to Caymans! And us only abidin and not sailin, we was layin her by! Seen dat land o'er and sung away as we was scuddin her into de broad day!

Restless, the Captain stands, then sits again.

Well, we got up under de island some ways, in sight of Georgetown. I put out two anchors at de same time, and neither one of dem two anchors held her. All two dragged, and she went off into de deep. And de first puff out of dat hurricane struck her, and it nigh blowed de blocks and rope off her. (*laughs uneasily*) Blowed every fraction of dat canvas away. She had started den to fall into de water, y'know, her gunwale was down into de water on de lee side. And I saw dat de two masts was gone to turn her over, so I took de ax and I started to chop de mast. But when I chopped de lanyards loose, de mast was decayed at de deck, and instead of it breaking off above de deck, it breaked onto de *edge* of de deck, and tore up dat side of de vessel ...

Oh, mon!

Oh, mon, dass it! (*leans toward galley door*) Give dese fellas johnnycake, den, Athens! (*sits back again*) Well, dass about it. Dat load of bird shit were blown all de way from Georgetown to Bragman's, and I never got home till January.

white sail

white clouds

white morning sky

He's dead, Papa!

Raib's cuffs hang, and his dry brown feet are scaly in the ocean sun.

He *ain't* dead, Copm Raib. No, mon. I gettin sign!

Wodie!

The old man's head is sunk onto his chest, the white hair blowing. Raib removes the thatch hat and stares at the papery scalp. Slowly he removes his own hat, standing there before his father. Behind him, Buddy removes his cap as the other men come forward.

Pity ye wouldn't eat.

He tries to cross the old man's hands, but they are hooked hard to the conch shell.

Papa? Is he dead?

Boy, death had to come to Copm Andrew more sooner den later, cause he past de age of eighty. He just dried up and blowed away.

Raib turns the white head by the chin; the eyes are clear. Frowning, he pauses, then presses his ear to his father's heart. He leaps backward, wide-mouthed.

Jesus! Why de hell you ain't spoke before!

He never spoke, Papa! I standin right here—

He spoke, I sayin! Right into my ear!

Raib replaces his father's hat, then his own; shaking his head in wonder, he begins to laugh.

Not yet! He say it slow like dat—*Not ... yet!*

All but Wodie watch the Captain's dance of glee. Wodie climbs to the galley roof and lies down on his back, shielding his eyes. His mirror glints.

The Captain throws his arms wide to the sky.

NOT ... YET!

The *Eden*'s course is south by east, 165 degrees, down the Main Cape Channel. Off to windward is the line of reefs: Half Moon Cay, Bobel, Hall Rocks, Cock Rocks, Edinburgh Reef, Cayo Muerto, known to turtlers as Dead Man Bar.

... forward of de cobberknife it tapers off. Dass where you shoot him, on de fall, just over de forward edge of his jalousies. One bullet dere kill a shark dead; eitherwise he don't pay much attention. So dis tiger took dat bullet and head straight down and bury his head so deep in dat sand dat he were standin straight up, and his tail stickin out de water so you could snare it without ever thinkin about gettin wet. And dis were in ten feet of water.

Now dem big sharks dat you seen dere at Edinburgh Reef, dat is de turtle enemy. Big turtle now, shark got to bite him right to get him, and de turtle is very fast, so de shark try to dismantle him so he can go to work on him. Take a fin off or go for de head. But I seen many times dat when de shark bite de head off of de turtle, he give up den and go way. And dat is cause in my opinion dat turtle head is still openin and closin inside of de shark, de way de turtle do when you chop his head off.

Make him uneasy.

Make him uneasy, and he abondon dat turtle.

Byrum best remember dat on de day dat big shark come for him. Just keep dat big mouth workin when he bite your head off, Byrum, and maybe he leave de rest of you alone.

Dass a very good plan, Athens. Thank you.

Rolling southward.

Lone white bird.

No, dat *not* a sprat bird—dat is a *egg* bird! Look
something like a nightingale! De sprat bird has
yellow bill and yellow feet!

You thinkin about de bos'n bird!

No, mon! *Sprat* bird! Dat one dere is called de *egg*
bird cause dem goddom Jamaicans theft de eggs
of it.

The northeasterly trades continue, bearing away heat
and humidity in a hard breeze; as the day wears on,
the wind increases.

See dat? Comin back at us again! I hoped dat wind
were done with us, but when I seen dat star,
I knew dat it were not!

The men stare somberly at the green seas and the
white sky of spring. The world is empty.

Look at dat! Calls hisself a seaman, and he pissin on de weather side de ship.

Who dat?

Athens! De cook dere! *(grunts) I* can cook better'n dat. I can *cook*, mon. I shipped as cook once, and I know how to cook good. I ain't shamed of it like some of dem; a mon can be proud of anything he know how to do.

Cook for *us*, den—we half starved, eatin dat shit.

Ain't got time to cook! If de coptin got to do dis mon's job and dat mon's job and de next mon's job, and watchin dem and carpin at dem—he can't do dat. But dat de way it is dese days, de crew you gets. And I hungry as hell myself.

Can't keep no steady crew, de way he treat dem. If he had a steady crew, he would had a first-class pilot in de port boat and den a first-class cook, like dey got on de *Adams*. Dem fellas on de *Adams*, de most of dem have been aboard a good while, and dey know dere jobs. Aboard of de *Adams*, a mon eat very good.

We *all* hungry, Copm Raib! Copm Raib?

De galley's gettin in a terrible shape. Nasty! And I got dem so much dishrags and soap and fresh water and all so forth—puddin pans. And dey take dat old salt water dere to wash de turtle grease off de pots! Jesus! Never take de time to do it right! But dat de kind of crew you get dese days. When all de boats was under sail, a mon had to be a sailor to get his job, but now any kind of half-ass fella call hisself a seaman! *(pause)* Dat Athens, dass a pretty one. I made a bad mistake when I sign him on. Dat were a very poor job I done.

Fuck'm. If de *Adams* still at Miskita Cay, I sailin home on her. I had enough of dis wind coptin. No equipment—I don't work dat way. No 'commodations. I worried about my baby—can't get he breath. Like me. He can't keep me aboard of here if my baby dyin, he got to sign me off.

A lot of de coptins now, dey have de same opinions of dere crews dat I haves, but dey scared to open dere mouth.

Dat one thing *you* not scared of, dat right, Copm Raib? I can hear you good all de way over here!

Dass okay, Athens, won't do you any hurt! Might learn something! It always best to speak de truth, like Speedy say!

Well, dey are times—

No! A mon got to have de guts of his opinion! And my opinion is, dey too many fellas like some dat I got aboard of dis vessel dat don't know nothin and don't *care*—no self-respect! Dass what it is—self-respect! Used to be dat in Caymans a mon respect hisself. He done his job, took care of his family, all of dat. He had his land and his own provision ground; he built his own catboat and hung his own nets. Things like dat. But now dey all gettin like de cook dere, like dat engineer I got—don't motter what de color is no more, dey *all* actin like colored people!

Colored people okay, Doddy. It us niggers dat takes hondlin.

Okay, den, Speedy, I be honest with you! You a very good mon, and I done a very good job dere when I sign you on down in Honduras! But I don't disagree entirely with discrimination! You know yourself dat colored people always kept dereselves in such a poor way, dey don't know to keep dereselves decent. We almost *need* some discrimination, we almost *need* some! When people comes around so goddom sloppy, hondlin de food like Athens dere with dem dirty shirt sleeves lickin down into de food—like dat engineer I got dere. Dass another one. Used to be de only place you see fellas like dis was in jail. Now dey all over de Caribbean Sea!

Athens, squatting, cap askew, eye squinted in the smoke of the damp cigarette hung from his mouth, is slicing turtle meat. His ragged arms move back and forth between his ragged knees. The big hickory-han-dled knife slides silently, twisting and winnowing. Despite the heat, Athens still wears his undershirt; its front is stained with turtle blood because his outer shirt, with only the top button fastened, is flying on the wind.

Brown and me hearin you good, Copm Raib. Loud and clear.

I hope you listenin—hearin ain't enough!

Athens holds up a piece of turtle meat and turns it in the sun.

Dat child Ronald—know de one? Ronald *your* child, ain't he, Copm Raib?

Raib stands up.

What de hell you mean by dat?

Oh, I know he *your* child, Copm Raib. I mean to say, he ain't nobody *else*'s.

What you mean, den?

Don't mean nothin. I just askin.

In an eddy of wind, an orange cigarette pack spins across the deck with a faint scratching sound. The men watch Athens' knife slide, slice, carve and pull and pare.

Cause he got bad hair—*dat* what you mean?

You sayin dat, not me.

A thick slap of meat on meat.

Vemon? H-ss-t. Vemon? Best tell your partner to go soft!

Look at Raib face. Look at dat *face* . . . !

Look at Athens! He *mad*, mon!

Got de nerve of de thief's callin, dat boy!

Raib stands over Athens, thick hands at his sides; the wind lifts the white strands in his iron hair.

You like a domn chameleon, know dat, Athens, de way you sneak around shiftin your color.

Oh, *my* color ain't shiftin, Copm Raib. I white as de driven snow, all cept my skin.

Athens tosses a piece of meat onto the stew pile, then looks up.

I kind of like Ronald, dat way.

He flinches when Raib moves. Raib reaches for the crumpled cigarette pack, but the wind skitters it beneath the catboat. He straightens again, panting.

I s'pose you meanin to steal dat knife from dat old mon? Now give it here!

Give you dis knife? *Now . . .? No*, mon! Not yet!

Athens crouches in the galley door. The big hickory-handled knife lies by his hand. His expression is guarded now as his rage wanes, and there is a twitch of merriment at the corner of his mouth; it twitches wildly as Raib himself begins to shake. Athens' laugh is a rapid sniggering that makes his nostrils flare; Raib, hooting and squealing, slaps his cupped hand against the mast.

Not yet! Dass de message dat dey *all* givin me— Not yet!

Raib wipes his eyes.

No, mon! Not yet! he say. (*coughs*) Well, you okay, Athens! I never figure you for dat kind of spirit, boy! (*a fit of coughing*) Mon, oh mon! I guess dey something in dat message dat you give me dere, okay; you got me dere! Don't motter whether Ronald my child or not, dey is a nigger in de woodpile *some*where! Oh, yes!

Raib rolls forward toward the shrouds. Halfway up the mast, hair crested by the wind, he gazes down at his men, regarding them a moment before speaking. He is still smiling, but the smile has turned.

Brown!

The engineer knocks his sombrero back and gazes at the Captain.

You keepin dat oil pressure too high! Know dat gauge you was askin me about? Well, dis mornin I took a little oil out of her, and right away de hand on dat gauge stop flitterin!

Raib climbs the shrouds to the masthead.

Will! Got to check dese ring bolts up and down de mast; dey workin in dere holes!

Will gets slowly to his feet.

Dey workin in dere holes cause de wood is punky. Dat whole domn mast is punky. (*sighs*) I tellin you, Athens, in dat mon's younger days, he keelhaul you.

He keelhaul him today, only dis boy got something on him—dat right, Athens?

So you say den, Byrum.

Land o'er! Dere Mahagans!

Reefs and mangrove islands of the Miskito Banks rise from the sea.

Port!

PORT!

Steady!

STEAD-DAY!

Copm Raib? We got cartons for dese boys on Dead Man Bar! We gone to speak dem?

Speak dem den, only keep movin!

The *Eden* rides down between Outer Mohegan and Cayo Muerto. Every little while she changes course, picking her way among the coral heads and shoals. Cayo Muerto is little more than a clump of giant mangrove, taken root on the shallow banks; from the northwest approaches, it shifts like a drifting forest on the sea.

Two miles west of the cay, the *Eden* slows her engines, and as if by signal, a small sailing craft takes wing at the mangrove wall and comes flying down the wind. The shallow banks are choppy, but rather than slack off on the sheet and give up speed, a man high on the weather side of the flying boat scampers to the end of a plank that serves as a makeshift outrigger; in the boat's silhouette as it bears down upon the *Eden*, the figure seems suspended in midair. Terns part before the boat, then snap together at a point over the sparkling sea where bait fish, pursued, rush to the surface.

Look at de way he slickin along—dat Melgreen
Powery!

Raib descends slowly from the crosstrees as his crew
lines up along the rail. On come the rangers, waving
and yelling, careening in on the *Eden*'s starboard side.
In seconds the sail is dropped and a line passed; the
rangers swarm aboard.

Come up, come up! Come up, mon, and be hoppy!

How you goin, Melgreen?

Not bad, Byrum. How yourself? Seen Desmond?

Yah, mon! Seen'm at Bobel! Got a pile of pan-heads
with'm.

Hoo, boy! Copm Desmond Eden! (*whispers*) Who
dat settin on de throne? Dat Copm Andrew?

Yah, mon. Won't eat. De poor old mon is dyin.

The *Eden* moves slowly on her course, east southeast
toward the Blue Channel. The rangers take their cigarettes and messages and cartons of provisions wrapped
in burlap; they are so glad to see new faces that they
keep yelling all the while they are aboard and after
they jump back into their boat.

Okay den, thank you!

Take care dere, Copm Andrew! Best eat something!

You kind to speak us, Copm Raib! We ain't seen
no mon pass dis way since Sat'day gone a week!

Though he has not eaten, and will not lie down, the old man moves easily with the long roll of the ship, and his liverish hands rest lightly on his conch. His mouth is firm, and his wide eyes are clear. Buddy stands behind the heavy chair, trying to see what the old man perceives.

Grandpapa? D'ye see the land? Cayo Muerto?

The old man is still. On his old thatch hat with its round crown there is a stain where in earlier days he had worn some sort of band, but the collar of his khaki shirt is clean. In the low sun of late afternoon, the silver hair over his ears dissolves in filaments of light against the sparkle of the water, and the ear lobes seem illumined from within, as if his skin had gone transparent.

From the companionway behind comes a faint sweet smell of manure. The green turtles lie belly up, each with a neat turd pile by its tail. One breathes its hollow gasp, and Buddy sinks beside it, on his knees.

You watchin us? Dat what Athens say. He say dat you watchin us die.

The turtle watches him, unblinking.

Dark noddies cross the swift colors of the coral bank, toward the cays. The cays astern disintegrate in the sun's mist.

Vemon and Athens slice, sort and salt the meat.

Calipatch and calipee!

You got de b'ilin water ready? Bring it here, den! I gone to make turtle stew! Gone to make turtle *stew*, I got to have b'ilin *water*!

Don't tell me nothin in dat bad voice, nigger. I told you once, I knock you on you ass.

Vemon showin Speedy something he didn't know to do: make turtle stew! After de first lesson, Speedy do it fastern' him—dass why dey calls him Speedy!

School days, mon. I learn my speed from school days.

Vemon stuffs meat into a sack, mixing salt in as he goes; Athens takes the rest into the galley.

Oh, he gone to scotch dat meat!

More salt! Got to get salt, you want salt *meat*!

A little brown sugar to put into it, dat be all right.

Brown sugar?

Give a better taste. Different color and better taste.

Crankcase? Well, dat oil got be changed

knots?

dis nigger think

        to make dat knot proper, you got to

No. off to de northward.

Listen! On a night like dis now you can *listen* for
turtle. You can hear . . . No,
de reef breakin

        red, red, red

Dat reef don't break no more now den it did

          get close

up to green turtle, you can hear
dem blowin

        know what he doin, but

he doin it wrong.

You think you can do dat better? *I* de one doin de
work—

He all right, y'know. Dis mon all right.

          de *bring* mon
who is called dat way cause he bring home de bacon:
den dere is de *sweet* mon, *(laughs)* what she call her
sweet mon—

Make her feel sweet.

Sweet, mon. Soft and mallow.

        through de Caribbean
here

    galley pot dere. I servin now.

Clank of tin pots.

Dis week gone have full moon light. Fore dis fortnight halfway done!

Green turtle see dat mesh in de full moon, steer off de nets.

Most de turtle gone south to de Bogue, and de rest too smart for us when de moon full.

April Fool Day, mon.

Fool Day, dass it. Next.

Clink of plates. A cockroach darts along the galley side.

Said I want more meat.

Okay, brother. Wait till we see if Copm Andrew take a little—

Can't do my work on no little piece like dat.

Brownie, you get any?

Byrum, you can stand dem nets in all dem channels out dere and get turtle.

I know it. Do very next two channel out dere—

Dat de last of de meat?

bullas? My woman make dose with ginger. And cornmeal cakes—

Got to do me better'n dat! Dat won't last me two minutes!

Vemon!

No domn good, y'know. (*silence*) Goddom sure
didn't get enough after my work. (*silence*) What one
mon get de next mon ought to get.

Give him de last piece dat I had, and listen to him!

Workin mon. Dat a hell of a thing. Why de one mon
get different from me?

You never eat better in your life!

Ain't nothin on dis bone! I don't go for dat shit,
mon!

Vemon? You cut dat out! No, mon! You not so big
as you think you is aboard of here!

I want something to eat! If I work, I want
something to eat, to pay for it!

You are not starvin aboard here! You would have
to be a hog if you are starvin! You were settin in dat
galley today, and you had a pot of rice dere and
a big old pot of fish! And de good-for-nothin mon,
do you see de way he goin on dere now?

Lot of people gettin better fed den me!

Shut up your mouth! You get more to eat den
anyone!

Athens speaks with his mouth full, spitting it on purpose as he talks.

You men eat like hogs! (*laughter*) I don't know
how you men sleep at night, eatin dis rich food!

Nemmine, Athens! Your partner don't have to go on
like dat! No call for dat!

You want porridge, Vemon?

No!

Give Vemon his coffee.

Coffee right dere by he foot.

I NEVER PUT IT DERE!

What you shoutin for, you goddom fool? Shut up!

Vemon rises and walks aft.

He open his mouth just to see if he can frighten
people, but de mouth is all dere is ... Buddy?
Copm Andrew eatin anything?

No, Papa.

Black coffee?

Now I can say, dear, you de worst of your kind ...

       hunk of meat and all, and bread, and take de
cookin trash and all and mix it right up with de
rest—look just like garbage. After dat, he put in dis
cake mix. And when he got it all done, he stand
back a little ways and look it over, and den he
call it a *cake*.

Dat sound like Vemon, okay.

Domn fool. I don't know how he find his bed. And
dat engineer I got, dass another one. I gone to
send him home after dis trip. I keep *dat* engineer,
I wouldn't have no engine left at all.

With his plate Brown has climbed onto his fuel drum,
where he squats on his heels, knees close to his ears;
under his hat, his eyes cannot be seen, but the rhythm
of his ear shows he is chewing.

Hey! Vemon!

Vemon Dilbert Evers!

He layin back dere thinkin up revenge.

He thinkin about obeah. He gone stick pins—

Obeah? I can do a little bit of dat myself.

Copm Desmond know about obeah good. He was down in Honduras, sleepin on all de graves.

Copm Desmond! Call *any* sonofabitch a coptin in dese goddom days—

How you work dat, Athens?

Oh, you got to pay me pretty dear to learn you obeah. (*laughs*) Gone to make Wodie's neighbors dere pay pretty dear for learnin it. When dey caught'm with all dat hair and shit, dey was complainin dat dey still had one more to kill. *Yes,* mon!

Kill?

You got to kill and do all dat! Why, you got to kill half a dozen, *learnin!*

You got to get what dey calls de Book of Moses, dat right, Athens?

Mm-hm. Book of Moses. Frogs' legs. All dem things like dat. Got to eat salt when you thirsty and coot with your sister and hang upside down in trees. Got to sleep on graves. Got to drown a child—dass what dey done dere in Caymans. Ain't dat right, Wodie? Dem obeah workers come from de East

End, y'know, and dat where de deed were done. Up
in de bushes over dere, by dem wild fig trees.

Athens pantomimes the murder of the child, and the
men laugh out of nervousness.

Dey only de two ways to protect yourself from
people dat is workin woe. One is, you goes to de
graveyard and dig yourself up some crumbly bones.
And de other is, you *kill* de obeah worker by
pushin her down on a sharp stake. (*laughs*) But
first you gots to pin her tongue to her chin with a
sharp thorn, so's she don't fix you with her last
curse. Dey do *dat* a few times down East End, dey
wouldn't have so much woe-workin, dat right,
Wodie?

Wodie grins; he looks at Raib, who sits against the
galley side, hat cocked over his eyes, wrists on his
knees.

Well, dem two ladies down East End, dey is my
neighbors. People like dat, dey just get caught up in
dere own foolishness! I don't think dey know what
would be good for a pain in de belly, but dey walk
around and try to fool people, make'm believe
things, and dey had all dat nonsense in dere house.
Well, after de death of dat child, dese things were
found in de house dat was knowed to be used by
people dat claimin to know obeah. Dey had black
candles, and clothes of different folk, and skulls of
animals and whatnot, and fingernails and hair
and bones, which people think is used in witchcraft
and workin obeah. And it be true dat de death of
dat child is very mysterious. Because de child had
no physical marks on it, like say, somebody kick it,
or lick it with a piece of wood, or choke it, and it
wasn't drowned; it died before it hit de water.
Because it didn't have one drop of water in de
lungs; dat child were floatin like a piece of

bobwood, with de air still into de lungs, floatin along under de beach dere in de mornin sun.

Never heard about poisonin? Bitter cassava? Don't have to be no jujuman to work with dat!

Who would poison dat child?

A long silence. The wind moves through the rigging, and the ragged clothes dance on the shrouds. Brown descends from his fuel drum and comes to the galley, squatting down next to Speedy.

Course I will say dem sisters is kind of unusual. Dey de ones dat drove dat nail into my footprint, and den accused me of de murder of dat child. Well, de night of de death, I were walkin home late, and I hear de sweet murmurin of a child in de nearby bushes. So dis were strange, and I wonderin if dis child were lost, so I call out but dere come no answer. So den, next mornin, I was over dere early to see if dese ladies want me to build dem gutterins so dat dey could collect a little water in de rainy season—it very dry out at East End, y'know —and when I come in de yard, dere was de sound of dis sweepin broom at de first cabin, and den dis broom stop even though my foots never made a sound in dat white dust. So dis sister, she very tall and got dese yeller-lookin eyes, she lean around de doorjamb, and she point to de other cabin dere, maybe eight fathoms away, a goodly distance, and when I turn towards dere she speak out so soft I can hardly hear. I turn back to see if she speakin me, but she not; she speaking dat other cabin over dere, and *dat* sister already standin in *her* door. Well, dat sister pretty wild-lookin, too, got de same yeller eyes, y'know, and Indian kind of face only very dark, and both of dem wearin all dese big kind of rags dat cling to dem some crazy way so dey don't fall. And de two of dose little voices in de wind dat if you did not know dey spoke, you would thought you had heard a breath of wind comin round de shutter, something like dat.

From under the rough slats of the galley side, a cockroach extends its feelers: the feelers twitch, hold still. From under the stove wood, the rat watches the big roach.

And it was den dat I turn and seen dat small boat out dere to de eastward, in de mornin channel. Couldn't make out just who de mon was, cause he black as a dead stick on dat early sun, just standin dere gazin in toward de shore, like he was waitin. Now dis were before I knowed de smallest thing about de death of dat child.

Wodie takes a breath, his good eye wide.

Raib has pushed his hat back. He opens his eyes slowly and whistles in disgust.

Now I know it be your opinion, Copm Raib, dat sign and duppies and obeah, all dat is nonsense, and you is an old sea coptin and a well-experienced mon. But I gone to tell you now dat I had *sign*. I want to tell you now dat lookin out dere at dat boat, I knowed something woeful had hoppen, and right den, it were like my heart had died. I looked back at dem two sisters, standin quiet with dere yeller eyes, and it were like dat de whole world had stopped. Mon! Dem two huts, I seen every speck of dat limestone on de walls and every straw in de thatch roof! Dey look like dey was dere two hundred years, dey were dat old and dat dry!

De one cabin has a kind of blue wash, faded to de same blue as de sky, and de other one white as bone, and both of dem bare, bare, bare, settin dere on dem old ironwood posts, with old gray narrow doors. A lizard were stuck to dat whitewash like a spot, and he never moved a scale. Dere was no wind, no air, nothin were movin, and all de same dis big leaf fall from de sea grape, just dis one, and come tumblin across de yard, big dead brown leaf, dry as de wind, and dat were de last thing in de wide world dat moved, cause den it fetch up on a post. So I turn my head slow, and all de palmetto and de grape and so, every plant were white with limestone dust dat de wind corries out dere at East End, but in all my years of livin in dat place, I never see things so white as what dey were dat mornin. De sky were white and de sea were white and all de island, too.

And quiet—dere were never a bird, although dis were just de time of dere mornin song. And out on de road dere was two dogs layin in de dust, white dogs laying in white dust, and dey lay like dey was dead, I seen black flies on dem, and across de road, in de jennifer and cocoes, dere was a very old donkey tethered dere, look like he *grew* dere. Dat donkey were de same silver color as a old piece of beach wood. (*sighs*) Well, I tellin you now, it were early still, in de first hour after de sunrise, but de light off dat white sand were something terrible. I had to shade my eyes to see dat stranger in dat boat.

And all dis time dat stranger never moved, and dat boat never drifted, no mon, not one foot, in de current and de wind. It were like de sun had stopped in its time of risin, and every livin thing had to stop and wait. De world was waitin. Den dat dead leaf jump free again, blowed down across de road, and I got my breath, and I turned my back on dem yeller eyes and I went down to de seashore. Oh, yes, I knew. I had felt de sign. I were right dere when he brought de body in. And you know something? I know every catboat on dat coast, and I never seen dat blue boat before. I never seen dat fella neither, never in my life. I never thought to ask his name, not den, and I never seen him after.

·11·

Near twilight, the *Eden* rounds the southwest point of Miskito Cay and comes up into the lee. The island, roughly two miles square, is the largest on the banks, but except for an acre of high ground where water of poor quality may be obtained, it consists mostly of red mangrove. There is no harbor at Miskito Cay, but ships can come in close on the south shore; in hurricane, they are run aground and lashed to the small trees.

There are two vessels in the anchorage. One is the rusty yacht called *Davy Jones*, the other a converted schooner like the *Eden* but much larger; she is trim in appearance, and her dark green paint is new. Turtles are being hoisted into the ship from two catboats that bob along her hull.

> Dere she is, mon! De *Alice H. Adams*, Speedy!
> She takin on her turtle now, gone sail directly to
> Key West!

Silhouetted on the fading sky are two thatched, ragged Indian shacks on sagging platforms. To avoid the sandflies that infest the cays, these shacks on stilts are built well off the shore. Trailing downwind from each shack are the small dugout *cayucas*, which in the turtle season bring the Indians across the forty miles of open water from the Mosquitia Coast.

The *Eden* moors inshore of the *Adams* and lowers her small catboat. Athens and Byrum go off to the *Adams*, and Byrum alone, trying to chew gum while he whistles, returns at nightfall for his supper.

Hey, Byrum! How de Indians?

Most of dem Wikas treats me nice. Don't treat me anything but nice. Dey give me dis nice sack of conchs.

Byrum drops a burlap sack onto the deck with a thick crunching sound.

Supper, Byrum, when you ready. No rush at all with me.

You back in de galley, Speedy?

Vemon? You ready for rice porridge?

Wait till I done! I still eatin dis hox-bill!

A catboat comes across the water, carrying Athens and three men of the *Adams* crew.

Cocinero!

Hey dere, Byrum! Gone to let us up?

Come up, come up! What say, Royal? Come up, mon!

The crews greet each other shyly.

Dis here Henry Bawden. From Old Providence.

Come up, Henry! When you fellas sailin?

Sail tomorrow, mon, if dat wind break with us.

Hey dere, Copm Raib?

Hey, mon! You talkin wind? We had a hell of a time! How many you get?

We full. Four hundred fifty—close to dat.

Hear dat, Speedy? De *Adams* got four hundred fifty, we got seventeen.

If dis wind moderate, you do okay. Dis last week, we didn't do much neither.

Dis a bad trip, Royal. Very poor trip. Boat leaks bad; no equipment. He ain't got de hang of dem motors—

frames is mahogany and de plankin is cypress, inch-and a quarter plankin on dat port boat—she pretty solid. I believe she a pretty good catboat. But somehow she keep right on leakin.

Will say she were launched dere without flowers— dat no good, mon.

We should have left dat boat at Half Moon Cay, and picked up Will's boat dat were left behind

business is a lot into de picture

rum, dat make a hard night of it.

Dat homemade stuff? Calls dat white lightnin!
More like *black* lightnin, by de color. Feel you
quick

mon dat is willin to take de

same hard farins dat we do

So Vemon tell me he got to have another half
share for comin along, and I tell him, if he got to
have *dat*, he best stay right on de dock

leave de nets
untended, mon, de log'reds
bear dem away

dat de *only* trip dat he got more turtle
den what we got! De only one!

speakin fair now, dat
fella don't deserve

New York,
y'know. Had papers and everything. You know any
of dem shippin lines up dere could use a mon?

So I went back to de seashore and kept watchin,
and I seen dat de waves were runnin smaller, and
I knew den dat de storm was goin *from* me,
passin over to de westward

de *Wilson*, de *Goldfield*, de
Adams, and den dis vessel, dey have a spoon bow.
De *Hustler*, de *Majestic*—all dose older vessels
had a figurehead, a real old-fashioned figurehead
bowsprit

de *Hustler* had a
one-piece bowsprit, no jib boom

by Alice-Agnes Rock
—big turtle, mon. We give dem hell dere.

Hon say to me: Precious—

I see four turtle into de one net. Dass right, four
turtle. And de way you do, you cotch one of dem
with de paddle and den de two men

                              soft, mon. Soft
and mallow

              midday I were takin
latitudes, and just at noon de sun covered up, and
she never come back out

Jamaicans? Way out dere?

Yah, mon! Desmond got a gang of pan-heads
dere livin like animals, *worse* den animals, drinkin
and fightin and all so forth. What dey done to
Bobel Cay—*worse* den a hurricane, cause at
least de hurricane is clean.

                              says, I can lay down any
minute dat I want and picture dose sets just as
natural as if I had used dem yesterday

                              use dat crawl to
de east of you, we could crawl dese
couple turtle we got here

                              were my chance in life and
den I lost it

              where we headed after Bragman's, won't
find no pan-heads *dere*, mon! Far Tortuga!

Mon, dat half-inch chain hold her
till Christ come

              sailin home
on de *Adams*. Don't like de way dese turtle watchin
me, no mon. I ain't stayin aboard of here.

Goldfield? Dey runned her ashore?

Oh, mon: I remember de year de *Goldfield* sailed
away, and now she gone!

She mashed up, mon. In miscalculation dey wrecked her

              a heavy beam sea when I left dere, oh God she was blowin hard. Dat wind blows de hairs out of ye

            he dyin, mon. Won't talk and he won't eat and he won't lay down. Just gone to sit like God on dat goddom throne dere till de wind dry him up, blow him away.

Captain Andrew Avers.

Copm Raib?

The figure of Wodie breaks the moonlight in the deckhouse door. Byrum sits up with a grunt.

Dat you, Wodie? What you wantin?

Raib lies still, his mouth wide, looking stunned.

Copm Raib? H-ss-t!

Raib opens his eyes and shuts his mouth, as a frown gathers; he gazes at the deckhouse ceiling.

It Copm Andrew! He gone!

Raib rises slowly in his bunk.

Dass what dey said de last time. You listen to his heart?

No, mon! Never went near him!

How you *know*, den?

As he speaks, Raib drags his pants on.

I see de fireball! In de hatchway overhead. So I poke my head out, and dat fireball dere by de mast!

Fireball! Never heard about St. Elmo's fire?

Dey ain't no storm, Copm, it full-moon light!

Raib goes out onto the deck.

I tellin you, Wodie, you got dis whole crew
thinkin you some kind of Jonah. If I'd have known
dat your head was filled with trash . . .

Raib falls silent. Rounding the forepart of the deckhouse, he pauses by the hatch. In the moonlight the
bony knees in their worn khaki emerge from the night
shadows of the port companionway. The rat retreats.

Ain't got no white suit, but we got his pockets
sewed.

Oh Jesus! You see how dat rat chew his shin?

In the yellow light the old man lies, knees up in rigor
mortis. While Will presses on the shoulders, Raib tries
to straighten out the legs, but every time the legs
contract, and the high black shoes lift slowly from the
deck.

See dat? Dey ain't no bendin de old fella, he just
as cranky as he ever was—domn! Know what we
gone do? Put him back on de throne dere and
corry him across de water in dat manner.
Eitherwise he be layin in de hole with his knees up
in dis woman's way—can't have *dat!* Got to bury
him chair and all!

Daybreak.

Light and sky.

The catboats from the *Eden* cross the anchorage, and a third boat slides out from the silhouette of the *A.M. Adams*. Lashed across the thwarts of the first boat, the dead man's chair rises and falls against the east horizon. The boats vanish in the shadow of the cay.

Men of the *Adams* and the *Eden* stand on either side of a dark pit, dug east and west. Buddy and Will are on their knees, pushing thin soil back into the hole with shards of board. Captain Andrew, in his chair, lies in the hole, his hat haloed around his head, his hands still folded in his lap, shoes to the eastward. His eyes, half open, are fixed upon branches overhead that flail at the gray sky.

An ant crosses his gray cheek.

Where's dat old conch shell dat he cherished? Did ye leave it aboard de vessel?

Holding his hat against his chest, Raib coughs to repress a smile.

Not ... yet! he say. Dem were de last words of *dis* old fella!

The branches creak.

Copm Andrew Avers! (*pause*) Well, Copm Andrew went and he went, and would not help hisself—wouldn't hardly rise one hand. But in de end he went away very well. He were not able to give testimony, but he went in peace, and we very hopeful for his soul. Amen.

Raib looks from one face to the other.

Amen.

Amen.

Amen.

Light scent of sweat and mangrove humus. Mosquito whine. Dried blood on a dark arm.

A cough.

At the sad demeanor of the men, Raib frowns, looks shy, tries not to laugh anew. He sees the catboat off the shore: through the twisting trees, an upright figure watches.

Desmond! Come ashore, den!

The figure stays the drifting boat by jamming an oar into the bottom on the downwind side. There is no answer.

Raib scrapes earth into the hole and offers the board to Vemon.

> Dis were de finish of a wind coptin, and a very good sailor mon. Sailed down to dese reefs all de days of his life, and now he died here at Miskita Cay! *(turns toward Desmond)* HIS LAST VOYAGE WERE HIS FINISH; DASS WHAT CORRIED HIM! IN HIS OLD AGE HE HAD TOO MUCH AMBITION; HE DIDN'T THINK OF HIS HEALTH, ONLY HIS WILL TO GO, AND DERE WERE DEM STANDIN READY TO TAKE ADVANTAGE OF HIS OLD AGE! *(more quietly)* Copm Andrew were a born seaman, one of de best. He one of de best seamen were in de island, and an expert on sailmakin; he could take a vessel and rig her from one end to de next. Knowed everything about it, and he learned me all he knew. Andrew Avers were a very good sailor mon.

A tear appears on Will's dry face.

> Oh, yes! A very good sailor mon!

Byrum and Speedy stack the turtles as they are lowered: the blue boat is nearly awash. A soft bump of old wood on wood as another catboat nudges alongside. Shifting a heavy turtle in the bilges, Byrum cocks his head: he sees tight kinks of hair on a section of pale heavy leg between black rubber boot and rusted swim shorts, and a stray testicle, and a red T-shirt.

Mis-tuh Desmond!

Yessuh! What say? (*grunts*) Couple turtle dere, I see.

Mon, you lookin at turtle but not turtlers. De turtlers is over dere aboard de *Adams*.

In the bow of Desmond's boat, a near-naked black boy stands on one elegant foot, balancing himself with a long sculling pole. In the stern squats a pregnant black girl no older than fourteen. Her hands are folded in the lap of a sack frock, and her eyes are fixed on pink broken conchs and twisted beer cans in the oily bilge that washes her short ankles.

Desmond belches, gazing up at the *Eden*'s deck.

Where you headed, Byrum?

Southern cays, I venture. De season very late. If de turtle gone, well, we work offshore—Misteriosa. Know dat place?

Desmond yawns, gazing up at the *Eden*'s deck.

Far Tortuga? Copm Andrew marked it careful on my chart. Long way out dere, mon. Bad reefs.

Dat so? Well, we desperate.

Plenty egg birds dere, dey say.

Birds, mon! And trees! Ain't one dese old mongrove

banks, y'know! (*whispers*) He got de idea dat some green turtle goes out dere to nest.

Dey plenty birds dere anyways, you know dat much.

Talkin about birds? Oh, mon! De sky is littered!

Desmond grins so suddenly that Byrum flinches.

Been out dere, Byrum?

No, mon! But I knows about it good!

Using the oars as paddles, Speedy and Byrum stand upright in bow and stern, one foot on the gunwales, the other balanced on the still, bamboo-colored bellies of the turtles. Slowly they start out toward the turtle crawls.

Raib comes to the rail, sees Desmond, steps back, is seen, stops. His face closes as Desmond grins at him; he squints toward the low sun.

What say dere, Copm Raib?

Not much. Not sayin much.

Keepin quiet, huh? Ain't like you, Copm Raib.

So you say, den. (*pause*) Got a Wika dere, I see.

No, mon. Dat Jamaica pussy, mon—cook on my boat now.

Desmond puffs his belly out and scratches it.

Yah, mon. Took her aboard to give her a rest (*winks*) from dem Jamaicans I got workin for me now—dey grindin her to death.

Nice bunch of fellas. Dat one dat got knifed dere at Bobel—did dat one die? I s'pose dem was more of your pan-heads dat we seen south of de cay.

Dem Niyamen? Dey very grudgeful cause you would not speak dem! (*grins*) Oh, dey *lookin* for you, mon!

Where you got dem now? Dead Man Mahagans?

Desmond Eden ignores the question. He contemplates Raib Avers.

Never asked me to de burial?

Never heard me holler, Come ashore—?

No, mon. Too late den.

Were not for you, dere would not have been a burial!

Desmond tucks his testicle into his shorts.

No, mon. Dat old mon were my doddy too, y'know.

I never swallered dat one, Desmond.

You de only one in Caymans, den—you gone to choke on it.

Copm Andrew's bush child! Desmond Eden!

No, mon. Outside child. I were acknowledged when he give me de *Clarinda*.

To see de ugly way you kept her! Call yourself Coptin—!

Look better dat way den burned down for de insurance, ain't dat so?

Is dat de tale you give to Copm Andrew? Dat why he would not talk?

How you like your new engines, Copm Raib? (*farts*) Gone ask your baby brother to come up?

Dat what you here for? (*contemptuously*) Come up, den.

No thank you kindly, brother—I too busy.

Athens comes forward, carrying a paper parcel; he hops down into Desmond's boat.

Goddom it, Athens, I never said you could go visitin dis mornin—!

Ain't goin visitin. I goin home. I sick, mon. I sick inside of my own self and I sick of de shit aboard of here.

You wantin to lose your share of dis voyage? Cause you jumpin ship! I never signed you off!

The boat moves away from the *Eden*'s hull.

Well, dat ain't much, on *dis* voyage, Copm Raib. But if you smart, you settle up with me when you come home.

Raib lifts his stubbled chin toward Athens' parcel.

If dey anything missin aboard of here, we know who got it, dat right, Athens?

You talk like dat, why, I might get to talkin too.

Rain clouds, rain-colored water. The *Eden*'s catboat, near awash, is poled slowly by Byrum and Speedy. Drifting downwind from the crawls come the gasps of the penned turtles and the sad plaint of a gull.

Speedy talks over his shoulder; his muscles jump beneath a bright white T-shirt.

Now de Coptin say he took a floggin dere in de Bay Islands. He say dem people cheat him, so dat is why he left dat place still owin dem money on de vessel. But dem people was always good to me, very fine. Dey had dat drydock down dere in French Harbour a long time, and dis is de first thing of dis kind dat ever I heard against dem. Old Doddy dere, he say dey kep'm dere to make more money, but maybe dey work de best when dey work slow. Maybe dass de way things go de best down in Honduras.

A soft-drink can bobs by in the gray dawn water; on the bottom lies a thick orange starfish. In pale patches between beds of turtle grass, bruise-colored medusae loom, seeming to breathe.

A scuttling fish.

Another thing: he put de blame on Brownie for de vibration in dat port engine, and de oil seals leakin, but it were nobody else den him dat struck dat shaft with a sledge hammer to straighten it, in de heat of de day, when he were angry—he were de one did *dat*.

Oh, I believe dat! He a mule, just like his doddy! You can't change him!

The mangrove walls of Miskito Cay close off the eastern sky.

Something about dat mon-grove, Speedy. Something lonely.

Lonely kind of day, mon.

I wish I could speak good. De things I *feelin* . . .

The turtle crawls are water pens constructed of long mangrove saplings stuck into the marly bottom in five feet of water and lashed with thatch rope, in pens twenty feet square. The saplings rise high above the surface as a protection against storm seas, and each crawl has a gate on one side that can be taken down to water level when turtles are put in or removed.

The gaunt poles of the crawls look bent in the gray wind, and the figures in the boats stand motionless against the sky. There is a catboat from the *Adams* and two Indian *cayucas*, which carry thalassia grass used as fodder for the turtles.

The turtlers wear plaited palm hats, the crawl tenders the sombreros of the coast. Most of the Wika men have Indian features in black skin.

Take he away!

The myriad bay-colored shells of the turtles in the crawl are scarred and dull, and the creatures have lost their gliding ocean flight: the crowded pen has made their movements jerky. Cornered, they rush against the stakes.

See dem turtle, Speedy? Some dem leany from bein so long into dat crawl—dey gettin watered. Meat get all kind of slimy. In Cayman we don't like dem dat way, we likes dem fat, but watered turtle sells fine at Key West.

A big Wika dives beneath the surface of the pen, where the turtles mill. Grasping a turtle by the carapace, behind the head, he slips a noose around the base of a fore flipper, singing out to the men at the crawl gate.

Take he away!

The *Adams* boat crew deals with the big turtle: the whole pen is a turmoil of white water. The Wika seizes a second turtle while waiting for a noose to be thrown back to him; he leans into a corner, holding it upright, from behind. In pompous strength, he watches, and his dripping head is grim. The upright turtle blinks.

... your two hands, mon! Grob her!

Switch her ass dis way! *Dis* way!

Easy do it—see my foot?

Up she goes!

The noose is slung back to the Wika.

   Take he away!

When the *Adams* boat is loaded and moves off, Byrum
secures his catboat. One by one, the *Eden*'s turtles are
hauled onto the gate, and Speedy cuts the flipper
thongs with quick hooks of his knife as the turtle is
shoved forward into the pen. Still upside down, each
turtle sinks thrashing toward the bottom but quickly
rights itself and rushes for the sea, striking so hard
against the stakes on the far side that the crawl sways.

   See dat? Won't be pretty long. Couple weeks into
   de crawl, all dat fine sea color be gone.

   Dey pretty, mon. Green turtle pretty. I like de
   way dey swims among de reef.

   Look out you don't cut dere throat, de way you
   swing dat knife—won't swim so pretty *den*.

Speedy slashes the last thong and shoves the turtle into
the pen.

   No, mon. I can cut, mon. From school days. If he
   can't do nothin else, dis boy can *cut*!

Byrum socks him on the biceps.

   You a hard nigger, mon! I very glad dat we in
   friendship!

   Oh, I a hard one, dass de truth! *Hard* nigger, mon!

Midmorning. The *Eden* moves offshore past the *Adams*, which is laying over one more day because of wind. Byrum bellows across the water to his former shipmates, who lift their hands or chins by way of parting.

Speedy looks for Athens on the *Adams* deck.

Funny thing he don't come out, wave us goodbye. (*sighs*) Havin a shipmate leave de vessel, never sayin goodbye—makes me feel funny.

Prob'ly he too sick of dis domn boat to look at it. You pick de wrong vessel, Speedy! You seein turtles but not turtlers!

Maybe de luck change tomorrow. I not worried, mon.

No, mon. Dis a very poor trip. Boat leaks bad; dis vessel need three thousand dollars just to make her seaworthy. No life jackets, no fire extinguisher, no runnin lights, and dat goddom radio-telephone dat don't send: I tellin you, it like de back-time days, bein aboard of here. Ain't like a freighter where you holler Mayday over de radio. Out on dese reefs you holler Mayday till you blue in de face, ain't nobody to hear. *Silent*, mon. Just like dem mongrove.

Well, de *Adams* look very nice.

Oh, she a *pretty* vessel! She got dat wind chute you seen dere dat suck wind down into de turtle hold; green turtle need dat, cause dey stacked maybe six-deep on dem racks. Pretty near every line on her you got nylon; you don't see all of dis old thatch rope. (*sighs*) Maybe if dis vessel had good blocks, wouldn't be so bad, but ain't a halyard here, or a sheet here, dat is rove properly. Since she got dose masts cut short, de *Eden* is ass over backward. All de riggin slack—you risk your neck just to climb up to de crosstrees. (*sighs*) Too bad you never work aboard of de *Adams*.

Old Doddy treat me pretty good. I work good so he treat me good. Nobody complainin about Speedy. I works on a drydock. Plenty boats. Work my property. Fifty-five acres, mon. Dey hate like hell for me to go off on dis vessel; dey not wantin me to go.

He always yellin about justice. But dey ain't only three of us does all de work aboard of dis vessel, and dey nine men gettin shares. Ain't no justice *dere*!

Speedy leans back, hands behind his head.

Dey gone to laugh like hell, dey be so hoppy when I gets back to dat sweet land of Roatán.

My intended dere, Miss Gwen, she de child of Copm Ossie. And Ossie, he de father-in-law of Acey Christian. Me and dem two fellas, we gone to get our own turtle boat, we gone to *build* her. Yah, mon. Dey some bush over dere in Ally Land dat got de last Cayman mahogany. We get in dere with donkeys, mon, and haul it out—dass de plan dat we got now.

Ain't you de one was tellin me dat dis fishery near finished?

Dass right. But we got it in de blood.

Okay. Dass good. Dass very very fine.

·12·

The *Eden* rolls down past the Nasa Cays and the
Alice-Agnes Rocks, bearing west-southwest, on a following wind, for Nicaragua.

South of the Rocks, a silhouette rises and falls in the
slow ocean as the green walls move one by one to
leeward.

See dat notch dere in de cobberknife? See it? Same
black tiger!

Don't know dat Copm Andrew gone.

I hope dass it. I hope so.

Listen to Mist' Byrum Watler! Jumpin at
shadders!

Vemon relieves Byrum.

Copm Raib? Copm Raib? Dat time I was down to
Bragman's, dem seas was so big dat we had to let go
de lines onto de pier. Seas like dat at Bragman's

every day, so de Sponnish say. So I was wonderin, Copm Raib, are we gone to tie up at the pier or are we gone to anchor off?

You had to let go de lines, you say? And dat was a ship of four, five hundred ton? So you would think den . . . god*dom*! *(incredulous)* So why in de hell would you ask if we gone to go in dis weather, in dis wind, in dis much smaller vessel, to tie up to dat dock? *Why*, I askin you!

Dat why I *askin*, Copm Raib—

Goddom it, Vemon, you a stupid mon, I tell you dat much! And dat partner of yours, dat Athens— know what he done? Stole Copm Andrew's knife! Stole a dead mon's knife!

A silence.

Bragman's. I been all around dat town. Oh, Speedy well-known *dere*! I used to run dere on a ship. And Bluefields. Used to run to New Orleans and Texas. Mahogany. And gold. Dey got a gold mine here, inland. Bonanza, call dat place. Plenty gold. Oh, yes. I been runnin down dere a very long time.

Got pussy dere?

Might be, Byrum. Prob'ly dey heard about it. *(smiles)* Oh, Bragman's a very fine town. Lots of fun. I dance. I am a *dancin* mon. I hang around de bar. A few drinks—not many. I not get drunk—just fun. Den I go back to my ship.

Well, you take Bluefields, dat a *big* town, mon, a very big town, and you look and see how sloppy de streets is kept. It de goddom Sponnish, dat is my opinion.

Might be I slip ashore. I got dis condrum I like to use.

I come down to Bragman's five straight year. I hang around de bar.

Hard to find pussy any more, y'know—get'm older den eight years of age, dey all got something in de oven.

Y'see dat one of Desmond dere? And Desmond tellin me dat his gang of pan-heads had three girls with dem and de whole three pregnant, only one of dem had her baby up dere at Bobel and got infected and died.

Fuck dem dat way.

When the men stare at him, Brown's lip lifts, baring his upper teeth.

How dat go, Brownie?

Colombia. *Igual* if dey fat—we fuck. Old one, young one. I fuck *una muerta* once; *después*, dey told me she dead by de time I fuck. *(shrugs) Igual.* I too drunk to know.

Dey all commonists down dere, ain't dey? Well, in Cayman we ain't got people acts like dat. In a democracy—

At Brown's expression, Vemon falls silent.

Ninguno tell me what I fuck. *Ninguno.* I fuck anything I want. *(spits at Vemon's feet)* I fuck *you, señor, hay nada de mejor.*

Brown looks from one man to the other; they stop laughing.

Ustedes. Tink you better den me? (*spits again*) **In** jail. In camp. *Claro?* Mon got to fuck, *verdad?*

Brown's gold teeth appear in a wild grin.

Verdad? Mon got to fuck, *verdad?*

Arms wrapped around himself, eyes closed, Byrum dances to the sound of his own voice; he makes a quick copulatory movement on each turn.

> *fun me, soldier mon, fun me . . .*

Speedy clears his throat.

What Brownie mean—well, in all dese countries now, we gettin quite a problem. Malaria got to be a thing of de past, all dem old kind sickness dere, so we got to de place where *nobody* dyin, and dey ain't enough of anything to go aroúnd. Den people start actin like wild animals. La Violencia. No work, no money, nothin. So all dey carin about is pussy, cause dat all dey got.

Dass it. Dey ain't even enough of *dat!*

Modern time, mon. Girls gets knocked up before you gets dere. Mon! De young fellas dey haves now, dey go around in gangs in de night time, and dey finds a girl, mon, dey *all* grinds her.

Well, Speedy, dey don't behave in dat manner in Caymans, I tellin you dat much—!

Cause you in de back time, Doddy, dey plenty of water between you and de world. But you just wait a while, you gone to see. Modern time, mon— dey ain't no place to hide.

> *Fun me, oh!*
> *Make me feel nice and cool!*

His song finished, Byrum laughs.

Dat one Brown grinded, she were cool already—

> Byrum? Don't mess with him, mon. Brown kind of
> sensitive, some way.

Bad thing about de *Goldfield,* Copm. Hear dat
news?

All de old fleet gone now, save dese ones dat was
converted. All de rest been sold away or sunk in
storm.

Every one?

Well, let's see now—keepin it to real turtle boats,
de sailin schooners, it was de *Goldfield,* it was de
Adams, it was de *Wilson,* and it was de *Armistice*—
all built by Arches. It was de *R. L. Hustler* built by
Roland Bodden, it was de *Rembro* and de *Antarus,*
both built by MacTaggarts. It was de *Jemsons,*
called dat for some of de Bodden children—de
"m" was for Melba, I think. Jim Bodden and Sons.
Called her de *Jemsons.* And de *E. L. Banks* and de
Majestic, dat was built by Boddens, too, and
another one from Cayman Brac dat dey calls de
Alsons, and de *Arbutus* dere dat used to trade over
to Turks Island.

Speakin about de *Arbutus* now, dere was dat
mystery about de way dat she mashed up.

Dass right. She was launched at Georgetown in
1939, de last of de Cayman sailin schooners dat

was ever built, and before she could put out, down
come de hurricane and wash her ashore right
where she had come from. Oh, mon. Well, dey got
skids and skidded her down, and after dat she
sailed for many years, and den she mashed up for
de last time, in a nor'wester. She drag her moorin
and she come ashore again, for good, right in dat
very same place dat she had come from twice
before.

Mystery, mon. Dey calls dat mystery.

Copm Raib, you sayin dere dat de *Jemsons* were a
schooner. De *Jemsons* were a ketch. Still is.

Dass right, Will. Anyways, de *Antarus* were sold over
to Colombia. Old Providence Island. De *Rembro*,
she were sold over to Old Providence. De *Banks*
were mashed up in West Bay, in a south wind; she
went ashore. De *Alsons* were lost up around de
Rosalind Bank—sunk in hurricane. Den de *Lydia
Ebanks Wilson* burned to de water line. (*pause*)
Now, den. De *Goldfield* wrecked dere at Old
Providence. And de *Armistice*, sunk down at
Miskita Cay.

In hurricane.

No, mon. She just sunk down. (*gins*) One day she
just sunk down. It was a plain motter of old age.

Raib laughs quietly by himself. Byrum winks at
Vemon.

And de *Clarinda*. Burned to de water line in de
North Sound.

Byrum cannot meet Raib's gaze. The men shift, or
pick at themselves. Hands behind his back, Raib rolls
with the ship as the Miskito Cays rise and fall in the
sea behind him. He is smiling.

And de *Clarinda*. Dat is correct.

Will say de *Clarinda* were like a wild horse, mon; you had to *hold* her.

Will couldn't say anything else but dat; dat were public knowledge. Den, continuin: de *Hustler* been sunk. Dat were my friend Copm Laurie Bodden. I was over dere to Verrella Cay in 1940, and he had already made one trip to Cristobal with lobsters. Now dat were late September, so I advised him dat he shouldn't make a second trip because it were into de hurricane time on dat ocean. But he corried a second load of lobsters down to Cristobal, and on his way home he got caught by a storm and was lost somewhere up around Misteriosa.

No, mon, dere was no storm reported. De *Hustler* just vanished, like de old *Nunoco* dere, in 1936. Dem two vessels lost in mystery.

Dat so, Will? You know better den me about Laurie Bodden? (*sucks his teeth*) Sometimes you a goddom idiot, know dat, Will?

A small boat, overloaded, broadside to the seas. Figures wave thin arms.

Gettin so you see dese boats most every voyage—dey crazy, mon!

The *Eden* circles the small boat. The figures crowding to the side nearest the *Eden* almost capsize her, and voices fly from round black holes in the staring heads.

Where dey come from? Where dey headed for?

Toss dem a line, den; we drag dem over to Bragman's.

The *Eden* wallows in the seas as a towline is bridled to the stern posts. In the boat, the refugees are yelling. On his fuel drum, Brown yells back, then turns away, disgusted.

Se dice que—got no gas!

God Almighty! In dat goddom flimsy cheap old thing, on de bleak ocean, in dis wind—dey crazy, mon!

Crazy or desperate, one. Gone to let dem come up? Look like dey wants water.

NO, mon! Let dem aboard, we gots to feed dem, and we ain't hardly got stores enough for ourselves! (*pause*) Dey get water at Bragman's!

... *buscandan ambiente!*

How dat go?

Dey *come* from Bragman's! Say dey huntin for a chance!

A solitary porpoise, black in the turquoise water. A sea mist in the west.

Parchin hot, mon.

Dass cause we scuddin with de wind.

Let her fall off to port, Vemon.

FALL OFF TO PORT!

What de hell you shoutin for? Ain't every mon aboard dis vessel settin right beside you?

I know my duty, Copm Raib!

You don't know *nothin*! You—DON'T LET HER FALL OFF ANY MORE!

You s'pose to holler, STEADY!

STOP DAT SHOUTIN, VEMON! YOU LETTIN HER FALL INTO DAT LAND TOO MUCH! NOW SAIL DE SAME COURSE DAT I TOLD YOU!

Vemon mutters for a while. When no one pay attention, his voice rises.

Gone to go ashore myself, get me some pussy. Mon want pussy, he got to go *ashore*.

Ain't pussy *you* after. You ain't goin.

I goin. I goin, brother. You can't keep me. I got my papers and I got my rights, ain't dat so, Byrum? De seaman's union! Byrum, you know any of dem shippin lines up in New York could use a good mon? Cause I sick of dis shit aboard of here. Should have gone with Athens.

Yo puedo shit *by de way you hold me, darlin!*

Dere de coast—can see it good.

See all dat smoke? New plontations, mon. Dem half-breeds swarmin over *dis* domn place, dat used to be de most Godforsakenist coast in all de world.

Late afternoon. Heat-thickened wind, and big bruised clouds.

Near the mile-long pier of Bragman's Bluff, the *Eden* casts loose the refugee boat. The refugees sit huddled, rising and falling on the swells; they do not wave.

The *Eden* anchors off the littered shore. Great seas driven by the trades across the whole reach of the south Caribbean rumble beneath the pier and crash on the stone beach. On the low bluffs, low huts trail away inland toward low scrub jungle.

The port catboat bangs and pitches alongside as the Captain screeches; he comes running from the deckhouse, still half dressed.

Who takin me in dere? Get in de domn boat!

Will takes the tiller, Byrum is at the bow oars. Byrum wears his turquoise shirt. Jumping down, Raib grabs the tiller from Will, who moves amidships.

Lookit de mate dere! Let's see can he row!

Row, mon? Will de island's best!

The catboat moves across the swells toward the pier, lifting and settling in the troughs as the seas pass.

At the seaward end, the pier is high and gaunt, dripping with brine as the wave passes. Each wave raises the three ships that are tied to the pier, heaving them back; the old soft hawsers creak. All the ships are headed seaward, so that their bows may part the heavy waves.

The catboat ties up to the stern of a freighter that is taking on fruit and timber.

Byrum follows Raib to the dockmaster's shack, halfway down the pier. Here, thin whores jeer at listless men who hang around a radio: the thin whistle and static of the radio nags at the rush of wind and sea. Byrum calls for Will to come, and the whores mimic his call: seated primly in the catboat, Will shrugs his shoulders, tries to grin, then stares away at the coast of Nicaragua.

It is near twilight when Raib and Byrum leave the Customs shed; the whores and idlers crowd forward, begging for work.

You fock me? I loaf you! *Amor!*

I sailor, Cap! I fishin boy! Go turkle boat!

The turtlers push through the throng and jump down to the catboat.

You know what dem Sponnish tellin me at Customs,
Will? Dey gone to close de turtle banks to Cayman
vessels! Close down dis fishery dat is de historical
fishery of de Cayman Islands! Yah, mon! Next year!

Close down de *turtle* banks!?

See dat, Will? Even de whores is pregnant!

...gone to charge me a fat fee for comin here, I
tell you dat! Outside de port fees, I got to pay de
medical officer and den de health officer, and after
dat de Customs officer and den maybe de Army
officer, none of which has done anything into dis
motter! Dey a bunch of thieves, just like
Honduras! And top of dat, we got to lay over till
de mornin to get de documents back, so dat we lost
another day on top of de days dat were lost at
Cape Gracias. Don't appear to be too much justice
into *dat*!

Will? Customs askin us, How many life jackets you
got aboard of dere? (*laughs*) And Copm say, he say,
Two! Answer sharp like dat, y'know, lookin angry
at de question. *Two*, de Copm say, I *think*.

I *think*. Dass about it. I thinkin about gettin one,
two dem jackets.

Best get enough for de whole crew or don't get any.

Goddom, how I hate dese Sponnish! Hate dere
women for de same reason. First time I ever get de
clap was here in Bragman's. (*groans*) See dem shack
dere at de pier head? Back of dat sign where dey got
de bar? Well, dass where I done it, right dere
on top of de ground, dere by dat hut. I never forgot
to dis day how dat woman stink. Domn! It were
terrible! You would have to be a dead person to
smell as bad as dat! So right away I knew I was in
trouble. I ate so much sulfa tablets I got sulfidized,
but it done no good. From here I went over to

Trinidad, and from Trindad I went over to Haiti, and I *still* got it. (*furious*) Dass what dey call a *dose!*

Speedy, Brown and Vemon are waiting at the rail. Speedy is wearing a striped suit and shiny shoes.

You ain't goin ashore, Vemon, I told you dat already. A mon go adrift in de lands of de Sponnish, dat de last you ever see of'm.

Got to get to a doctor, Copm Raib. A mon dat sick, he got to see a *doctor!*

You sick, okay, but ain't no doctor in dis world can help you. Dat take self-knowledge, which you ain't got.

Raib and Will climb aboard the *Eden*; Speedy and Brown descend into the boat.

> *I miss me, oh I miss shit miss me*
> *At your house last night . . .*

How come you singin? Don't *look* hoppy.

Es posible I sing *por el publico, entiende?*

Buddy comes to the rail with his hair water-slicked, in a flowered tourist shirt, clean pants and hard shoes, but makes no move toward the boat.

Buddy? Come with us? We dance, boy! Sing! We hang around de bar! Den we come back to de ship!

No, thank you, Speedy.

Buddy? What you all dressed up for if you ain't goin ashore?

No, Papa. I don't like dem goddom Sponnish.

How do you know? (*contemptuous*) How in de hell you *know*? You just heard *me* say dat! You never even *been* dere! And prob'ly dis be your last chance in life, cause dem goddom Sponnish closin down dis Cayman fishery in de next year!

Huh? Closin it down?

Yah, mon! Waited till I got dem goddom diesels, and den closed her down!

When Raib goes astern, into the deckhouse, Vemon slips down into the boat. At the bow oar, Byrum laughs.

Look de stowaway!

Come back up, Vemon!

Nemmine, Will, we watch him. He ain't much but he our shipmate, dat right, Vemon?

Let's go, mon! Let's go!

Copm give de orders, Byrum—dat be de rule of de sea!

Just pretend like you never heard it—*you* be okay, Will.

I tellin you, he be vexed, mon! Copm Raib be fightin mad!

Let him fly up all he want—he ain't gone to fire nobody. Not off *dis* vessel. Not on *dis* trip. Ain't we one mon short already?

The boat moves off on the long swells. Vemon is crouched down in the bilges, so low in the boat that the crown of his striped cap barely shows over the gunwales.

Night.

The boat returns over big slow seas, parting reflections of the light from shore. The man sculling in the stern scampers forward over the seats at the last moment to keep the bow from banging the *Eden*'s hull.

A line is slung down without warning, stinging his face.

Where in de hell is Vemon?

Nemmine, Copm Raib.

Nemmine tellin me Nemmine! I say, Where de hell is Vemon? Who dat in de bilges?

Brown ain't feelin very good. Told dem girls he sing a song for dem, and dey laugh at him cause of his teared clothes.

Sing a song of love, *amor*, and de fuckin bitches *laugh*! I take my knife, I cut dere fuckin t'roat!

Where Byrum? He drunk too?

He say he go find Vemon. He say tell you de two of dem be dere bright and early on de dock when you go get de documents.

I TAKE MY KNIFE, I CUT DERE FUCKIN T'ROAT!

The two haul Brown aboard.

> Now who de fool took Vemon into de boat? Who *done* dat?
>
> We did.
>
> You lyin dere! It were Byrum!
>
> You know so much, Doddy, why you askin, den?

Raib dumps Brown by the engine hatch.

> Who paid de rum for dis one?
>
> I paid. You never give him his money yet.
>
> Dat a very good thing! See what he do with it?
>
> Ain't your business, Doddy. (*pause*) Keep people down too much, you got to have trouble. Modern time, mon.

A silence.

> You drunk, too, I see.
>
> No, mon. I tell you de same thing tomorrow
>
> > > > fuckin T'ROAT!

Wrenching free, Brown lunges for the ladder head, grasps it and swings out wide over the engine hatch; he loses his footing and falls, landing hard on the iron floor. With ragged breaths, still conscious, he lies there on his back, the sombrero a torn circle around his head. Swinging slowly with the ship's motion, the light plays back and forth on his soiled face. His mustachio is drawn back, baring his teeth in a kind of snarl as he gasps for breath, and his wet, canine eyes look broken.

You okay dere, Brownie?

Brown spits and mutters, staring vacantly; the heads of Raib and Speedy roll across the stars.

Magdalena! Dem bitches! Cut dere fuckin t'roat!

What he tellin dere?

La Violencia. He talkin about old *bandito* days in de province of Magdalena.

Sí! Magdalena! Don't b'lieve dat, old mon? Don't b'lieve dat? Where my knife?

Raib straightens. Speedy is starting down the ladder.

Speedy? Do dat fella have a knife hid some place?

When he turn up in Roatán, he had one dem street knives with de spring in it, but he sold dat in French Harbour.

You see dat fella with a knife, you let me know.

Speedy sinks to his knees and lifts Brown's head into his lap. Brown's eyes fill with tears.

Brownie? How you feelin? You okay dere, Brownie?

I sing a song of love for dem. *Amor.*

Brown stares straight up at the rolling stars. The rawhide chin strap falls and rises on his stubbled throat.

I hurtin, Speedy. Oh, I hurtin.

Daybreak.

The swift fire of the rising sun strikes the dirty beach under the pier head, where thin hogs root at peels and rotten fruit. Above, whores nag at Byrum, who sits on the pier head beside a sprawling sack of oranges. He gnaws angrily at a whole orange, spitting skin and seeds into the sea.

Near the waterfront bar, on a hard barren ground, Vemon is swaying. He has lost his cap, and the trade winds shift the lank hair on his skull.

Raib faces Vemon at a little distance.

You comin, Vemon?

Just give de word, I grob him.

Vemon?

Can't leave him with de Sponnish, mon. He *die* here.

Shut your mouth! Why you didn't think of dat last evenin? Why dey fire you off de *Adams* for? Why? I try to be a gentleman dere and not ask a mon what is his own business, but by Jesus, now I wants to *know*!

Insubordernation. Know what dat is?

Boy, you learned me it good if I hadn't knowed it! Domn drunken fool—you broke de stem dere on de catboat!

Byrum spits orange seeds at the Captain's feet.

You best fire me, den, Raib.

You forgettin yourself, mon! (*sucks his teeth*) You de worst of all dese fellas, Byrum, cause you know better den what you doin. You de *worst* one.

Dat so? Now let's grob him and let's go.

Vemon retreats a little.

Forty year, Copm Raib! We been in friendship forty year, and never a wry word!

Byrum lurches to his feet.

Listen to *dat* bullshit! De way you got dis fool and Will kissin your ass, I tell you, it turn my stomach. And de boy. And Speedy. *Four* of dem ...

Byrum's voice dies as Raib turns.

Get de hell back down dat dock and get into dat boat.

Shouldering his big sack of fruit, Byrum attempts a salute, but the Captain has already turned back again to Vemon.

Vemon salutes.

Reportin for duty, Copm Raib!

Let's go den, darlin, cause we sailin.

You never treats me with respect! A mon gots to have *respect*! Dass why I stayin, Copm Raib!

You a turtler or ain't you? I ain't goin to shanghai you.

I got *papers*, Copm Raib! You show me no respect for dat—dass why I stayin!

Raib contemplates him for so long that Vemon nervously salutes again. Then he extends his hand, which Vemon stares at.

Stay den, mon. You gettin de respect you wants: I respectin your decision. And I wish you all de luck of it.

Copm Raib? Copm Raib?

Walking away, lugging his documents, Raib limps a little in his shoes. On the long pier, he looks small. Ahead of him, Byrum lurches around to yell at Vemon; because he is drunk, the heavy fruit sack, swinging, makes him stagger.

Vemon! Come *on*, mon! De goddom *guardias*—

Vemon follows at a distance, placing his feet carefully; he has lost his shoes, and his feet are pale and soft under the dirt line at his ankles. The pale feet limp on the dead bottle caps. Uneasy, he glances behind him, then hobbles out onto the pier.

Byrum turns back a final time, as Raib passes him and goes down into the boat. Vemon has stopped, raising his hand to shield his eyes against the Caribbean sunrise at the pier end.

Vemon!

red morning sun

trade wind, rain glitter

waving cocal

sweet stink, tin music   shinging leaves

rust, insects, weeds   mango   banana

dead bottle caps, a bright red rag

thin livestock, wandering

bony mission church

far rain

a man

blowing paper, urine tang

dark circling birds, inland

isolated huts, and blue smoke rising

wind   wind

sun   sun

wind   wind

VEMON!

·13·

The *Eden* bound outward, west-northwest, into the wind.

At the pier end stands a figure in a flying shirt.

We ain't goin back for him, den?

NO, MON!

Vemon Dilbert Evers! Mon! Dem papers he always talkin about ain't de papers he need here. Dem *guardias* gone to pick'm up and he rot in jail.

Lucky if dey don't shoot'm for a spy.

Lucky if dey *do*—you seen dem Sponnish jail! Better off dead.

DAT MUTTERIN DON'T DO NO GOOD. YOU HADN'T TOOK HIM ASHORE, HE BE HERE NOW!

Copm Raib, I could had grobbed him dere! He wanted to come with us!

Don't you tell me about Vemon! I corried dat
fella all my life, and corryin never done him a bit
of good; he just waitin on dat. So dis time I tellin
him he got to take de responsibility: either he
back up dat big mouth he got or back up his
common knowledge of dis life. And de fool back
up his mouth.

He never b'lieve you leave him dere!

Raib gazes somberly toward shore.

He b'lieve it now. Old Vemon b'lieve it now.
(*grunts*) He were my neighbor in dis life—dey
called him Vemon. God done a bad job when he
give me something like dat man to be my neighbor.

The Witties and London Reef.

Still the wind blows, and turtle are few. In the next
fortnight, the *Eden* takes twenty-three green turtle and
four hawksbill. Slowly she beats eastward.

We come too late. Dey gone south to de Bogue.

Dis a bad trip, mon. A bad trip. Dis wind gettin me.

I not worry, mon. Never worry, dat is me. But I
givin up de sea, work on de land. De sea always
treat me pretty good, but now I gone to give her up,
work on de land. Fifty-five acres, mon, all free and
clear. And I don't have to go lookin for my job.
Oh, dey laugh like hell dey be so hoppy when I
go back dere!

Speedy-mon? Try dese oranges? Something *good*!

Misteriosa! Dat way out dere, ain't it? Queena way?
(*sighs*) Oh, Queena got plenty fish, Copm Allie say,
but dey very few turtle, and dey not very easy
caught. Too much tides and currents around dere.
It just layin out in de open sea. Very bad reef. It a
great place for cotchin up wrecks.

Dass why de Sponnish calls it Quita Sueño—get
no sleep dere.

If dis wind don't moderate, den we ain't gone to
do much anywhere, cause de season has come up
with us—we gettin into de May time. So our last
chance is Misteriosa Reefs. Cause I got de theory dat
green turtles makes dere nests at Far Tortuga, and
dat would mean dat quite a few could be driftin
out dat way already. Oh, yes! Dey good turtle spots
out on dem reefs, boys, but you got to know'm—
can't set just any old white hole or pan shoal or
channel. You got to *know*.

If dey egg birds dere, dey Jamaicans dere. Domn
pan-heads all over de place.

No, mon. It hard to find and it hard to fish. It
too far south for dem, and too far off de coast.
Far off de shippin lanes, even when dis were de
Sponnish Main—dass why dey called it Far
Tortuga. So when dem old-time turtlers come across
it once again, back dere in de last century, why, dey
just kept dat secret for dereselves. (*sighs*) Dat
island is a very nice place. A *very* nice place. And
dere good shelter in de lee, cause it high enough so
it got trees—grape trees and jennifer trees, and
den logwood and mongrove: got a little water dere
if you know how to dig for it. Plenty birds. I
thinkin one day I might build a little shack out
dere on Far Tortuga. Dass my dream.

Got no dream, mon. I got fifty-five acres, mon,
and cows. I go along every day, do what I got to
do, and den I lays down to my rest.

Feel bad about Vemon. He ain't much, but he our
shipmate.

Never do *dat* in de back time! Maroon a shipmate
on de Sponnish coast! Might's well leave him off in
hell!

Mon come and go, I guess. Like Brown dere. Modern
time, mon.

A blue catboat, rag sail luffing.

Dey only de one fella—I can see him!

Tackin to de eastward! Where in de hell he think
he bound?

Maybe he sunstruck. Copm Raib? We speak him,
den?

He can see us and he ain't wavin. (*winces*) Ain't
nothin de motter with *dat* fella, he just crazy.

S'posin he too sick to wave.

Well, speak him, den! Dass all we need aboard of
here! Another crazy mon!

The Captain points at Wodie, who stands with both
hands on the rail, staring at the small boat as the

Eden comes astern of her. At the tiller is a black man, near-naked. When the *Eden* rolls up alongside, the stranger looks away to the east horizon.

You okay? Need water?

Got a compass? You very far from land!

A line looped out to the boat falls across the thwarts, within reach of the man's hand. The man turns slowly, watching the line drag overboard as the *Eden* passes.

Shit, mon! Grob de line!

Slowly the man in the boat raises his hand; he waves, and his mouth opens. Wodie screeches.

Shut up, Wodie! What dat fella sayin, Will?

He tellin us goodbye! I heard him good: *goodbye!*

No, mon! He not so crazy as all *dat!* Come up on him again!

Will recoils the line as the *Eden* circles, rolling heavily in the blue chop; she comes abreast of the small boat a second time. Again the mate loops the line across the boat, and again the voyager ignores it. When its end slides off into the sea, the man raises his gaze to the faces at the *Eden*'s rail, regarding them one by one. His face is clear and his eyes bright. Again his mouth forms just one word—

Goodbye!

The *Eden*'s men do not answer, nor do they speak or look at one another. All stand silent but for Wodie, who has retreated to the galley roof. Eyes shut, he lies there on his side, arms wrapped around his knees. Speedy goes and lays his hand on Wodie's foot, and Wodie moans.

Speedy? Dass him, Speedy! De mon in de blue boat!

Blue boat?

Yah, mon! De child in de mornin sea!

What de motter with you, Wodie?

Dey drove dat nail into my footprint—now I done.

With an old machete, Speedy chips the crest of a big conch: a hollow metallic *tonk*. Then the crown cracks off, and he slices the muscle and drags the animal out of its shell, rolling the body off the warm pink inner spiral. Flecks of pink shell and livid entrail glisten in the sun on his black hands. He pares away the mollusk guts, horns, radula and spleen; with a length of pipe, he pounds the meat to break the fibers, then tosses it into a bent pot of citrus juice to cut away the slime.

See dis, Wodie? I boil dis just a little bit, den more juice, den black pepper. Plenty black pepper, mon— learn dat from school days.

Wodie rocks a little, saying nothing.

Conch salad, mon; good for de nerves. I give you some of dis, you gone feel *better*.

Will relieves Buddy, Byrum relieves Will, Wodie relieves Byrum.

Noon.

Start dis voyage with one man too many. Now we one too few.

Afternoon. Speedy relieves Wodie. The crumpled cigarette pack blows aft along the scuppers, and Raib grabs at it and misses.

Goddom thing! I never can come up with it!

Raib chases the orange packet to the stern, where he gets down on hands and knees to extricate it from beneath a turtle.

Domn Athens gone a fortnight, and he *still* litterin de ship, dat de kind of slob he is!

Wind clouds. Hastening birds.

A shadow in the eastern distance, under a sunken sky, like a memory in the ocean emptiness.

Land o'er! See dere? EAST-SOU'EAST!

EAST-SOU'EAST!

The cay is stranded among reefs, broken white to
windward.

Oh, mon! Look at dem blowers!

Well, we gone to get more weather here. See de
uneasy way dem birds is flyin? To and fro, low to
the water, like dey huntin something?

Now *you* de one soundin like Wodie, Copm Raib!

Dat ain't duppy talk! Dat is common knowledge!

The *Eden* is several miles to leeward when the first
terns come shrieking to her masts; the swarms of nesting birds circle the cay as if it might withdraw beneath the sea.

I never see birds as thick as dat! Dey look like
smoke!

Dat cause we scarin dem.

Raib, yelling, runs toward the mast.

Ain't *us* dat scarin dem! No mon! Ain't us! You,
Speedy! Port!

PORT!

Steady!

STEAD-*DAY*!

The island has formed in the corner of a reef, built up
slowly over decades from a drift of storm sand and
detritus: an eddy, a shoal of coral sand, tide pools, sea
wrack, a floating mangrove radicel, hot humus of sargassum and red algae.

On the high ground at its northern end stands a small
wood of sea grape, logwood, jennifer trees. On the
open sand a thatch shelter is visible and a fire burns
nearby. The flame and smoke are transparent in the
sunlight, but the rising heat blurs the patterns of the
bird multitudes above. The shadow of wings dapples
the island, and the bird voice dims the sea sound on
the windward shore.

Dis a pretty place, Copm Raib!

It were! Dey foulin dis one, too!

We let go de hook, den?

I disgusted! I tellin you, *I disgusted*! I so disgusted
I would sail dis evenin except de reefs so bad in dis
domned place dat I needs high sun to see dat
channel!

The Captain climbs down slowly from the mast. His
face is terrible.

We stuck here till de mornin.

The *Eden* anchors a quarter-mile offshore, under the lee. Raib moves past the silent men into the deckhouse.

Dey got two skiffs dere, Copm Raib.

Think I ain't seen dem? Get out de way.

A narrow long black skiff, powered by outboard, leaves the island. It veers toward the *Eden*, coming fast, and circles the schooner at full speed, bow slamming down hard on the chop, old motor roaring. The eight figures in the skiff, all of them standing, yell and gesticulate. Over motor and wind, no message comes, only harsh desolate human cries and the single word "Cay-*mahn*!" howled in derision.

The skiff's circle tightens; the eight figures sway. The skiff carries big baskets full of tern eggs.

Dat de same gang we seen up dere toward Bobel. See dat black skiff?

Yah, mon. And dey more of dem on de beach. Dey never come way out here in dem small boats, not in *dis* weather. Were Desmond brought'm.

Got'm reapin de bird eggs while he out scourin de cays for more. Den he take de whole swarm over dere to de land of opportunity.

If dey lucky. Might land dem on de coast of Cuba, tell dem it Florida. Save fuel dat way.

Dey be lucky if he come back for dem at all.

Hope dey don't know *dat* yet.

Yah, mon. Got any idea like dat, den we in trouble.

Slowly the men eat their rice and beans, all except Raib, who is still in the deckhouse. Brown takes his plate and climbs onto his fuel drum. Squatting there, he stares at the circling skiff, his food uneaten. He grins a little.

The men speak in near whispers.

I tellin you, dese pan-heads gone to condemn dese banks for turtle. Mon go high-seain now, can't crawl his turtle at Bobel cause de sons of bitches all around. Got to leave de crawl minded, or dey corry de turtle away.

Corry de *mon* away, too. I give dis fella ten pound ten to take up de street in Kingston Town, and dere was a gang dat grob de fella ahead of him and took his money, so he turn back. I don't want to see *dat* place again, not in dis life, mon. I was up dere one time, layin over, and by Christ you could not leave a porthole open. Oh, dey mean bastards, I tellin you. Dey kill you on de docks dere and not think a thing about it.

Dere heads is filled with nothin—goddom pan-heads.

See dat spiky hair? Calls dereselves dreadlocks. Niyamen. Dey livin in de garbage of de towns, and dey smokin weed.

Dass it. Ganja. When dey on dat, dey gets hostile— hear dem yellin? Don't like white people, *no* mon!

The skiff disappears under the stern.

> Got to feel sorry for dem all de same, for dey been kept down too much. I been in a lot of dem big towns—Bragman's, Bluefields—and I been to Port-of-Spain. *(shakes head)* Oo, mon! *(whistles)* Rats lives better den de people livin at de outskirts of de town! Dey got no song dere and dey got no hope. De onliest thing dey got and dat is anger— oh, dey got plenty *dat*.

> Yah, mon. See dem fellas? Prob'ly dey West Kingston boys, or Sponnish Town.

A brutal bang against the hull, on the port side, amidships, brings Raib out of the deckhouse; he comes forward to the galley. The crew of the *Eden*, standing now, mouths full, not chewing, are ranged opposite the eight Jamaicans, who have swarmed aboard.

The eight are big wild mongrel blacks, near-naked in remnant shorts and dirty singlets, with wild hair twisted into spikes and eyes burnt red by rum and sun. Wet muscles twitch in thick dark skins that are scaly with salt spray. One wears a beard and big dark glasses and a mean street hat with tight brim, cocked forward.

The eight sway softly with the slow roll of the ship.

> Who tell dem come aboard of here?

> Nobody tell dem.

> Nobody tell dem to clear off, neither. Cause dey might say no.

Raib steps forward.

You fellas clear off now, till we eats our supper.

The eggers are nudging one another. They have recognized Raib from Bobel Cay, and wear bad grins.

Without looking at it, Raib takes the plate that Speedy hands to him in warning; when he puts food into his mouth, his men sit again and resume eating—all but Speedy, who leans against the galley side.

The man with the dark glasses jerks his chin toward Raib and speaks.

Tuttle mahn! H-ss-t! See Desmun any place?

No!

Desmun s'pose to come. We waitin.

You be domn lucky if he ever come at all!

A silence.

The eggers look at one another.

Dat so, Cap?

Easing forward across the deck, the Jamaicans form a half-circle around the turtlers; they mutter and scowl at Wodie's blind eye, and his shard of mirror. The turtlers stare at nothing and eat carefully.

—goozoo!

S-ss-t! Unca John-John! Gib us rice!

Bes gib us boo-nus rice, boy, cause we starbin.

Still squatting on his fuel drum, Brown utters a small aimless laugh; he tips his sombrero back onto his neck and begins to eat.

S-ss-t! Tuttle boy! Doan like Jamaica fella? S-ss-t!

Ras! Dey boog, mahn!

The eggers rail at the *Eden*'s crew; their jabber grows chaotic, with wild laughter. They nag at the turtlers for cigarettes and food, cursing shrilly when the crew ignores them.

Forks click thinly on tin plates.

The man with the black glasses feints toward Will, as if to take his food. Will is cutting turtle gristle and his knife turns upward, though he keeps the knife hand on his thigh. The jabber quickens; the angrier the eggers get, the more they laugh. They dart their hands at other plates, hooting in glee as the knives rise.

Brown disappears below.

The man with dark glasses scowls at Speedy.

What say, Short Boy?

Speedy chews.

The eggers go ranging through the ship. Taking their plates as an excuse to carry knives, the crew move aft to guard the deckhouse. Raib stands with one hand on the helm. His squint is cold and tight and mean; the eggers circle him. Hooting and jabbering, they pick around the bunks and duffels; one finds a pack of cigarettes and points a finger at himself in mock entreaty. Raib shakes his head, and the man drops the cigarettes with a sharp screech of frustration.

One has found the stove wood hatchet, another has the conch machete: he tests the old blade with his thumb as the jabber grows more strident. The man with dark glasses leans toward Raib and shouts angrily at his face; he leans still further, to touch Raib's chest, and then thinks better of it. Between yells, they chatter rapidly among themselves.

H-ss-t! Buddy? Get into de deckhouse and stay dere.

Papa?

When his father shoves him, Buddy drops his book. It falls open on the deck; the pages tatter.

Brown reappears and squats under the taffrail: he picks his toes.

S-ss-t, you, Sponnish! What say, boy? S-ss-t!

Gone gib us cigarette? We *hungry*, mahn!

His shipmates look at Brown, who shrugs his shoulders, gold-toothed, grinning; still squatted on his heels, he hunkers sideways to see better. He pulls out the shreds of his torn pockets, and laughs when the eggers hoot. They turn to Speedy.

Short Boy! You Caymahn tuttle boy? Doan look like dem!

Dey boog, mon! Ras clot!

Short Boy! S-ss-t! What you tink bout dis mecky bo-att?

Why you go wit dese kanakee tuttle boy on dis ol fuckin bo-att?

S-ss-t! Hey! (*snaps fingers*) Sponnish!

Both sides turn toward Brown, who squats there grinning; he looks proud of the big knife that he has drawn from inside his shirt. He winks at Speedy, giggling. The eggers fall silent. When Brown rises, they back away.

Dat Copm Andrew's knife! Were *him* dat took it!

Give dat knife here! Goddom thief!

Brown spins toward Raib, lip curled, incredulous.

Ladrón?

The eggers gaze at the big knife. The scales of salt spray are drying on their skin, which has turned a dirty gray.

Dese boog walla mahn doan like you, Sponnish, you go wit us! Got *pussy*, mahn! Got *rum!*

Yah, mahn! You, too, Short Boy! We all of de same color!

Let see dat knife! We gib it back!

What say, Short Boy!

Nemmine dem, Brownie. No, mon.

Brown points at Raib.

Call me mon-fool! Call me *ladrón*!

Best stay with Speedy, mon. We go home to Roatán.

S-st! Sponnish!

Sí! We go with dem, Speedy! Call me *ladrón*!

No, mon. I stayin. I signed de articles.

S-st! Gib us dat knife, Sponnish, till we see somet'ing!

I never sign!

You made de X. Dis is our ship—we stuck with it.

Raib moves toward Brown.

Go den, and good riddance! But I want dat knife!

Panting, Brown whirls, then swoops and rises, knife tip trembling; at his feet, a red line wells on the white throat of a turtle. The turtle blinks.

Brown confronts Raib with the bloody point.

Speedy and Will grab the Captain from behind. The man with the black glasses extends his hand to Brown, who puts the knife in it. The eggers sigh.

In the scuppers, the old conch of Andrew Avers rocks with a small *thump* as the ship rolls. A tatter of dried turtle grass, blown aft, hangs for a second on the taffrail, then whips into the sea.

The man with Brown's knife enters the deckhouse and takes the cigarettes from Byrum's suitcase. He strikes a match.

Goddom it, dem my cigarette!

Dem my cigarette! We jus *smokin* dem for you, muthafuck (*inhaling*) Booo-nus, boo-noo-noo!

Oh, mahn! *Hungry*! All we eat is bird eggs, dis lahst fortnight! Bird eggs and rum!

Raib speaks in a guttural thick burst:

Wharf rat bastards! You are nothin but beggars and thieves!

Pity, pity, Cap. Poor starbin niggers!

Cap gone be cocksure as dat, I break he bumbo!

The eggers loot the suitcases and duffels; they fill a sack with coffee, cigarettes, rice, flour, beans.

Gone gib us tuttle, Cap?

T'row dem down longside de bo-att!

Two turtles are dragged to the port rail and heaved overboard in quick succession; because their flippers are still tied, they sink slowly out of sight.

Ras! Dey *sunk*!

You lost two tuttle, Cap! Ain't got no fish?

Dem muthafucka *sunk*! Why dey don't float?

Shit, mahn, t'row two down into de bo-att!

Dey break de bo-att, mahn!

Ain't *you* bo-att, black mahn—*t'row* dem!

A third turtle is lifted to the rail and toppled into the boat, cracking the bow seat. A fourth is dropped; its weight splits the shell of the third turtle, and it caroms into a basket, crushing tern eggs.

We gone take dis salt meat, dat okay, Cap?

Oh, dat okay by *Cap*—tell by de face! Same mecky face he show us at Bobel!

We take dis hatchet and machete, okay, Cap? We bring dem back!

Grob dat rice pot on de stove!

Les go, den! T'ank you, Cap!

We be back, Cap!

See dem egg dere, Cap? Dem for de poor starbin niggers of Jamaica. But bein you so kind to us, we gib you one, two for you breakfahst!

The man wings two eggs at Raib's head; the eggs splatter on the cabin side. Raib turns toward Brown, and Speedy steps between them.

Go den, Brownie.

Brown follows the eggers down into their boat. They make a place for him, indifferent. A bottle is hurled at the men along the rail; as the rest dodge, Speedy blocks, fumbles, and retrieves it.

Short Boy! Oh, you *good* nigger, mahn!

Started while in gear, the skiff leaps forward, and one man falls over the side. The boat circles at full speed, and the man grabs the gunwale as it runs him down; howling, he is dragged aboard. The skiff veers in toward the cay, striking the sand hard at the north point.

Wodie retrieves Buddy's book; he pats the wind-torn pages. Byrum, at the rail, opens the bottle.

Never even stop to get his gear; just go.

Got no gear, mon—he went de way he come aboard.

The crew crouch at the galley, watching the fire on the shore. Overhead, black rain squalls hang as the earth turns east beneath them. On the hull and cabin sides, the tern eggs are congealing. The turtle with the slashed throat blinks a last time, opening its mouth, and the mouth stays wide.

Will and Buddy butcher the slashed turtle.

Byrum, in his turquoise shirt, brings another bottle from the cabin.

> Smuggled *dis* rum aboard at Bragman's—'member dat big sack of fruit?

For a time the crewmen drink in silence, avoiding one another's eyes. Shrieks come from shore.

Speedy sets his cup down on the deck.

> If dey been here a fortnight, den dey gettin
> short of water.

> Dat fuckin Desmond overdue. Dey desperate.

> Dass it. We ain't seen de last of *dem*, no mon.

In a wind gust, the ship veers, and in the scuppers the old conch shell rocks.

Wodie speaks, in singsong.

> Last night I dreamin dat de sun rose up out of de
> west, and dat we livin on de wrong side of de

night. I dreamed dat we was dead and did not know it.

Just a gang of duppies settin by de stove, dass us.

Byrum drains his cup and comes up gasping.

Know something, Wodie? You a fuckin Jonah.

Easy, mon. He only wanderin. Wanderin and wonderin.

Will lobs the head of the dead turtle over the side.

I dreamin, too. I dreamin dat I were all alone in dat port catboat, and no land anywhere. And I hearin de drowned of de *Majestic* callin out dere names—what do dat mean, Wodie?

Weak light from the stove fire casts Raib's face in a poor color; his mouth hangs wide but his windburnt eyes are tight.

You never heard me tellin Vemon dat I don't stand for none of dat aboard of here?

Slowly Will gets to his feet; Byrum, Speedy, Wodie remain squatted. Buddy, perched upon the rail, is outlined on the night shine from the shore. Then Byrum, rising, picks the old conch shell from the scuppers, tosses it once on his big hand, and hurls it out into the night.

Triumphant, drunken, he confronts the Captain.

Copm Raib, de voyage done. You lost three de crew, and now it done.

The Captain stands expressionless, without movement.

Byrum holds out a red plastic cup. Slowly Raib's hand extends and takes it. Byrum pours rum into the cup, grinning at Raib as the rum overflows and pours onto Raib's hand.

Got enough, old mon?

The Captain is silent. Byrum snorting, turns his back on him, sitting down again among the men.

Raib stands there, broad face in a mask. Then he drinks off half a cup, gasps, coughs, starts to laugh, stops short. The men watch him. For one instant, he looks bewildered, studying the cup.

Dis cup stink like hell, de plastic in it. In times gone back we used to have dem good old blue tin coffee cups ...

He is silent again as Byrum laughs. Taking rum into his mouth, he holds it a moment, then spits on Byrum's feet.

Mon dat drink dis log'red piss has got no self-respect.

He tosses the red cup overboard and moves aft toward the deckhouse.

You finished, Copm Raib, know dat, old mon? YOU FINISHED!

·14·

Midnight.

Low murmuring. A cough.

One A.M.

Black rain squalls to eastward of the cay, black upon black. High in the dark, pale terns circle the masthead, their cries piercing the wind creak of the ship. Ashore, black figures fall across the firelight; the fire flares and dies.

By the *Eden*'s galley, sparks blow from a loose cigarette.

Mon, mon. What could dey be doin over dere!

Dis a bad night. See dat black water?

Yah, mon, dat tiger down dere somewhere.

Where dat Wodie get to? Gone below?

Don't know, mon. (*spits*) Domn fuckin Jonah.

Wodie okay, y'know. Nice fella. He just kind of fufu.

Dogwatch.

The Captain comes, unseen.

Throw dat boat overboard! I goin ashore!

Huh? All by yourself?

I ain't sailin without Copm Andrew's knife!

Copm, it no good to fly up now! You askin to get dat knife back in de belly!

Lower de boat, I tellin you!

Speedy and Byrum get slowly to their feet; they do not help Buddy and Will swing the boat over the rails.

Watch dat—HOLD HER OFF!

The catboat smacks onto the sea, and the short chop heaves it back against the hull with a hollow *boom*.

Now Byrum sways unsteadily before the Captain.

> So you abondonin dis vessel without no pilot and
> without no kind of crew, in time of storm, with
> bad reefs all around dis place—s'pose dey·knifin
> you in dere?

> *boom*

> Why den, de best thing, Byrum, de *best* thing to do,
> boy, is notify de Union! Yah, mon! Call de seaman's
> union! Ask dem what to do (*shouts*) ON DE
> BLEAK OCEAN!

Speedy points at Will and Buddy. He looks sleepy.

> Dem two takin you ashore? (*softly*) You ready to
> get dem two killed just cause you sick of life?

> And leavin only three aboard de vessel? We *never*
> get dat anchor up!

Raib starts to speak, stops; he turns toward the rail.

> Get out de way, Will. I take her in myself.

> You ain't goin dere alone.

> Dass right, Papa!

> Will? (*gently*) You a goddom idiot, know dat, Will?

Speedy has moved between Will and the rail; he puts
light fingertips on Will's chest.

Ain't *no* crew goin down into dat boat, Mist' Will. Maybe Doddy dere got nothin to lose, but I got fifty-five acres, mon, and cows. I goin home.

Speedy! You been drinkin!

Raib watches both through squinted eyes; he is not quite smiling. When Will picks up a marlin spike, Speedy taps his knife.

Mist' Will? I fast, mon. Very very fast.

To disobey de Coptin, dat is mutiny!

I ain't disobeyed de Coptin. Not yet, anyways.

All wait for Raib, who is gazing at the cay.

Okay den, darlins, put dat rum away. Get set to sail.

Byrum howls.

In de *night* time? You sayin yourself dat Misteriosa Reefs ain't no place to navigate in de night!

Well, speakin fair now, I de one mon left in de Cayman Islands dat would try it. But if dis crew ain't too domn drunk, I believe I manage it.

Can't wait till first light? *Shit!*

On the cay, wild shapes move back and forth across the firelight.

We could lose dis vessel between dis time and first light. I ain't sailin before daybreak less dey force me to it, but we gots to be ready for no motter what—don't hear dem pirates?

You always tellin us dat *we* are stupid! But *you* de one told dem domn pan-heads dat Desmond would not come! And *you* de one called Brown a thief just when he try to help us!

Speedy casts a spray of rum across the rail.

Dem dreadlocks tell us dey be back. No tellin when.

Dey be back soon's dey find out from Brown dat he can run dese engines.

The men look at one another. Then Speedy steps forward, hitching his pants; one by one, the others form a line. The Captain nods.

You a fine-lookin crew of fellas. (*sighs*) We ready? Where's dat Wodie?

WODIE!

When you start de motors, Copm Raib, ride forward over de hook—save time dat way.

Ain't gone to start no motors, Will.

Huh?

No, mon. (*laughs*) Winchin dat chain against dis wind might get you fellas sober. (*shakes his head*) No, mon. Got to feel my way—can't do dat with motors. I got to listen to de sea fall on dem reefs to get my bearins, cause I sailin by remembrance—ain't no moon.

So you takin dis schooner through night reefs with

dem short masts and patchy sails and no goddom
sea room, and no moon! Mon, dat is crazy!

Raib turns toward Byrum.

Dat is crazy, okay, if us six here thinks we can
hondle maybe sixteen pan-heads like dem ones we
seen tonight. (*pause*) Nothin more to say? Okay den,
boy, de talkin time is done.

He walks up and down the deck.

Now maybe dey too drunk to come out after us,
or maybe dey just drunk enough to try. But I
believe dat dey will try, because dey desperate.
Probably dey slip out here without dem outboards,
take us by surprise, so I wants two men on watch.

What if—

DE TALKIN TIME IS DONE! (*resumes
walking*) First thing, we winch dat chain right to de
place where de anchor barely holdin, and de two
on watch can slack her off a little if de vessel
start to drag; den we unlash dem sails and clear de
lines. After dat, we waits for daybreak light.

The fire ashore casts a glint on the black water.

Soon's de hook is up, she gone to fall off by de head,
but even with dis goddom wind, dere is plenty of
reach before we would strike into de reefs, and in
dat time we h'ist de sail and bear away to de
sout'westward. (*pause*) I be up on de mast. Speedy
take de helm, and mind you holler back loud
whenever I yell de change of course. Will and
Byrum managin de sheets—till you hears me sing
out, let her run before de wind.

Wodie emerges from the fo'c's'le; he stands entranced.

> You okay, Wodie? You still with us? Cause I wants you to keep dat stove wood burnin so dey sees it good, right until dat hook is clear; den damp her down quick as if some mon had shut de galley door, so dey don't see dat fire movin. Got dat? I say, Got dat?

> Got dat, Jonah?

When Byrum smacks Wodie hard across the back, Speedy steps between them. Byrum is cursing.

> Tonight you men are crewin on a sailin boat dat finds herself in a very ugly corner of de reefs. If dey any mon here dat don't understand his job, den speak up now.

> Speak up, den, you fuckin Jonah!

> Papa? Where you want me, Papa?

> Copm? How about dat boat? We take her back aboard?

> No, mon. Leave her astern, and rig de other to de block and fall so's we can throw her over quick, if de ship strike.

Raib looks once at each tense face.

> I believe we make it okay, but it never hurt to have things ready. Soon's de vessel under way, den Wodie and Buddy prepares stores and water for both dem boats. Okay? I make a crew out of you yet!

4 A.M.

The crew is huddled by the galley. No man sleeps.

See dere, Copm Raib? Down by de point? Dey up to something.

Yah. Takin dem outboards off—dass *dere* mistake!

We lift de hook, den?

No, mon. Let dem come a little way downwind. Once dey see us underway, dey got to row back into dat breeze to get dem motors, and den dey ain't no way dey can come up with us.

Okay. Dey comin. In two boats. You ready?

Yessir.

I goin aloft. You fellas raise dat hook when I raise my hand.

Black wind.

The ship heels as the wind takes her, and the sea quickens; across the wind fly shards of human voice.

The skiffs turn back toward the cay.

LET HER RUN FREE!

Black clouds in a black sky, and the reef booming.

At the blind helm, Speedy is alone: he can see no man but the Captain, who swings to all four quarters on the masthead, holding a shroud with one hand and cupping his ear with the other.

SOU'WEST BY SOUTH!

SOU'WEST BY SOUTH!

                            dancin on dat masthead
like a child!

          de wind in reefs like dis! He crazy, Will, he crazy! Hear dat surf? We never—COPM RAIB! WE SAILIN TOO FREE, COPM RAIB!

He got to keep steerage way

                BYRUM!

                      laughin up
dere! We in de mouth of hell, and dat mon *laughin*!

BYRUM? CALL DE SEAMAN'S UNION, BYRUM! TELL DEM I SAILED TOO FREE ON DE BLEAK OCEAN!

YOU A CRAZY MON, KNOW DAT?

Hush, Byrum, hush! Dat mon de *Coptin*!

YOU HEAR ME, RAIB, YOU HEAR ME?

GET DE HELL BACK ON DAT LINE! HAUL HER UP CLOSE!

CRAZY OLD WIND COPTIN
SONOFABITCH!

HAUL HER UP CLOSE, I SAY!

Wodie and Buddy crouch in the galley door. They
stare at the deck, not daring to look outboard.

SHE NOT FAR FROM DE OPEN WATER,
BOYS! NOW FALL OFF A LITTLE
TOWARD DE SOUTHWARD!

SOUTHWARD!

Byrum and Will, exhausted, stare into the blackness.
The ship is encircled by white wraiths of reef.

Oh *Jesus*, Will—!

Hush, mon, hush! We got to trust him!

WEST-SOU'WEST!

WEST-SOU'WEST!

HOLD HER ON DAT POINT! SHE GONE
TO MAKE IT!

Black clouds rush past the mast; the sail is ghostly. On
the crosstrees, the Captain flings his free arm wide, ex-
alted.

SHE CLEAR, SHE CLEAR! WE IN DE
CLEAR!

The ship strikes.

A shriek of twisting timbers.

The gear in the galley crashes, and bound turtles slide overboard.

Shuddering, the *Eden* rights herself, and in a din of flopping canvas, screeching blocks, drifts downwind from the reefs.

Black wind and rush of water. Figures running.

—*Shit!* My shoulder!

—Christ A'mighty!

Hear dat water? *Shit!* Get dat boat *over*board!

Got him, Speedy?

We got most of him.

Got enough to start dese engines? *Shit!* I *told* him! Domn old rotten riggin! *Shit!*

Never mind dem engines, Byrum, mon! Dey flooded out!

A gathering of oceans.

The *Eden* drifts downwind in the black seas.

The crewmen hunch in a circle around the Captain, who lies on deck beneath a soiled gray blanket. They eat rapidly and gulp down water.

What you think, Will?

Maybe she got till daylight. Maybe not.

The Captain's eyes are wide, but they see nothing. His mouth opens.

Copm Raib? You hearin us?

Ain't no rock dere. Ain't no coral in dat reach at all. We in de clear now, boys, we in de open water.

Lie easy, Copm Raib—don't stress yourself.

He right, y'know. I knocked down dere by de rails, nearly went overboard when she heeled over, and I look down to see what she had struck on, and all I seen was darkness. And de next moment she had righted herself in good deep water—

It were dark, mon, with no moon! How in de hell—

Mon, mon, don't matter how she mashed up. I knew she were gone soon's I heard dat water rushin.

first light

She goin now—dere go de stern. Dem diesels gone
to corry her down fast—

Dere! She slidin! Oh! She gone! De *Eden* gone!

Drifting.

Far Tortuga, in the east, is a shimmering black burning
in the sunrise.

The catboats bump together in the seas.

In the starboard boat, Byrum grips the tiller, his big
face shocked by pain. Wodie hunches on the seat
amidships, Speedy is in the bow. In the port boat, the
Captain lies eyes wide to the fired sky, his head in his
son's lap. Will Parchment bails doggedly with a half
coconut. In the bilges of each boat lies a green turtle.

Will? Goddom it, Will, it's a pity you never changed
dat boat for de one dat Conwell left at Half
Moon Cay!

Will looks up at Byrum, then resumes bailing.

How de Coptin, Will?

He breathin peaceful, Speedy, dass about it.

Know something? With de high old masts dat was
on dat vessel when she come dere to French
Harbour, he would have cleared dat rail!

Yah, mon! See him strike? Back must be broke,
de way he lie so still.

Between the boats a dark-haired face swims round
and round in the gray sea; salt water slopes across
hard bright black eyes.

Look dere! A rat!

Just de one? Old hulk like dat, I s'prise de sea
ain't littered with'm.

From Buddy rises a low whine of dread; Will pats his
knee.

Well now, Jim Eden, your doddy done what he
said he would do; he could not have known about
dat one wild rock. We de first ones ever sailed out
of Misteriosa Reefs in de night time and lived to
tell de tale.

Jumping up, Byrum drives the rat down with an oar
blade, scattering water across the other boat.

Tell de tale to *who*? Goddom wild mon! He never
cared if he sailed us straight to hell!

With his shirttail, Buddy mops his father's face.

Wodie straightens; the new sun glints on the mirror
shard on his black chest.

I hearin dem wonderin at East End! Dey wonderin
what was de fate of Wodie Greaves!

Hush up, Wodie.

Oh my! It seem like de thing for me to do was to sail away down to de cays, and now I dyin!

Ain't nothin de motter with you, Wodie.

Nothin de motter, no! Just crazy!

Hush up, Byrum.

The boats drift steadily downwind. The sea increases.

Well, den, best take advantage of dis wind, start for de coast.

Dis all de water, boy?

Each boat got dis one big bottle, Byrum. One bottle and one turtle and one box of breads, and fishhooks.

Shit! I a big mon, and I needs water!

Dere weren't no kegs!

No kegs, no! And no fire equipment, no life jackets, no *nothin*!

The rat swims back and forth between the boats.

Will? Call dat fair? Dey three men in dis boat!

Water laps around Will's ankles. He stops bailing.

Three here, too.

Can't count dat old mon dere! He dyin!

Raib's iron hair strays on his forehead. His mouth is gaunt.

Not ... yet!

The brief choked laugh turns to a cough of pain, and the eyes water.

Lie easy, Copm Raib, mon—you gone hurt yourself.

Raib's voice comes in a series of harsh breaths.

We best sail back to Bragman's, pick up Vemon.

Papa?

Dat you, Sonny?

Raib's hand gropes in the air, and Buddy takes it.

No, Papa, dis is Buddy. Dis is Jim Eden.

Sonny and dem other boys would never sail no more down to de cays ... Jim Eden? Best pick up Vemon, den, Jim Eden, and set sail for home, cause de season has got away from us, and de turtles have all gone to Turtle Bogue.

A silence. Raib looks straight up at the sun. Tears glisten in his eyes.

Too late now, ain't it. It's too late.

Papa? Lie easy, Papa.

Oh, dat sun wild. Oh, dat sun wild.

Far Tortuga sinks beneath the sea.

We got de good boat, Byrum. Dass enough.

The two boats drift apart. Speedy steps the mast.

Now don't be fearful, Buddy! We be lookin out for you! Good luck, Mist' Will! Take care of dat old wind coptin you got dere!

Will nods. The soot on Buddy's face is streaked.

The starboard boat falls rapidly downwind. In the port boat, the two stiff figures are black sticks on the white sky.

Late afternoon.

On the horizon, the sail of the port boat rises and falls, tilting and luffing in the gathering seas.

Ain't ridin right. She wallerin.

She shippin too much water, Byrum. Best take dem fellas with us in dis boat, before de night fall.

Never heard what de mate said? Long's dat old log'red still alive, dem two never leave him, and dey ain't no room here for de three.

Best take dem in before de sea do.

You de one in charge of dis boat now? (*grunts*) Dat mon be dead before de mornin, maybe we take dem fellas with us den. (*groans*) Christ! Dis shoulder killin me!

Sundown.

Never took time to set dem turtles free. Never took time.

Domn one-eye Jonah! Just when we needin every hand we got, you runnin around cuttin de lashins on dem turtle—!

Sea turtle must go back into de sea . . .

De most of dem went down with de vessel! Dem turtles *drowned*!

Searching the rough seas to the eastward, Speedy speaks across his tattered shoulder.

Byrum? Easy, mon. You fellas help me look for dat port boat.

Captain Raib Avers.

night rain

the wind rises

the wind dies

squall

In sleep, Wodie whimpers once and sleeps again.

Jim Eden Avers.
Will Parchment.

Daybreak.

The sea is still. In the starboard boat two figures hunch, awaiting sun; the third is curled under the seats.

No sign of dem.

We should have took dem in with us—dat what you sayin?

Easy, mon. Maybe dey off dere to de sout'ward.

Wodie rises and, in singsong, speaks.

Copm Raib die in de twilight time, de boy and de mate drown in de night.

SHUT UP DAT FUCKIN MOUTH!

Chin rested on the silvered splinters of the gunwale, Wodie stares sightlessly into the east.

Last night I dreamin dat I see Will Parchment's grave. And in de dream I smellin graveyard jasmie. Not de wild jasmie dat grow so sweet—

SHUT UP DAT MOUTH, OR YOU GOIN OVER DE SIDE!

Nemmine now, Byrum—he just wanderin. Wanderin and wonderin.

horizon

Noon.

The catboat lifts and falls on long smooth swells.

Resting on his oars, Byrum glares around the mute horizon.

See dat? Empty! Howlin dis last fortnight like de winds of hell, and now when we needs dat wind to make de coast, dere is dead calm!

Wodie giggles.

Oh, wind die, too. De wind die, too. De sun just a pure ball of light, and dat mean dry dry weather.

Speedy pours one mouthful from the bottle.

Dere's your portion, Wodie. Don't go spillin.

Midafternoon.

A noddy lights upon the tiller. It cocks its silvered head.

See dere? It waitin.

How you *know* dat? How you *know*?

I see birds flyin in de corners of de sky, dey towardin de last light to de west, and I get feelins, and I *know*!

The bird raises its wings, and the wind lifts it; it flies away westward, into bright wastes of ocean afternoon.

Dusk.

One day I was in de bushes nearby what dey calls de Shadow Pond cause dey ain't but de shadow of water in it, and dat day I found dis old coconut tree dat I knew never belonged dere, and beside it dis nut with a young sprout comin out, so I say to myself, De old people put dis coconut tree down so a mon could get a drink, and I gone to do de same. So I plont dat tree, and so de story end.

Tell him stop talkin about WATER!—

Dass good, Wodie. I plont some young trees when I get home, small plonts. On my own ground. In de Bay Islands.

Oh, I know everything dat grows, cause I were reared up in de Island, and by dat I come to know things. De old people tellin dat fore de hurricane of '32, all de sea front dere in Bodden Town were jennifer and sea grape and coco-plum and lavender. Oh, coco-plum! Dey tastes so nice, boys! Cocoes!

When Wodie sits up straight and claps, Byrum slaps his big hand on the tiller, then cries out, clutching his shoulder.

Pig food! Maybe de niggers eats dat at East End, but back home in West Bay we calls dat pig food!

Noon.

My grandmother dat were a slave woman dat a white mon got by his cook over dere by Prospect, she seen dis pirate standin in de Gun Bay road dat had no head—

Give me dat water for you knock it over!

Let him do what he want with it, Byrum.

Never heard Will say dat I in charge of dis boat? Never heard dat?

Speedy does not answer. They gauge each other, red-eyed, dry lips parted. Byrum's big face is loose, on the point of tears.

Dis Jonah say he dyin! He admit it! He givin up on life!

Maybe two more days of no wind and dis heat, you find a reason to take my water too. Ain't hard to find a reason when you thirsty.

Well, givin dis one water is a waste! He spillin it!

Speedy shrugs.

Ain't we in friendship, Speedy-mon? I *needin* it!

Darkness.

You too quick dere with dat knife.

Best back up, Byrum. Best sit right up dere in de bow where we can see you.

I ONLY SAYIN DAT HE SHOULD NOT GO TALKIN ABOUT DYIN WHEN HE DO NOT *KNOW*!

Maybe he know. Maybe you so wild cause you b'lieve him.

Oh, yes! I seen de night birds flyin to de moon.

Noon.

Wodie's hand lies on the turtle's belly, black fingers taut on the pale calipee.

Where one old wreck struck on de reef was de flat we calls Old Anchor Flat, but dat growin up again long years ahead of me. Oh, yes! De corals is fillin it in.

Don't spill dat, Wodie. Wodie? Dat little cup is all you gets today.

Course dere is duppies dat is facey enough to show dereselves—one dem rusty cats or a ruffly hen, sometimes a goat—and dere is times you will see one if you look back quick over your left shoulder, or rub your eyes with de eye water of a dog . . .

Shit! (*spits*) Ain't gone to eat dis turtle?

Got to eat her raw. You ready to do dat?

Speedy splashes sea water on the turtle.

When we ready to eat her raw, why, den we eat her.

Noon.

In the parching sun, Byrum's caked lips are caught on his dry teeth.

The water bottle stands in the shade of Speedy's seat. Speedy whispers.

You touch dat bottle once more, mon, just once, I gone to move, mon, very very fast. So you got your own self to deal with, Byrum.

On the cracked blue paint of the thwart, Speedy lays down his knife with a hard rap.

I goin home, mon. Dat land in Roatán waitin for Speedy, fifty-five acres, mon, and cows. I take anybody with me dat don't get in my way. If Wodie die, den I am sorry. If Byrum die, den I am sorry. But Speedy goin home.

Noon.

Dis de bad time of de day. Oh, yes.

Huh?

Oh, yes. Mon got no shadder. Very dangerous time.
Cause de shadders of de dead is flyin round, lookin
for people dat don't have no shadder.

'Afternoon.

De old people, dey taught me. I was just a boy dat
loved to keep old people company. I loved to know
something about de old people and de old ways.
I loved . . .

Wodie sits up smiling, starts to speak again, sees
Byrum, stops. He lies back again beside the turtle.

I dyin, Speedy.

Not Speedy, mon. Not dis year, anyways. I goin
home.

Speedy winks at Byrum, but Byrum turns away.

Yah, mon. Been goin home all of my life, seem like,
and dis time I meanin to remain.

Dark.

Byrum?

Course in de night, if you cotch a spider web
across de face, or if you might hear an old cow
lowin where no cow belongin, den you know dat
dey are dere . . .

Face forward into de bow, Byrum. And stay dat way.

Fuckin black Honduran!

Dass me, okay. I nigger to de bone. (*sighs*) Wodie
mon? Shut up, okay? I got to sleep a little, so lay
down all across de thwart, tween me and Byrum.

Maybe he get me in de night!

No, mon. He get *you*, den he know I get *him*. De
only way he gone get you is if he get me first.

Polaris

The turtle sighs.

Wodie lies flat on his back on the middle thwart, fingertips trailing in the bilges, blind eye rolled upward to the dying stars.

In the bow Byrum shifts a little, settles down again, body twisted aft. Soon one eye opens, and when he draws a breath and holds it, Speedy's eyelid trembles. The knife lies by Speedy's hand, wet with sea dew.

The universe is still.

Go in de water, Byrum.

NO!

Go in de water, mon.

Byrum Watler.

White sky.

Two figures in a boat. The world is empty.

I hearin birdsong but dere be no bird. Seem like I
dreamin.

No, mon.

Speedy—?

No, mon. Ain't no goin back.

You a hard mon, Speedy.

No, mon. I go ahead every day, do what I got to do.

Oh! I dyin here dis day! Gone to foller Byrum
Watler into de sea!

Go den, Wodie. I can't keep you.

Daybreak. High in the west, a lone cloud following
the night is caught by the sun still under the horizon.
The cloud turns pink.

Shark got him! Drawn to de blood! I *feels* it!

Hush, Wodie, hush.

I never walked de left-hand path, danced
widdershins, nor worked nobody woe. But dey will

say dat Wodie Greaves took de life of Byrum
Watler out in de cays!

The hard line of the sky, surrounding.

It was a holiday in de month of May . . . oh, yes!
Call dat de maypole, and de gumbo limbo, dat is
called red birch. Oh, I was raised up in de island,
and know everything dat grows dere, cause dat
Old Rock is my home.

Wodie follows Speedy's gaze to the wind banks in the
eastern sky. His eye is staring.

Oh, yes! De corals is fillin it in!

I hoppy to see you hoppy again, Wodie.

Oh, we be hoppy in de bushes, too.

Best drink dis little water, mon. Cause we get wind
out of dat sky, we gone to make it, hear me, mon?

One mon in a blue boat and de child face down in
de mornin sea. One mon in a blue boat dat say
goodbye, settin dere at de tiller in de manner dat
you doin and lookin at me like de way you lookin.
(*weeps*) Remember de way dat his eyes shine?
I knew right away den, I had sign.

What you sayin, Wodie? Just drink dis little water.

De people, de people will be sorry to see
De graveyard for Bonnie and de gallows for
me . . .

Dat is a sad song, Wodie, but you got a pretty voice.

Dat mon in de blue boat, dat mon is you.

The last light glances from the wings of a white tropic bird high in the south.

Night falling.

wild stars

horizon

night-blue sea

Wodie Greaves.

Noon.

White sun, white sky.

slap

slap

Parting the water, the great mantas catapult into the sky, spinning white bellies to the sun—black, white, white, black. Slowly they fall into the sea. In the windlessness the falls resound from the horizons.

Near the silent boat, a solitary ray rolls over and over in backward arcs, wings rippling, white belly with its eye-like gills revolving slowly just beneath the surface.

Nemmine, Speedy-mon. (*sighs*) My oh my.

Twin wing tips part the leaden surface, holding a moment as if listening. Then water rushes softly and is still.

Noon.

A man in a blue boat. Blue sky and breeze.

A loggerhead, rude shell awash, holds its ancient head at a hard angle; its eye reflect the sun as the blue boat passes.

Gone.

evening star

morning star

The sun, coming hard around the world.

Green seas of the continental shelf roll west toward the mainland.

At first light the trade wind freshens and the solitary man raises his head. Mangrove radicels, copra husks and half-sunk fronds of palm float in a milky sea.

   black triangle—a fin

                        dark west horizon

The man balances the turtle on the gunwales. He rests a little, then cuts the flipper thongs and eases the turtle over the side.

   Don't cry, girl. Swim. Dass very very fine.

Still upside down, the turtle sinks, the blank face of its calipee pale in the deep. When it rights itself, the pale face vanishes.

the shadow of the coast

sun shaft and silence

old morning sea

bird cry and thundering

black beach

a figure alongshore, and white birds towarding

About the Author

PETER MATTHIESSEN is considered the finest nature writer of our time. Born into a wealthy family in New York City on May 22, 1927, he was educated at Hotchkiss, the Sorbonne, and Yale (B.A. 1950). In 1951 he married Patsy Southgate, settled in Paris, and became part of a group of literary expatriates that included James Baldwin, William Styron, Terry Southern, Irwin Shaw, and George Plimpton. Together with Harold L. Humes, he founded the *Paris Review*. In Paris he also wrote his first novel, *Race Rock* (1954). Returning to the States, Matthiessen settled in East Hampton, working as a fisherman and captain of a charter boat during good weather and writing during bad. In 1956 Matthiessen was divorced from his wife and then began the series of travels that dominated the next twenty-five years of his life. Three years of study and observation in wildlife refuges produced *Wildlife in North America* (1959). Treks into South America and New Guinea (the same 1961 expedition in which Michael Rockefeller died) led to his writing *The Cloud Forest* (1961), *Under the Mountain Wall* (1962), and *At Play in the Fields of the Lord* (1965). In 1967 Matthiessen's *The Shore-birds of North America* was called by Peter Farb, "among the finest nature books ever to come off the presses of this country." *Oomingmak* (1967) chronicled Matthiessen's 1964 expedition to the Bering Sea to bring back specimens of the musk ox; *Blue Meridan* (1971) described his search for the great white shark; and *The Tree Where Man Was Born* (1972) gave his reflections on East Africa. *Far Tortuga* (1975), set on a turtle fishing boat in the Caribbean, is generally considered his finest novel. In 1972 the death of his second wife, Deborah Love Matthiessen, and his growing commitment to Zen Buddhism prompted him to join George Schaller's Himalayan search for the rare snow leopard, a trip which became a profound journey into himself and a confrontation with the mysteries of life and death. The resulting book, *The Snow Leopard* (1978), won the National Book Award in 1979.

Peter Matthiessen's most recent work is *Sand Rivers*, an account of his travels in the Selous Game Reserve in southern Tanzania.